12.95

D1145335

ANTARCTICA
THE LAST GREAT WILDERNESS

STANLEY JOHNSON

ANTARCTICA

The Last Great Wilderness

FOREWORD BY SIR PETER SCOTT

WEIDENFELD AND NICOLSON

LONDON

First published in Great Britain in 1985 by
George Weidenfeld & Nicolson Ltd,
91 Clapham High Street, London SW4 7TA

Copyright © Cadena, 1985

ISBN 0 297 78676 8
Typeset at the Spartan Press Limited
Lymington, Hants
Printed and bound in Great Britain by
Butler & Tanner Ltd
Frome and London
Jacket photographs by the author

Contents

Acknowledgements

I would like to express my profound gratitude to the British Antarctic Survey. Without BAS, this book would not have existed. *The Last Great Wilderness* is about Antarctica, but it is also about BAS, and the men and women who work for BAS. I hope I have done them justice. Wherever possible, I have quoted the remarks and explanations of BAS personnel – on ship or shore – because I felt that these were authentic voices.

I should also like to thank British Petroleum for a grant which enabled me to buy as much film as I needed. Short of falling down a crevasse or getting frostbite, running out of film is about the worst thing that can happen to the Antarctic visitor.

John Curtis, of Weidenfeld and Nicolson, has given valuable encouragement to this project, while my wife, Jenny, has had to accept my more than usually protracted absence. My thanks to both of them, and to Cassandra Phillips, Chairman of Wildlife Link's Cetacean and Antarctic Group, for her comments on the draft.

Finally, I would like to express my appreciation to Sir Peter Scott for agreeing to write the introduction to this book. To most of us the name 'Scott' is virtually synonymous with Antarctica. But Sir Peter is not only the son of a famous father; his writing and painting and his work for wildlife (including Antarctic wildlife) are known and appreciated all over the world. If I had a fraction of his understanding of the way nature works, this would have been a much better book.

Stanley Johnson

Foreword

by Sir Peter Scott

When I was two years old, in 1911, my father with four companions walked 800 miles across the polar ice-cap to the South Pole, only to find that the great Norwegian explorer Amundsen had reached it before them. My father's party completed 700 miles of the return journey, but died still one hundred miles short of their base camp. This family connection with Antarctica has not unnaturally given me an even stronger interest in that part of the world than I would probably have developed in any case as an artist, a naturalist and a conservationist.

In 1966 I first visited Antarctica myself, and I have had the great good fortune to return there four more times since then. Each time I have found it a place of awe-inspiring beauty and have been enthralled by what Stanley Johnson describes as the 'unbelievable biological abundance' one encounters in the vast colonies of seals, penguins and other sea-birds.

Stanley Johnson's lively and entertaining account of his journey in 1984 to the Antarctic Peninsula, the Falkland Islands, the South Orkneys and South Georgia provides a very topical commentary on what these places are like now and on what may be in store for them before the end of the century. He describes the fantastic beauty of the mountains, coasts and ice almost completely untouched by man, the thrill of seeing some of the few remaining whales, and the extraordinary numbers of seals and penguins, and he goes on to discuss the threats that are now hanging over what is frequently but nevertheless accurately described as the last great wilderness on earth.

As the author points out, one of the main threats to the Antarctic ecosystem in the closing years of the century is the indiscriminate harvesting of the fish and particularly the krill on which all the higher species depend – the penguins, sea-birds, seals and whales. A treaty exists to control their harvesting, but so far it is proving sadly ineffective. Another serious threat to Antarctica is the prospect of its oil and minerals being exploited. The Antarctic Treaty Consultative Parties are holding a series of meetings to discuss how, rather than whether, this should happen. They acknowledge that the risks of catastrophic pollution from oil spill, blow-outs and the increased human occupation of the few ice-free areas (which are also the most important areas for wildlife) are very real, but they seem to regard them as acceptable if the world can be given perhaps another four or five years' supply of oil. I entirely agree with Stanley Johnson that this is a most distorted order of priorities. Will our children and grandchildren ever forgive us if we allow our short-sighted greed to despoil the beauty and the teeming wildlife of the last great wilderness on earth?

Peter Scott
Slimbridge, 1985

ANTARCTICA
THE LAST GREAT WILDERNESS

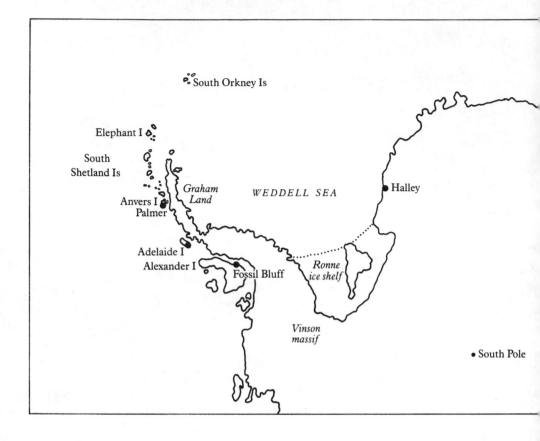

South Orkney Is

Elephant I

South
Shetland Is

*Graham
Land*

WEDDELL SEA

Halley

Anvers I
Palmer

Adelaide I
Alexander I

Fossil Bluff

*Ronne
ice shelf*

*Vinson
massif*

• South Pole

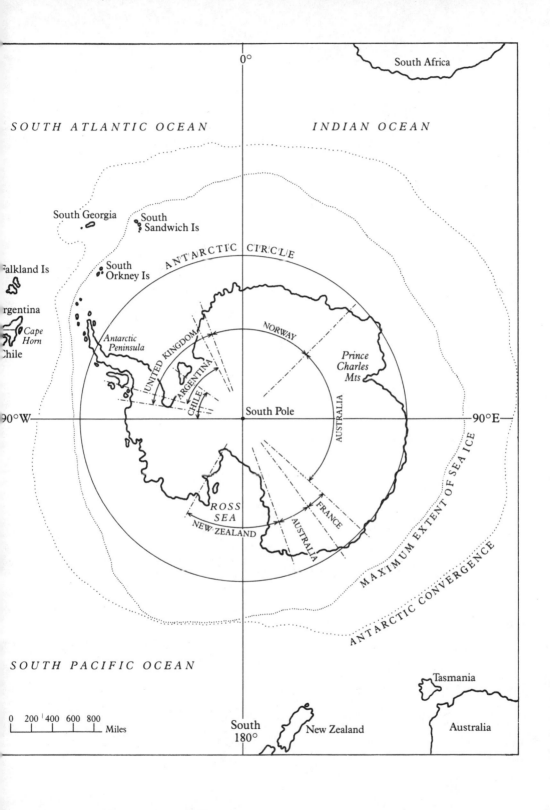

I

Preparations

Antarctica is the world's last great wilderness. There is no place like it on earth. It covers 13.5 million square kilometres (or 5.5 million square miles) which is one-tenth of the earth's land surface. It is the sixth continent, split into unequal parts by a mountain range (whose highest peak in the Vinson Massif soars to 5,000 metres), and covered by a mighty icecap which averages 2,000 metres (over a mile) in thickness and which at some points exceeds 4,500 metres. The weight of this icecap is so great that it has depressed about one-third of the landmass of the continent to below sea-level. It extends offshore in the form of vast ice-shelves up to 600 metres thick. The sheer immensity boggles the imagination. The ice-shelf in the Ross Sea is the size of France. When the seas around Antarctica freeze in the winter, the area of the continent is almost doubled.

It is a cold place, as one might expect. The average annual temperature is minus 50°C on the polar plateau and minus 15°C in coastal areas. And it is the windiest continent on earth with winds up to 320 kilometres per hour (200 mph) – catabatic is a word you learn to use when describing these great downward draughts. Antarctica is also drier than most deserts. Annual snowfall at the South Pole is equivalent to less than one inch of water. There are dry valleys, devoid of moisture, whose physical characteristics seem more properly to belong to some other planet – and which indeed were used by American astronauts for their lunar preparations.

Yet, though the environment is a harsh one, the sheer physical beauty of this ice-bound landmass is without parallel. The vision of that majestic landscape of ice and cliff, mountain and nunatak*, will haunt me as long as I live. What William Wordsworth saw from Westminster Bridge, magnificent though it must have been and magnificently described ('never saw I, never felt, a calm so deep'), could not, I am sure, have held a candle to the majesty of Antarctica. Wordsworth! thou shouldst be living at this hour!

Add to the physical splendour of the place the fact that the Antarctic coasts and the seas that lie within the Antarctic convergence contain an abundance of

* An isolated rocky peak.

wildlife – whales, seals, penguins, seabirds, fish, squid – unsurpassed anywhere in the world. As we left South Georgia on the last leg of our voyage, we passed tiny Willis Island, home to 6,000,000 penguins. The sight and sound of just one penguin rookery are something that has to be seen and heard to be believed. When the elephant seals and the fur seals mass alongside those penguins on the beaches; when the albatross and petrels and blue-eyed shags beat their way across the icy waves; when you glimpse at close quarters – as I did one manky morning in the Le Maire Channel – the blurred shape of a whale, you can quite easily believe that you are in paradise, and a very special paradise at that.

The point about Antarctica is that it is not only an enchanted and enchanting wilderness constructed on an epic scale but also a place which has so far avoided desecration and degradation by the activities of the human race. There are precious few other places about which this can be said; where they do exist, the dimensions are not the same.

Of course, there have been human interventions in Antarctica. According to Rarotongan legend, Antarctica was discovered by a Polynesian, Ui-te-Rangoria, in about AD 650. The period from 1739 to 1848 saw early French, Russian, British and US exploration by ship. The 'heroic' period of polar exploration which took place at the beginning of this century – the period of Scott and Shackleton from Britain, of Amundsen from Norway – was succeeded by the age of scientific discovery.

The first New Zealand expedition took place between 1929 and 1931; the first expeditions by Argentina and Chile were in 1942. The establishment by the Royal Navy of Operation Tabarin in 1943 marked the beginning of the scientific programme now being carried out in Antarctica by the British Antarctic Survey. The US Navy's post-war Operation Highjump (1946–7) represented the largest expedition ever to visit Antarctica. It was composed of thirteen ships, twenty-five aircraft and more than 4,000 personnel.

The International Geophysical Year (IGY), which took place from 1957 to 1958, provided a stimulus to international cooperation, with major research efforts focused on Antarctica as well as on the first crossing of the continent via the Pole. IGY led to the signing in 1959 of the Antarctic Treaty, which came into force on 23 June 1961 with twelve original participants, while a further fifteen states have since acceded. Some of the participant countries are 'claimant' states in the sense that they have asserted sovereignty over sections of Antarctica (United Kingdom, New Zealand, France, Australia, Norway, Chile and Argentina). Fifteen per cent of the Antarctic continent is unclaimed. The USA and the USSR have not made claims but maintain a right to do so.

The 1959 Antarctic Treaty provides that Antarctica shall be used for peaceful purposes only and that any measures of a military nature shall be prohibited; that there shall be freedom of scientific investigation and that the results of such investigation shall be exchanged among all the parties and made freely available; that any nuclear explosions and the disposal of radioactive material in the Antarctic shall be prohibited; that all parties shall notify each other in advance of all expeditions to the Antarctic and of stations occupied by their nationals; and that each party shall ensure that no one engages in any activity in Antarctica contrary to the principles and purposes of the Treaty.

This, then, is the present situation. On the whole these activities – whether of the heroic age or of the scientific – have been environmentally benign, or what the Germans would call *umweltfreundlich*. The status of the world's last great wilderness has not been seriously threatened. That marvellous and awesome combination of remoteness and beauty with supreme biological abundance has remained intact. There are at present thirty-four year-round scientific stations populated by approximately 800 science and logistics personnel in winter, increasing to more than 2,000 during the Antarctic summer. But it probably takes more than this to dent a continent.

Today the precious status quo, as defined and protected by the Antarctic Treaty and by the raft of agreements and conventions that have grown out of it, such as the Convention on the Conservation of Antarctic Seals and the Convention on the Conservation of Antarctic Marine Living Resources, is under attack from several sides. The reason is not far to seek. At a time when scarce resources are becoming scarcer (when are they not?), Antarctica – it is supposed – may contain wealth which should be put at the service of mankind.

Sizeable beds of low-grade coal are known to exist in the Transantarctic and Prince Charles Mountains. Even though no deposits have been found that could be developed economically, the identification of minerals such as iron, copper, molybdenum, chromium, nickel, platinum, gold, lead, silver, tin and zinc might lead to the discovery of larger concentrations. And on the deep seabed surrounding the Antarctic continental margin, manganese nodules are known to exist, though technical and commercial aspects have still to be assessed. As part of the international deep-sea drilling project, the American ship *Glomar Challenger* discovered traces of methane, ethane and ethylene in the Ross Sea in the early 1970s. Circumstantial evidence of oil is compelling, based on the Gondwanaland hypothesis (Antarctica is thought to have formed part of a supercontinent together with Africa, India, Australia and South America), *Glomar Challenger*'s discoveries and what is known about the nature of the sediments.

Similarly, Antarctic seas – as I have already observed – are among the most biologically productive areas in the world, particularly in those parts, such as the Scotia arc, where the cold waters from the south meet the warmer waters from the north with a resulting upsurge in nutrients. At the base of this productivity is the Antarctic krill – the critical link in the Antarctic food chain. It feeds on microscopic floating plants and is in turn fed upon directly by numerous species of fish, squid, birds, whales, seals, and other marine mammals. Estimates of total krill population vary; in the two areas surveyed, it is believed to be about 80 million tonnes.

If winter comes, can spring be far behind? If resources – mineral or biological – are known to exist, is there any chance at all that humankind will somehow exercise a self-restraining ordinance and refrain from exploitation, recognizing that the consequences of exploitation may be the destruction of this last great wilderness? The omens at the moment look bad. The pressures on Antarctic marine living resources are steadily growing (and we have already seen in the course of this century the drastic depletion of whale and seal populations in Antarctica): now there is the prospect of large-scale exploitation of fish and krill. Moreover, the Antarctic Treaty partners are busy negotiating a 'minerals regime' which would permit development of the continent and its off-shore areas, something which is not at present envisaged by the Treaty, while the United Nations, frustrated by the seemingly exclusive nature of the Antarctic Club, seems to be determined to proclaim Antarctica as the 'common heritage of mankind', a high-sounding concept which will not necessarily lead to effective conservation. The United Nations General Assembly had its first ever debate about the future of Antarctica at the end of 1983; the UN Secretary-General is now preparing a study and the world organization will be returning to the subject in the near future, notwithstanding the tacit and sometimes not-so-tacit resistance of members of the Antarctic Club who sense the threat to their privileged status that 'internationalization' will imply.

Does it actually matter if the magnificence of Antarctica is maimed and mutilated? Does it matter if, where once one might have seen a line of blue-eyed shags atop an ice-floe, we now see an oilrig? Does it matter if, in the share-out of *Lebensraum* between the human and other species on the few ice-free shores of the Antarctic continent, we find that man occupies the prime sites – as he already has in most other parts of the globe? Does it matter if pollution and contamination, and the new scale of human activities, change irredeemably the character of this wilderness?

My own view is that it does matter. It matters tremendously. The preservation of Antarctica ranks among the great issues of our time. I put it alongside the protection of the remaining tropical rain-forest, the control of population growth, the elimination of chemical pollution, and even the maintenance of peace itself – indeed it is not too fanciful to imagine new wars, perhaps more severe than the Falklands conflict, being sparked by competing claims down there in the Deep South. That is why I want to hear the President of the United States, the British Prime Minister and the Head of the EEC Commission, as well as the Chinese and the Soviets proclaiming the need to save Antarctica – not for mankind, but from mankind. And I want to see those speeches followed by action.

Looking back, I can recognize that for me in recent years the very word Antarctica has been like a bell summoning forth childhood memories and a host of other images. On Mercator's projection of the world, the continent occupies a grossly disproportionate share of the available space, lying ragged and white as a shroud along the bottom edge of the map. As a small boy one noticed such things. Later on, though not much later since I was still at school, I remember watching the film 'Scott of the Antarctic' with John Mills in the title role. On that particular occasion the raw evening outside with the rain beating down on the moors above Tiverton was more than matched by the blizzard which raged within the classroom. Eyes narrowed against the elements, ice riming their beards, Scott and his men plodded determinedly, desperately onwards only to be beaten to the Pole by a Norwegian, the wily, unsporting Amundsen who had had the cheek to equip himself with dogs and more dogs; whereas Scott, after dabbling unsatisfactorily with ponies, had had to resort to stout, old-fashioned manhaulage half-way to hell and back again.

No one who watched that film in the early 1950s, as I did, could have had any doubt about where the sympathies of the director lay. Scott was a national hero and that was the beginning and end of it. Antarctica was the convenient backdrop against which heroic deeds could be performed. I am sure that, *mutatis mutandis*, a film entitled 'Scott of the Gobi Desert' would not have made as considerable an impact. What counted was raw courage, a touch of masochism here and there and, most movingly, the three bodies found side by side in a snow-buried tent together with the letters and the journals which became the stuff of legend. Antarctica itself, as I say, was incidental. Or at least that is my recollection and I have not seen the film since. I certainly do not think that it portrayed Scott's serious *scientific* interest in Antarctica or hinted that there were other objectives apart from the race for the Pole. If these aspects *were* covered, I missed them at the time.

After Ravenswood School, Devon, came Sherborne School, Dorset. After Sherborne, Oxford. After Oxford, jobs with the World Bank, the EEC Commission and later, as a Member of the first directly-elected European Parliament, where I was a Vice-Chairman of the Parliament's Committee on Environment, Public Health and Consumer Protection. I don't suggest that during the more-than-thirty-year interval between seeing the film and making the trip, Antarctica had been constantly on my mind. Other responsibilities, other interests had intervened. But many of these had been environmental in nature, had involved dealing with environmental issues and problems. During the decade that followed the United Nations' Conference on the Human Environment (it took place in Stockholm in June 1972), I became aware that the theme of Antarctica – particularly the protection and preservation of that continent from sundry looming threats – was more and more in the minds and on the lips of those whose motives and judgements I respected.

As a Euro-MP I put down – quite early on in my mandate – a couple of questions to the Council about EEC policy towards Antarctica and received unsatisfactory replies. The Council, I was informed, had never discussed

Antarctica and seemed to have no intention of doing so – which answers I took with a pinch of salt. Then, in October 1981, I was asked to represent Mme Simone Veil, the Parliament's President, at the biennial meeting of the International Union for Conservation of Nature and Natural Resources (IUCN) which was to take place in Christchurch, New Zealand. I made a brief speech on behalf of the President at the opening session ('the reason Mme Veil is not here is because she is there') and, otherwise, made the most of an all too brief visit to the southern hemisphere.

One thing that struck me forcefully was that Antarctica was very much the 'hot' topic among the delegates to the Conference. Christchurch, of course, has long had connections with the White Continent. Scott put in here to a hero's welcome on his way south (his statue still stands in the town); the American Antarctic base at McMurdo is supplied via New Zealand; the ill-fated tourist flight which crashed on Mount Erebus on 28 November 1979 with loss of all 257 people on board took off from here. But relative proximity alone could not have accounted for the interest which delegates of every nationality, whether governmental or non-governmental, were showing in the Antarctic question. In the halls and meeting-rooms, people were busy drafting and redrafting position papers and resolutions, all of them designed to reconcile potentially irreconcilable positions. As a fully-fledged world issue, Antarctica had come of age. The question in a nutshell was this: could Antarctica be 'saved' or was it to be 'ruined'? Could it be 'exploited' without losing its apparently unique character – its wildlife, its wilderness, its advantages for scientific research?

When I returned to England I wrote a letter, as people do, to the editor of *The Times* which he kindly printed under the heading 'What may flow from Antarctic oil'. I argued, with the benefit of my brief Antipodean insights, that many consequences might result from the exploitation of oil and minerals in Antarctica and that very few if any of them would be good. I suggested that whatever it was Antarctica had was something the world could perfectly well do without given the risks involved (not least the Weddell Sea 'gyre' – a Yeatsian swirl that would carry pollution round and round the continent in a clockwise motion for ever and a day). I ended by advocating a 'hands off Antarctica!' policy and then, having fired that shot, returned to the more parochial concerns of my committee.

In due course *The Times* printed a rejoinder from Dr R. M. Laws, Director of the British Antarctic Survey in Cambridge. Dr Laws was clearly pained by what he took to be the intemperate tone of my letter and pointed out that much useful scientific research was being done by BAS and other nations in Antarctica. He added that the 1959 Antarctic Treaty provided a sound basis for regulating activities down there (this side of exploitation, on which the Treaty was silent). In brief Dr Laws seemed to imply that when men of good will get together to hammer things out, preferably about a million miles away from enthusiasts of every kind, including 'environmentalists', rational and acceptable solutions will emerge to seemingly intractable problems.

That was more or less where things stood when the Falklands War intervened. With the outbreak of hostilities in the Southern Atlantic, the Antarctic question which, as I have indicated, already occupied the attention of conservationists, moved very much more to the forefront of the political stage.

The Falklands War was not, of course, fought about Antarctica. No one suggests that. But the Governor of the Falklands is also the Commissioner for British Antarctic Territories. In a real sense, the Falklands and South Georgia are the forward base for British Antarctic operations. The fact that soon after the Falklands War the budget of the British Antarctic Survey received a dramatic increase was by no means coincidental. Blood and treasure have been expended by both sides in the Falklands conflict. Anything that can be put in the other pan of the scale may be welcomed, if only unconsciously, as providing one more justification for the Falklands operation and Britain's continued heavy investment in those islands. (The same goes, of course, for Argentina though it can be argued that Argentina's proximity to Antarctica makes 'springboards' like the Falklands and South Georgia less important than they are for Britain.)

I decided in November 1983, while the Treaty partners were busy trying to hammer out a 'minerals regime' on one side and the United Nations was gearing up on the other, that I wanted to write a book about Antarctica – a personal account based on first-hand observation – which would put the case for conservation rather more comprehensively than could be achieved in the context of a letter to *The Times*. The moment was ripe, I believed. The pressures in favour of exploiting Antarctica, of developing its resources, were growing steadily. Soon those pressures might prove irresistible. Having committed myself to the project, I was left with the minor problem of getting to Antarctica and back. Speed was of the essence, as they say. The Antarctic summer had already begun and quite soon, like the nightingale's song, it would be over. Once the pack-ice began to harden over the surrounding seas, I could say goodbye to the idea of visiting the Deep South at least for another year.

Leafing through my Antarctic clippings, I came across Dr Laws's reply to my letter in *The Times*. I dialled directory enquiries and asked for the number of the British Antarctic Survey in Cambridge. Dr Laws, it turned out when I was put through to his office, had already 'gone south', by which was meant that he had left for the Antarctic.

The expression 'gone south' was irresistibly romantic – so much more romantic than for example 'gone to seed' or 'gone to ground'. It reminded me of the man in the poem by T. S. Eliot who says 'I read much of the night and go south in winter'. With that very first telephone call a thin layer of excitement was forming in my mind like, I supposed, the first hint of ice on the southern seas.

Dr Laws being unavailable – indeed a man could hardly be more unavailable than being in Antarctica when you were hoping to see him in Cambridge – I learned that Dr Raymond Adie, BAS's Deputy Director, would be in his office on Monday (that day was Friday) and why didn't I ring back then?

I didn't ring back on Monday. I drove to Cambridge instead at the crack of dawn. I have learned over the years that it is much more difficult to put someone off when they are actually sitting on the doorstep. Ray Adie, a burly soft-spoken man who had wintered in the Antarctic a good many times himself, was politely sceptical. It would be very difficult, he thought, to find space on board a BAS vessel bound for Antarctica. There were only two ships – the *Bransfield* and the *John Biscoe*. Even if their itineraries happened to coincide with the timing of my projected visit, it would be very unlikely that there would be space for me on board.

'Frankly' – Dr Adie spoke kindly but there was no mistaking his meaning – 'BAS is not running a tourist operation. This is science. Our ships are there to service BAS bases in Antarctica and to carry out their own scientific programmes.'

His desk, on the first floor of BAS headquarters in Madingley Road on the outskirts of Cambridge, a stone's throw from the motorway, was piled high with papers. Scientific reports, I assumed; geological surveys; atmospheric charts all bearing the stamp, or so it seemed to me, 'NOT FOR LAYMEN OR ANTARCTIC TOURISTS'. Deep down he dug, under one of the piles, and surfaced with two brochures from companies running commercial tours, which he handed over to me.

As I left, Dr Adie – friendly and helpful as ever – had one last suggestion. 'You could always try to get hold of the *Endurance*,' he said. 'Colin Gilbert – that's the captain's name. He might be able to take you to Antarctica. It would be cheaper than going by Lindblad or World Society. Of course, you'd have to get yourself to the Falklands somehow.'

When I pressed Dr Adie about precisely how one would set about getting hold of the captain of a Royal Navy ship at the bottom of the world, he became studiously vague. 'You're a politician. You'll have contacts to help you with that kind of thing, won't you?'

I spent that afternoon in the Scott Polar Research Institute. Even if I never reached Antarctica, at least I would be able to say that I had visited SPRI which is probably the next best thing. On the ground floor of the Institute's building in Cambridge was a permanent exhibition of documents and photographs from the heroic days of Polar exploration. Epic moments from those epic journeys were faithfully recorded – pages from Scott's diaries, Wilson's last letters home, a snow-shoe or two, even a Nansen sledge. Though one was ten thousand miles away – in comfortable Cambridge – from where it all happened, something of the Polar atmosphere came across. I stood in front of the glass case and looked at that final entry from Scott's little leather-bound book found so many months later by Apsley Cherry-Garrard: 'I pray God look after our people.' Of course, I had read it before, twenty times if once, but even so the prickle was there behind the eyelids.

The books are upstairs, in the library of the Institute. Thousands of them; tens of thousands. Every period of Polar exploration is covered from Captain Cook's earliest circumpolar voyages, through the 'heroic' days of Scott and Amundsen, Shackleton and Mawson (the great Australian explorer) and on into the modern era of Admiral Richard Byrd, the American who wintered alone near the Pole in 1934 and nearly died as a result of carbon-monoxide produced by the generator in his hut; of Vivian Fuchs and Edmund Hillary who crossed the continent from sea to shining sea at the start of the International Geophysical Year in 1957; of Ranulph Twisleton-Wykeham-Fiennes whose *Journey to the Ends of the Earth* – an account of the recently completed Trans-Globe expedition – appeared on the 'new acquisitions' shelf.

Every aspect of Antarctic science seemed to be covered too. Learned journals, in every language, including Russian and Chinese, were ranged on the shelves; papers and treatises of every kind were piled on tables waiting to be catalogued. The Institute, it was clear to me, was the hub and focus of the international research effort in Antarctica, the repository of most – if not all – worthwhile knowledge. (Later I was to find that the Institute's own journal, *Polar Record*, was an invaluable source of information and insight in its own right.) I couldn't help asking myself, as I left Cambridge, whether there was really space for one more book on the shelves.

Back in London that evening, I rang the Ministry of Defence and spoke to the duty officer. How could I reach the captain of HMS *Endurance* by telephone?

'Try dialling 100,' said the duty officer.

In due course the telephone operator put me through to the ship-to-shore radio telephone service based at Portishead near Bristol.

'Do you know where the HMS *Endurance* is?' the radio-operator asked.

'Somewhere in Antarctica, I expect,' I replied.

'Has your call been cleared with the Ministry of Defence?'

'It was MOD who told me to dial 100.'

'I'm afraid we shall have to clear the call, caller.'

I could well understand why. You couldn't have every Tom, Dick or Stanley ringing up ships of the Royal Navy wherever they happen to be. And the case of HMS *Endurance* was rather special anyway. Exactly two years earlier the British Government's decision to withdraw the *Endurance*, our only ice-strengthened vessel in southern waters, from its permanent station had apparently been taken by the Argentines as a signal – among others no doubt – that we were not really serious about defending the Falklands. The 'Argies' had thus been encouraged in their invasion plans. In the event, the *Endurance* had not been withdrawn (there had been cries of protest on all sides) – in fact the ship had been used to bring marine reinforcements to Port Stanley just before the Argentine landings took place. Since then the *Endurance* had stayed on patrol, the cost of keeping her down south (which had once seemed to the Treasury to be unacceptably high) now being absorbed as part of the infinitely greater expense of the Fortress Falklands concept. Given the background, it was not surprising that the Portishead operator had standing instructions to clear calls to the *Endurance* with the Ministry of Defence.

'If they say yes, we'll call you back,' she said. 'It may take an hour or two.'

Exactly two hours later the telephone rang.

'Your call to the *Endurance*,' the operator said.

'Hello,' I said. 'Is that Captain Gilbert?'

'It is,' said a voice enlivened by static. 'What can I do for you?'

I must admit that I was taken aback by the drama of it. There I was in the kitchen in our house in London pretending to help with the washing up and then suddenly I'm talking on the telephone to someone on a ship in the Antarctic as though, to coin a phrase, he was in the very next room.

'What's the weather like down there?' I asked.

'I'm afraid I can't tell you that,' replied the Captain.

'Oh,' I nodded sagely into the telephone. Talking about the weather on an open line could, I suppose, give away a ship's position to the enemy.

Eventually I came to the point. Was Captain Gilbert, was the *Endurance*, by any chance going to be visiting Antarctica itself in the near future? If I was able to get myself to the Falklands, could I hitch a ride as it were on his vessel?

The Captain crackled away, polite but firm. 'I can't tell you when we are going or whether we are going. As for taking a passenger, that's something for the Ministry of Defence. You'll have to get in touch with them. Good luck.'

Captain Gilbert, I imagined, went back to the bridge to stare at icebergs. I was wrong. Seconds later the telephone rang again and the operator said, 'Have you finished your call to the Bahamas?'

'Bahamas? I thought I was talking to Antarctica.'

'You were talking to HMS *Endurance*, that's what you asked for, didn't you? HMS *Endurance* is currently in the Caribbean on her way south.'

It was clear that the telephone operator didn't work for the Ministry of Defence.

After the washing up I went to my study and wrote a letter to Michael Heseltine, then (and still at the time of writing) Secretary of State for Defence. I knew Mr Heseltine. In a previous incarnation he had been the Secretary of State for the Environment and in that capacity I had badgered him unmercifully about seals. Saving seals. Eventually he did. (Others badgered him about badgers but that is another story.)

'Dear Michael,' I wrote. 'Is there any possibility of getting down to the Falklands on the air-bridge via Ascension Island and then on to Antarctica with

HMS *Endurance* if that ship is going?' If we had any ham, we could have ham and eggs if we had any eggs.

A few days later I received a most friendly note from Lord Trefgarne, Minister of State at the Ministry of Defence. No stones were being left unturned and so forth. A day or two after that a man in the Private Office rang to say that there was absolutely no problem about my getting down to the Falklands on the air-bridge though he was bound to point out that since this was not as it were an officially-sponsored trip more like, how should he say, a private . . . er . . . initiative . . . not to say jaunt . . . they would regrettably have to charge me the full non-IATA fare for flying in a VC10 to Ascension followed by thirteen hours sitting on a packing case in an unheated Hercules from Ascension to Stanley and that would come to – I could hear him totting it up on his pocket calculator – yes, approximately £4,000 sterling give or take a few pounds here or there.

'How', I murmured, 'do the Falkland Islanders manage to get to and from the mother-country if it costs them £4,000 a go.'

'They're not Members of the European Parliament,' the voice at the other end replied diplomatically.

Later in the conversation I asked the man from Lord Trefgarne's office whether, assuming I reached the Falklands in one piece, I would find the *Endurance* in the harbour at Stanley ready to weigh anchor for the realms of ice. Unfortunately he had no information on that score and there our discussion ended.

The first week of December passed with no clear decision being taken by me – or indeed anybody else.

Fortunately I was saved by the telephone bell. On 12 December my daughter, Rachel, came to tell me that Dr Adie was on the line from Cambridge.

Dr Adie came straight to the point. 'We've been looking at the schedule of our ships', he said, 'and we think after all that we may be able to help you. The *John Biscoe** will be leaving Punta Arenas in Southern Chile on 12 January for Antarctica. It will be visiting two BAS bases on the Antarctic Peninsula. Those are Rothera and Faraday. Then it will be coming up to take on supplies in the Falklands at the end of January before going south again to our base at Signy in the South Orkneys. From Signy the *Biscoe* will go to Bird Island which is just off South Georgia and then steam on to Rio de Janeiro. You can fly home from Rio if you like. Or else you can stay on board the *Biscoe* until it returns to the UK in the middle of March. I'm afraid we'll have to charge you a nominal victualling charge of £4 a day while you're on board the *Biscoe*. And you'll be responsible for your own airfare to Punta Arenas in Chile going, and back from Rio on the way home. Mind you, you'll get a discount agreed by the airlines

---

* Named after John Biscoe (1794–1849), a British sealer who spent the years 1830–32 in Antarctic waters working for Enderby Bros and died in Australia.

because you can be considered as crew leaving or joining a ship – that's if there are no stopovers on the way. Does all this sound all right?'

Did it sound all right? I was thrilled. I wrote to the Ministry of Defence thanking them for their very kind offer of a passage on the airbridge to the Falklands, indicating that it would no longer be necessary since I would be visiting those islands by way of Antarctica – a slightly more roundabout route perhaps but one which met my requirements nicely. In the end I booked my own ticket on the way out including stopovers, because there were people I wanted to talk to in America, but I relied on the BAS travel agent to get me back from Rio at the end of the voyage.

Shortly before Christmas I went back to Cambridge to be isued with my Antarctic clothing which would be air-freighted to South America ahead of me. Key items included: a bright orange anorak (the colour to stand out against the ice and snow thereby assisting rescue parties in the event of mishap); woolly balaclava hat and gloves; waterproof trousers, Antarctic boots and long thermal underwear, two pairs, men's.

I had the pleasure of meeting Ray Adie for a second time and he explained the background to his invitation.

'Our OBP people – that's the Offshore Biological Programme – ' he said, 'did a winter season this year. This means they won't be on board the *Biscoe* for this particular trip, so there are some cabins free. There'll be three other guests beside yourself from outside BAS. "Steve" Stephenson and Colin Bertram – they were on the British Graham Land Expedition fifty years ago and we thought we'd offer them a chance to revisit the area where they worked before. The BGLE was the last great Antarctic expedition to operate with sailing-ships and dogs. And it also made a very important scientific contribution, you know. For example, they were the first to demonstrate that the Antarctic Peninsula was attached to the mainland, in other words that it was a peninsula and not an island. Then there'll be Adrian Berry as well. He's the science correspondent of the *Daily Telegraph*. He wrote some good pieces some time back about the Antarctic, so we thought he might be interested to come along.'

In addition to the four of us, Adie explained that BAS was taking the unprecedented step of offering three of its female staff from headquarters the chance to visit Antarctica for the first (and possibly last) time in their lives.

'This is very much a one-off occasion,' Adie said. 'It may never happen again that we have space in this way. We've never really taken women down to our bases before.'

One of the three women in question, Adie explained, was Anne Todd who had joined BAS in the 1950s when Vivian ('Bunny') Fuchs was the director and had stayed with it ever since.

'She's an absolute mine of information about Antarctica – places and people, projects and programmes, even though she's never been there.'

Besides Anne Todd, our female travelling companions from BAS Cambridge were Rowena Harris, currently working with the director, and Carys Williams, a BAS personnel officer.

'If you have any problems between now and departure, just ring up and ask for Carys. The switchboard will put you through.'

Ray Adie had one final piece of advice. In fact, more instruction than advice: 'Remember when you're aboard the ship, you'll be under the command of the Captain at all times. On shore, the Base Commander – wherever you are – is in charge.'

Before I left Cambridge, we (Rachel had come with me for the day) saw an Antarctic slide show in the BAS projection room. It was (for me) the first demonstration of the spectacular environment which was to greet our small party as some weeks later we headed south on board the *Biscoe* towards and then across the Antarctic circle. I still found it hard to believe that less than a month after my initial enquiries all the necessary preliminary steps had been taken, short of actually boarding the plane for the South Atlantic. One thing we didn't need was visas. Depending on which way you looked at it, the slice of Antarctica we would be visiting belonged either to Britain or to the world.

I met Adrian Berry at a party in London before Christmas. His wife, Marina, predicted that we would be sharing a cabin, a prospect which she found hilariously funny.

'Adrian is fantastically untidy,' she explained.

'Does he snore?' (It turned out that Adrian and I did indeed share a cabin, at least for the first part of the journey. Adrian had to leave us when we reached the Falklands; he explained that the editor felt a three-week absence on the part of the *Telegraph*'s science correspondent could be justified in the circumstances. However, extending the period to six weeks might involve the risk of major scientific developments going unreported by one of Britain's leading newspapers.)

'Actually,' Adrian added more plausibly, 'Marina will kill me if I'm away for six weeks on the trot but, no, I don't snore. Do you?'

In the event, it was the most friendly relationship. Adrian, two or three years older than I, tall, dark-haired, whereas I am blonde and of medium height (less than six foot), is what I think of as a technological optimist. He is deeply convinced that the world is a marvellous place and that it is getting better all the time. Because he has a total scepticism about environmentalists and conservationists and resents their wingeing on about insignificant little problems such as pollution and world population growth when in reality extraordinarily wonderful and life-enhancing things are happening all the time like computers, especially and particularly computers, he was a wonderful travelling companion to have on a voyage to Antarctica. When, some way south of Tierra del Fuego, our first albatross wheeled overhead, Adrian – standing next to me on deck – instinctively raised his arms and swung with the bird as though taking aim with a twelve-bore. And, as the White Continent hove into sight, he cited with apparent approval Marshal Blücher's comment when visiting London for the first time: 'What a place to plunder!'

Deep down I am sure that Adrian believed, and believes, that Antarctica is such a vast and inhospitable place that either large-scale exploitation is going to prove impossible or the damage is going to be insignificant, or that anyway, if neither of these applies, a price has always to be paid for progress. I don't think Antarctica was a moral issue for Adrian as it was for me, a gut feeling that here was an environment quite unlike any other environment. And precisely because it wasn't a moral (or mystical) issue he was a good man to have alongside in the Gemini or the Zodiacs, our rubber dinghies, as we zipped through the icy spray from ship to shore. It meant that I had to 'fight my corner', as Mrs Thatcher puts it, if the opposing viewpoint was to have any kind of a hearing. It wasn't like sharing a cabin with someone from Greenpeace or Friends of the Earth.

On the Thursday before Christmas I gave John Heap lunch at the Savile. We talked until well into the afternoon, long after the clink of ivory from the billiard-room had ceased. We sat in the worn leather armchairs at the side of the blazing fire while Heap told me what he thought I needed to know. I use the expression 'needed to know' advisedly. For almost twenty years John Heap has worked in the Foreign and Commonwealth Office. Telling people what they need to know (and not much else) is very much the house tradition.

Unusually, Heap had spent the whole of his time in the FCO working with Antarctic issues. If not our man in Antarctica, he was most certainly our man on Antarctica. Before joining the Office, he had worked with the British Antarctic Survey, including spending a couple of 'winters' down south. In a real sense, Antarctica was his life and his life's work. If any man was entitled to wear the coveted Antarctic tie with its two crossed penguins, John Heap was. (For those who have somehow managed to play tennis south of the Antarctic circle, a pair of tennis rackets complete the emblem!) The flicker of the fire was reflected in Heap's broad, honest face as he tried to put me straight on some of the essentials. Poor sod, I thought. Here he is, a decent man, thoroughly committed no doubt to the propagation of all that is true and good and lively and of honest report and yet his place of work is precisely where the most turbulent waters meet. The environmentalists attack him because they think he and the Government are committed to exploitation, come what may. His superiors probably give him a hard time because they think he spends too much time with people like me. Third World activists get at him because they see him (and his fellow representatives on the Antarctic Treaty) as part of a rich man's club, determined to prevent at all costs the 'internationalization' of Antarctica. His wife probably grumbles because he works too hard and travels too much – particularly now as the rhythm of meetings to discuss Antarctica accelerates; and they don't all take place in London or Cambridge.

'As far as I'm concerned,' said John Heap, 'there are two essential principles. The first is that Antarctica must be protected and preserved. The second is that scientific research – and this is one of the most successful aspects of the operation of the Antarctic Treaty – must be able to continue.'

He readily admitted that there might be a conflict between these two principles. Realistically speaking, one reason – though not the only reason – why continuing large sums of money were being spent on Antarctic research (BAS's budget for example now exceeds ten million pounds a year) was the prospect, however distant it might be, of the actual exploitation of Antarctic resources.

In John Heap's view the Antarctic Treaty which had flourished since 1959 had done a remarkable job in 'finessing' the difficulties inherent in the situation.

'The sovereignty issue has been neatly side-stepped. Since the Treaty came into force, claimant states and non-claimant states have all agreed that the situation should be frozen. That's Article 4. Scientific research has continued and there has been an unprecedented degree of international cooperation. Antarctica, for example, is the only place in the world where the Russians have accepted the principle of open inspection – and without advance warning.'

Heap believed that it should be possible to build on the existing framework of the Antarctic Treaty to ensure that the right safeguards were laid down for the future. And he pointed to the successes which had already been achieved, the raft of international agreements which had grown out of, and which now complemented, the initial Treaty concept: the agreed measures for the Conservation of Antarctic Fauna and Flora, the Convention for the Protection of Antarctic Seals, the Convention on the Conservation of Antarctic Marine Living Resources. There was no overriding reason, he believed, why it should not be possible to devise an appropriate regime for minerals as well, including oil.

I asked him how he viewed recent developments in the United Nations. Now that the debate in the first Committee of the General Assembly had been concluded, the Secretary-General of the United Nations had been instructed to make a study of the Antarctic question and to report back within the year. Won't there be irresistible pressure, I suggested, from the countries of Asia, Africa and Latin America who are not yet members of the Antarctic Club to open up the Treaty on the grounds that Antarctica and its resources are, by analogy with the seabed, the 'common heritage of mankind'?

Heap wasn't so keen on analogies, least of all with the seabed (Britain, like the US, still refuses to accept the new United Nations Law of the Sea Treaty). Though he was too much of a diplomat to say so openly, it was clear that he viewed recent developments in the United Nations with gloom and despondency. Fragile ecosystems, he seemed to suggest, came in different shapes and sizes. Some were biological; others could be legal and juridical in nature, a complex amalgam of customs and conventions, principles and practice. The Antarctic Treaty and its associated instruments were a delicate affair. Knock it in the wrong place and the whole damn thing could fall apart.

Heap illustrated just how well the Treaty structure worked by referring to 14 June 1982. 'That was the very day Port Stanley fell, the day the Argentines surrendered. It also saw the opening of discussions about the minerals regime in Wellington, New Zealand. The New Zealanders were insisting that the Conference should be postponed but Britain and Argentina wanted it to go ahead. Both Britain and Argentina ended up by sitting down side by side.'

I left London at the beginning of January and flew to the US. As I had told Ray Adie there were people I wanted to talk to in Washington before going south. One of these was Craig Van Note. Craig runs Monitor. In fact he *is* Monitor. From a small upstairs office half a block from Dupont Circle in Washington DC he keeps track of a consortium of non-governmental bodies (NGOS), both in the United States and abroad, all of whom are concerned with environmental and animal welfare issues.

The key instrument is the twice-monthly mailing of articles and press cuttings *from* all parts of the world *to* all parts of the world. Craig knows that half the battle is keeping people informed. You can't mobilize the NGOS – and in his view it doesn't do to underestimate the force of concerned public opinion – unless they know what the issues are.

I met Craig first in Botswana in May 1983 at the Fourth Meeting of the Convention for International Trade in Endangered Species of Fauna and Flora, known as CITES for short. He was concerned then with lobbying delegates about the fate of migratory animals in the Kalahari. Wildebeest and hartebeest, eland and zebra were dying by the thousand because veterinary cordon fences, intended to provide a buffer against the spread of foot-and-mouth disease, had been constructed across their traditional migration routes, thus blocking their access to water and forage.

But many other issues excited his interest and sympathy: seal-culling in Canada; 'roo'-bashing in Australia; Philippine dogs; Amazonian highways. The large buff manila envelopes which dropped through the letterbox every two weeks contained the latest update, as he would put it, on the key environmental issues of the day. Antarctica was one of his – and Monitor's – major concerns. If you wanted the most recent 'secret' draft of the minerals regime (it was known as the Beeby Draft because it was largely the work of a New Zealand delegate to the meetings of the Antarctic Treaty partners – Chris Beeby), Craig Van Note would be able to supply it via one of his numerous contacts in the NGO world. If you wanted to ensure an international audience for the latest scare story (for example a recent *Observer* article on the way the French were jeopardizing an important penguin colony in Antarctica in order to build an airstrip), then the best thing was to send the clipping to Craig and he would get his Xerox machine working overtime.

He was a large man, broad-shouldered with heavy black spectacles and a soft drawl. I found him between meetings with about ten minutes to spare.

'Basically, its geopolitics,' he told me. 'The oil industry rules the world. Terrestrial, i.e. land-based, oil supplies are running down which means the future lies offshore. The Arctic is going to be the place for exploitation in the 1990s; by the late 1990s the focus will have shifted to the Antarctic and it could stay that way up to the twenty-first century. It's the world's last great pool of oil.'

The prospect clearly appalled him. 'We've got to convince people that the marine ecosystem down there is much more valuable than any oil we could extract. That is the message we have to put across. That is the justification for protecting Antarctica which will really appeal to people.

'Look at the ships which are down there already. All the major fishing fleets are there – East Germany, Japan, USSR, West Germany. Vast quantities of fish are being taken. Remember when countries started bringing in two-hundred-mile limits for their own coastal waters in the late 1970s the world's fishing fleets went down to Antarctica instead. Down there it's a free-for-all. There are no 200-mile limits. This is a classic case of the tragedy of unprotected common lands. In two seasons the Russians destroyed the halibut.'

It was hard not to be impressed by the urgency with which Craig spoke.

'Look,' he said, 'we have already hammered the top of the food chain with what we have done to the whales. We have had a crack at the middle of the food chain with what we are doing at the moment to the fin-fish and now the plan is to smash the bottom of the food chain as well by going after the krill. Can you beat it?'

I said: 'What about the Convention on the Conservation of Antarctic Marine Living Resources? Isn't the plan there to set catch-limits on an ecosystem basis, taking into account the interaction of the different trophic levels?'

Craig Van Note paused in mid flow, registering the fact that I had obviously picked up some of the jargon already and was prepared to use it if I had to.

'That's fine in theory,' he scoffed. 'But by the time they get round to setting catch-limits and quotas on a multispecies basis, it will probably be too late. They haven't even fixed *global* limits yet, let alone worked out how to split them up between countries and regions. And it's not just the quantities being taken out. It's the methods too. The monofilament nets which are being used are wreaking havoc on fish stocks. They're being left down there and they're also drifting down to the Antarctic from other parts of the world. Net entanglement is a real problem.'

Before he hurried on to Capitol Hill where he was planning to brief a gathering of Congressmen about the plight of gorillas in Rwanda (or vice versa), Craig had a parting shot about oil and minerals.

'South Georgia is going to be the key place if you're planning to develop Antarctic oil. You're going to see workings on the sea floor with pipelines or even submarines taking the oil away. The Japanese are down there already. There are good hydrocarbon indications. As for the minerals, the geology is fascinating. South Africa, you know, was once attached to Antarctica. You've got gold in them thar hills!'

Jim Barnes, whom I talked to later that same day also in Washington, was quite a contrast. I had met him before, as I had Craig, but in New Zealand rather than Africa. Jim Barnes was part of the reason why that IUCN gathering in Christchurch, New Zealand, had become so interested in the Antarctica issue. Where Craig Van Note had Monitor, Barnes had ASOC – the Antarctica and Southern Oceans Coalition. ASOC represented people and organizations from all over the world who believed that the future of Antarctica was too important to be left to governments alone.

Jim Barnes and his team at Christchurch nobbled delegates, put on films and slide-shows, distributed literature and in the end helped ensure that the Resolution adopted by the IUCN Assembly on the subject of Antarctica and Antarctic resources was at least ambivalent. Though it didn't come out clearly and straightforwardly in favour of the 'hands off Antarctica' policy, at least it indicated that developments shouldn't take place without stringent environmental safeguards. This was progress of a sort.

Jim Barnes had written a book entitled *Let's Save Antarctica*, and using the book as a kind of manifesto had started the Antarctica Project, dedicated to the political goal of ensuring that Antarctica's unique wilderness was able to survive for all time.

As I talked to him in his office in downtown Washington he came across as the very image of a passionate, committed environmentalist. There were maps of Antarctica and pictures of whales and penguins on the wall; he himself wore jeans and a T-shirt and looked younger than his thirty-eight years.

He told me that in the mid 1970s he had decided as a lawyer to specialize in international environmental issues such as acid rain and the export of toxic chemicals. He worked for the Center for Law and Social Policy, which was a public-interest law firm, funded by foundations and taking on work which others weren't prepared to handle. There was about him an air of moral fervour which is peculiarly American. You don't find public-interest law firms in Britain or indeed anywhere in Europe.

'Antarctica represents 10% of the surface of the earth. It is the main feeding-ground for the large whales. Millions of birds either live in or migrate to Antarctica. Two-thirds of the world's seas are linked to it.'

Jim Barnes saw the moral and philosophical dimension to his work. 'If we don't have the vision to put aside a few parts of the earth, what kind of people are we? We ought to see ourselves as the trustees of this earth. Let future generations have a chance to decide what *they* want. We shouldn't pre-empt all their choices. If we don't have this kind of vision, then our moral stature is rather poor. What rights do future generations have? And by generations I mean generations not just of human beings but of all kinds of creatures. Look at the blue whale, the largest creature ever to live upon the earth. Once – around the turn of the century – there were two hundred thousand of them; now they're down to two thousand or three thousand. No one knows what impact the present level of krill fishing may be having on the blue whale's chances of making a recovery. Yet no government is ready to propose a whale sanctuary, let alone an international park in the southern ocean.

'The governments are driving themselves berserk trying to negotiate a minerals regime. I think we should say, "Let's put it off-limits for this generation, let's give it a chance, and think about it again later."'

We talked about the scientific research which was being carried on in Antarctica. Science, said Jim Barnes, was the basis of true international cooperation. But he had one caveat about the current working of the Antarctic Treaty. There was no cooperative evaluation of projects built into the Treaty.

'The French want to build that airstrip in their part of Antarctica. They state their view and that's all there is to it. Some scientists say this will affect the emperor penguins there – it certainly *will* affect them if you start blowing them up. But the fact is there is no means of having the French evaluation, if they make one, counter-checked by other people. We need to build an environmental protection mechanism into the current Treaty; there should be an international secretariat to insist that proper environmental impact assessment procedures are carried out.'

The memory of Jim Barnes's vision, and the fervour of his commitment, were to stay with me throughout the *Biscoe*'s voyage through the Antarctic.

2

Joining the John Biscoe

Out to Kennedy airport, this ninth day of January, in time to catch the flight to Santiago via Miami and Lima – the first step of the long journey south. It was a comfortable flight if a protracted one: I found five empty seats in a row and woke up to see the sun rising over Lima. The Andes reared over the port wing; the Pacific Ocean stretched away to starboard. We landed at Santiago in shirt-sleeve weather with Chilean fighter planes taking off like starlings as we approached.

A man from the Pacific Steam Navigation Company – one of those centuries-old businesses which have somehow miraculously managed to stay abreast of the times – met me and took me into town. We drove down what seemed to be the main street, Alameda Bernardo O'Higgins. (O'Higgins was the first President of Chile; his father came from Co. Meath – and like George Washington in the United States, he crops up everywhere. For example, if you look at a Chilean map of Antarctica you see that a large slice of what we think of as British Antarctic territory is called Tierra de Bernardo O'Higgins – in other words O'Higgins Land.) On the right, the man from PSNC pointed out the railway station – a splendid example of industrial architecture, designed by Monsieur Eiffel of Eiffel Tower fame. It's not only the trains which run in Santiago; there's a metro too now, which there wasn't when I was last here in 1968. We passed Government House on the left which is where General Pinochet now lives.

My flight to Punta Arenas was not till the following day. It seemed sensible to see as much as possible. Chile is a country with a big say in Antarctica, if only because of its geographical proximity. At the end of an otherwise leisurely day, I went off to see the British Ambassador, Mr John Higman.

'You've got to take seriously what the Chileans say about Antarctica,' His Excellency advised. 'They're certainly planning a colonization programme down there. Indeed it's already started. They have an effective logistical operation – Chilean airforce C130s shuttling back and forth between Punta Arenas and their base in Graham Land.'

'O'Higgins Land, surely?'

The Ambassador, smiling, spoke of the almost religious intensity with which Chileans and Argentines and Latin Americans generally regard their national territory.

'We may think of the Falklands as British. But we don't think of it as British in the same way that the Chileans or the Argentines think of their territories belonging to them. The Chileans even organized it so that a meeting of the Antarctic Treaty partners could take place actually on their base in Antarctica. Men like Vivian Fuchs were flown down specially in Chilean airforce planes.'

The Ambassador looked wistful. He would clearly have liked to visit Antarctica himself, but it was not to be.

'The Foreign Office took the view that, as Ambassador, I shouldn't fly down there on a Chilean plane because that would be tantamount to admitting Chilean claims to Antarctica.'

'What about the *Biscoe*? Couldn't you come down with us?'

Higman shook his head. 'Ambassadors can't be away from their posts for weeks on end.'

Thank heavens, I thought as I left his office for a late swim at the nearby Sheraton, that I was only a humble Euro-MP.

The next morning we took off from Santiago in a Ladeco jet bound for Punta Arenas, Chile's most southerly town. It is clear from the maps that 'Punta', as the place is familiarly called, is already half-way to Antarctica – at least if you are starting from Santiago.

On board the plane, I am handed a copy of *El Mercurio*, one of Santiago's leading newspapers. As we fly south, once more keeping to the narrow corridor between the mountains and the sea, I am able to read – on the front page – of progress being made in the current dispute between Argentina and Chile over the Beagle Channel. Ambassadors from both countries are meeting the Pope's representatives in Rome, the Vatican having agreed to act as an arbitrator. On the inside page is an article – my Spanish is good enough to get the gist of it – which contains the text of the speech given by Ambassador Zegers, Chile's representative at the Antarctic Treaty meetings, to a recent seminar on the subject of Antarctic resources held at the University of Chile.

Zegers, I can see, does not mince his words. He speaks about strengthening the air-bridge between Punta Arenas and Antarctica, a two-and-a-half-hour flight; and of the necessity 'to penetrate further into the interior of the Chilean sector right up to the Polar Circle'. He goes on to call for the reinforcement of the Chilean bases in Antarctica, for full-scale investigation of the continent's resources both mineral and biological. The article ends with Ambassador Zegers's plea for the 'visionary project, the visionary programme of human settlement' (*asentamientos humanos*), by which he means Chilean settlement, of the continent.

I tear the article out and put it in my briefcase. Zegers seems to represent the 'maximalist' position but it is good to know what we are up against. I walk up and down the plane looking with greater interest at my fellow travellers. Are these, I wonder, the new *colons*, the *pieds-noirs* about to be airlifted from Punta Arenas into the icy wilderness, the frozen continent – *el continente helado*, as Zegers puts it?

After an hour and a quarter we land at Puerto Montt. For the time being both mountains and sea seem to have disappeared. We descend toward a wide grassy plain. Cattle country. The cows seem unperturbed by the passage of the aircraft a few feet above their heads. There are helicopters and tanks on the airstrip, and some military transport planes and hangars camouflaged with green and brown paint.

When we take off again, half an hour later, I find myself sitting next to a Chilean oilman. He tells me that the Chilean National Oil Company, his employer, already has a rig in the straits of Magellan and they are looking for oil even further south. The sheer extent of Chilean territory, in terms of longitude at least, comes across to me when he says we have still two thousand kilometres to fly before we reach Punta Arenas.

Around noon the plane banks sharply to the left. I am sitting on the port side so am able to catch a glimpse of some stupendous scenery, funnels and chimneys of ice, blue frozen lakes, soaring pinnacles of rock.

'That is the Parque Nacional Torres de Paine,' the pilot announces. And the oilman, sitting next to me, explains: 'It is a land of great beauty, one of the finest in our country. Sometimes, with friends, I have gone up in a Cessna from Punta Arenas. That is an experience, I can tell you, flying in a small plane in and out of those mountains.'

Twenty minutes later the theme tune of *Dr Zhivago* comes across the plane's intercom so I know we must be about to land. I dash across to the starboard side and have time to catch a glimpse of the Straits of Magellan opening up to meet the Pacific Ocean. I am thrilled. I have been almost everywhere else in the world, but I have never seen the Straits of Magellan before. There are oil installations on the northern side of the Strait. I suppose they belong to the Chilean National Oil Company. Across the water, as we come in to land, I see the low dark hills of Tierra del Fuego – the land of fire.

Punta Arenas is a frontier town. If the description had not already been worked into the ground I would even go so far as to say it is the last frontier town. Where else can you go before dropping off the edge of the world? I shared a taxi from the small airport into town with a schoolteacher and a construction worker. We had the kind of conversation one usually has with people in taxis. English – good! Argentines – bad! I hadn't quite realized how many friends Mrs Thatcher has in the southern hemisphere.

Twenty kilometres' ride along the shore of the Magellan Straits, past grazing sheep and some rundown houses lying between the road and the water, brings us to the town. Rows of bungalows with corrugated iron roofs of various colours mark the outskirts of Punta Arenas. Towards the centre there are two-storey or three-storey buildings. The post office in the main street has a sign outside saying 'Telegrams and telexes can be sent to Chilean Antarctica'. A strong wind blows and the water in the harbour, reached when the taxi brings me through the town to the dock, looks decidedly choppy. Riding about half a mile off shore, her bright red hull contrasting with the waves and the sombre background of Tierra del Fuego, I can see the *John Biscoe*.

Sr Calderón, the long-suffering BAS agent in Punta Arenas, counsels patience when I corner him in his office. 'There's no point in trying to swim out to the ship,' he says. 'The weather's too rough for the *Biscoe* to put in to the quay at the moment. But she'll come in tomorrow or the next day or the next. She's late arriving anyway.' He explained that because of the difficulties Britain was having with Argentina BAS vessels were not using the Magellan Straits even though it was an international waterway, but were passing round Cape Horn instead, which of course added considerably to the length of the journey.

Taking up one whole wall behind his desk is a magnificent old map of the southern ocean, charting the winds and the waves as well as the lands and islands of these parts. I can see that Punta Arenas lies further south than any other town in the world. Further south than Christchurch, New Zealand. Much further south than Cape Town. I have to content myself for the time being with tracing the *Biscoe*'s intended route, while hoping that the wind will drop at least sufficiently for the passengers to join ship.

'Why don't you go to the hotel for the night?' Sr Calderón advises. 'We'll telephone you there as soon as there's any news.'

The dining-room of Hotel Los Navegantes was, it seemed to me, full of stranded BAS passengers. Though I had met Adrian Berry at the party in London and (briefly in the course of my visit to Cambridge before Christmas) Anne, Rowena and Carys, this was the first time I had encountered Steve Stephenson and Colin Bertram, those legendary figures from the annals of Antarctic exploration. Fifty years earlier Colin and Steve had headed for the Antarctic on board the *Penola*, a wooden three-masted schooner which the British Graham Land Expedition had bought for £3,000. She had covered the 7,500 miles to the Falklands in seventy-four days even though only five of her thirteen-man crew had had previous sea-going experience. The *Penola* spent the first winter frozen in; in the spring the members of the expedition worked day-and-night shifts for three days sawing the ice up to free the ship. Having Colin and Steve on board during the *Biscoe*'s voyage through the Antarctic was an extraordinary privilege. It was a palpable link with the 'heroic' age.

The tone of that first meal was, of course, subdued as befitted the occasion. I was not the only one to have flown half-way round the world to be separated from destiny by half a mile of choppy water. Conversation consisted mainly of 'I say, would you mind passing the butter. No, after you of course, help yourself', or, 'Do you think they have any pickles here?'

That day, as well as meeting Bertram and Stephenson, I met Munro Sievewright for the first time. Munro, a former BAS scientific officer who had moved over to the administrative side, was taking advantage of the *Biscoe*'s almost unprecedented tour of four out of five BAS bases (we *weren't* visiting Halley on the Weddell Sea ice-shelf because the distances to be covered were altogether too great) to conduct his own brief tour of inspection.

In the course of our voyage we all came to know each other fairly well. That is the way things are on voyages. One thing that came over to me quite clearly, even at that first lunch, was how much my fellow passengers all knew about the subject and how little I knew myself. When Anne Todd, for example, quoted the *bon mot*, 'For science, trust Scott, for sport, go for Amundsen; but if you want someone to help you out of a hole, call for Shackleton', there was a small knowledgeable chuckle from the assembled party – all men and women who knew their Antarctic onions.

I had been reading on the long flight down from New York Roland Huntford's book *Scott and Amundsen: The Race to the South Pole.* Scott, according to Huntford, was an incompetent bungler or a dangerous egocentric or both.

'What do you think about the Huntford view of Scott?' I addressed my remarks to no one in particular. 'I have just finished the book.'

The temperature in the dining-room of Los Navegantes descended a perceptible notch or two. Colin Bertram, ahead of the field and already on the cheese course, snorted something which sounded like 'disgusting', pushed back his chair and said he was off.

I decided to shove Huntford's book under my mattress once we were on board the *Biscoe* – if we ever got on board the *Biscoe* and if I indeed had a mattress.

Late that afternoon I climbed up the hills behind the town in the general direction of Santiago. An hour's steady walking brought me to a vantage-point from which I could see the corrugated expanse of Punta Arenas spread out below me at the water's edge and, beyond the town, the still troubled water of the Magellan Straits. The *Biscoe* rode at anchor out to sea, just as she had that morning. From the distance the ship was a mere pinprick of red, a round barrel being tossed capriciously by the waves.

She finally came into harbour around 9 p.m. We were advised to spend the night in the hotel before boarding the next day. In the hotel bar somewhere around midnight, I ran into a BAS pilot who had just come up from the Antarctic on board the *Biscoe*, having completed his tour of duty. He said he would be flying back to the UK from Chile.

'How did you get down there?' I asked.

'We flew from Britain.' He told me the route the De Havilland Twin Otter had taken. Iceland, Greenland, the North of Canada, then down across the

United States to Peru and along the spine of South America until it was time for the last jump across the Drake Passage to Antarctica itself. Three weeks' flying in all. Later, when we ourselves reached Antarctica, we would fly around in BAS Twin Otter aircraft (Twotters for short). Sturdy enough planes though they may be, they are a far cry from a Boeing 747. Going to Antarctica in one of the 'red jobs' (BAS planes, like BAS ships, are painted bright red) is no mean feat.

'We were forced down in Peru,' the pilot told me over a drink in the bar. 'I think they may have put sugar in the petrol because the engines failed soon after they let us leave.' He spoke nonchalantly. Nonchalance becomes a habit with such men.

There is a blonde, bronzed woman in the bar as well. She, like the pilot, has come in to Punta on the *Biscoe*. I learn that she is the first British female geologist to have wintered in Antarctica. Actually, the first British female *tout court* to have stayed down there through the long dark night. I wanted to ask her what it was like, but the party broke up before I had a chance.

I went to bed finally with a certain sense of relief. If the *Biscoe* had been able to put in to Punta Arenas, presumably she should be able to put out again as well.

The agent's minibus came to pick us up the next morning and we drove down to the dock. A Chilean soldier waved us through the gates. 'Don't photograph the warships,' he warned. The *Biscoe*'s captain, Chris Elliott, welcomed us on board at the head of the gangway, shaking eight hands in turn. He was a young man, with light brown hair and eyes of that pale grey steely colour which comes from a lifetime spent squinting at far horizons.

'Hello,' he said when it was my turn. 'I think we've got a telex for you.'

The telex, it turned out, was for Adrian Berry from the foreign desk of the *Daily Telegraph*. They wanted a piece about the Chilean reaction to the Beagle Channel business.

'What Beagle Channel business?' asked Adrian. 'What Chilean reaction?'

I had read *El Mercurio* in the plane.

'The Pope is about to sort it all out. Or at least that's what the paper said yesterday.'

'We had better get today's paper if they have one. Do you read Spanish?'

'*Más o menos*,' I replied.

There was a blackboard slung from the railing beside the gang-plank. It said: '*John Biscoe* sails 1700 hours for the DEEP SOUTH today. Shore leave ends 1600 hours.'

We walked back into town, from the dock. Adrian found a pair of shoes which fitted his extra-large feet – for some reason he had arrived without shoes – and a copy of the local Punta rag. We found a reference to the Beagle Channel settlement on an inside page. It actually turned out not to be a settlement as such, more an announcement of the intention to settle.

'That'll do.' Adrian knew that he had enough material for a story.

Back on the ship – I quickly learned not to call the *Biscoe* a boat with so many serious sailors around – Adrian bashed out his piece. It was date-lined from Adrian Berry, science correspondent on board the *John Biscoe* in the Beagle Channel. 'Chileans rejoiced today', Adrian began, 'at the news that the Pope has finally decided to recognize the justice of their claim to the long-disputed islands in the Beagle Channel and to the fabulous wealth of the Antarctic seas beyond . . . '

When Adrian showed me his completed copy before handing it over to the ship's radio-operator, a good woman called Dallas who had quite enough of both of us by the end of the voyage ('I say, Dallas, you couldn't possibly transmit this two-thousand-word telex before breakfast for me, could you?'), I tried feebly to remonstrate.

'Actually, Adrian, we're not in the Beagle Channel. We're in the Straits of Magellan. And the Pope hasn't actually found in favour of the Chileans yet. All it says is that he is going to give his decision.'

'He will,' Adrian replied firmly, as one who knew the mind of God.

Shore leave ended as planned. At the last minute a local taxi drew up to the ship's side containing about sixteen people who jumped out and stood alternately waving and dabbing their eyes with handkerchiefs.

Munro Sievewright, standing next to me, explained in a Scottish accent which years in the south, including the farthest south, had barely modified: 'That'll be Miriam Booth's family. She's BAS's agent in Stanley. Her people come from here. She's been visiting friends and relatives in Punta. She'll come on to Antarctica with us and back to the Falklands that way.'

In the event, poor Miriam spent much of the journey to Antarctica and on up to the Falklands in her cabin prostrate with sea-sickness. But all that was still ahead of us.

At seven minutes past five the crew raised the gang-plank. I stood with Colin Bertram by the rail watching the gap between the ship and the quay widen. The cars on the dock hooted and the *Biscoe* responded with two long blasts from her funnel. As we steamed out into the Strait, several storm petrels took up their position astern, following in our wake. Colin, whom I had discovered to be a mine of information on almost any subject, told me that in the course of the great naval battle fought off the Falklands in 1914, sailors who found themselves in the water after their ship had been sunk were 'picked off' by giant petrels. What a way to go!

'Mind you,' adds Colin, 'petrels are extraordinary birds. I worked with them. Did you know that they will mate for a lifetime? They can fly around the world and a year later come back to nest at exactly the same spot.'

While we stood there watching the seabirds (the first of many hours spent in that manner), a young man called Adrian Henderson introduced himself. He was the ship's doctor and would stay with the *Biscoe* throughout her voyage. Though the sea was calm that evening – after all we were in the relatively sheltered waters of the Strait – Henderson said that when we came out into the open ocean, about 180 miles to the west, we should be hitting some of the roughest waters in the world. He advised a prophylactic Dramamine or two.

Dinner that first night was at 6.30 and thus it would be throughout the voyage. The ship's officers and BAS guests ate in the wardroom, a large light room two floors (or, I suppose, decks) down from the bridge. At one end of the room there was a large picture painted at the time HRH Prince Philip visited BAS stations in Antarctica and subsequently presented to the ship by the artist. It shows the *Biscoe* surrounded by bleak and menacing icebergs. There are also several framed photographs of the *Biscoe* – one shows the ship being 'rescued' by an American ice-breaker after she had been 'packed in' during particularly severe weather.

'Talking of which,' says the Captain, sitting in the 'lounge' part of the wardroom with a pre-dinner glass of sherry in his hand, 'the *West Wind* has ripped a hole in her side. They've had to bring all the geologists home. A Chilean Airforce Hercules is flying down to their base at Rodolfo Marsh with sheets of metal. They're going to try to repair the *West Wind* down there.'

The *West Wind*, I learned, was the United States ice-breaker, a vessel of giant strength which could push through ice which the little fifteen-hundred-ton *Biscoe* wouldn't even sniff at. This time obviously something had gone wrong.

Chris Elliott looked around. Officers and passengers seemed to be all present and correct, most of us like him with a glass in our hands. When the weather became rougher there would be a certain amount of absenteeism as people came to the decision that three square meals a day was altogether too much for a churning stomach. But that first night we were in an optimistic frame of mind. Let the galley do its damnedest. We would be equal to the occasion.

The Captain rose, draining his glass. 'Shall we . . .?' he murmured. The party moved about ten feet across the room to where the tables were already set for dinner.

If I am to tell the plain unvarnished truth – and after all why shouldn't I? – I shall have to admit that the *Biscoe* did us proud *sur le plan gastronomique*, as the French would say. Steve Jesson, the officer in charge of catering, a cheerful individual, regarded it as a point of honour and professional pride not to repeat the same menu (breakfast excepted) in the course of a long voyage – and I believe he succeeded. And even at breakfast, a meal which does not naturally lend itself to variety and intrigue, he often threw in a surprising and unexpected twirl or twiddle, e.g. French bread as opposed to fried bread ('French' in Steve's recipe book meant that the bread was dipped in egg before being fried). Or again, most mornings the three white-coated stewards who looked after us would serve real grapefruit but sometimes, just for a change, Steve would insist that 'chilled grapefruit segments' appeared on the menu.

If I seem to digress for a moment on the subject of ships' food, it is because ships' meals – as anyone who has been on a long voyage knows – assume an important role in the daily rhythm of life. Once breakfast is over there is lunch to look forward to; after lunch, dinner. In the interstices of time, just in case anyone is feeling hungry or bored, the wardroom is open for coffee in the morning and tea in the afternoon – and the pantry next to the wardroom is always available to do-it-yourself activists who wish at unstated moments of day or night to manufacture their own *tartines*.

From a purely logistical point of view, ship's catering on Antarctic voyages is an exercise demanding much competence and preparation. You can't pop in to the nearest supermarket to stock up on Nescafé and tomatoes. Once you've left the last port-of-call – in our case Punta Arenas – you either have what you need on board or you go without.

Most important of all, the regular assembling of our company for meals gave us all a chance to know each other and, in my case at least, to listen and learn. At any one meal there was a great deal of Antarctic experience gathered in the *Biscoe*'s wardroom.

For example the Captain, that first evening, talked about ice. Ice, for him, is not what it is for most of us – something you get out of the fridge and put in your drink. Ice, for Chris Elliott, is the working environment, something you live and breathe.

'Ice has many different forms,' I heard him say down his end of the table, with Bertram and Stephenson, as was proper, in close attendance. 'When it's ten/tenths and packing with an onshore wind, you've not a hope of getting through it. It's easy to be trapped, even on the edge of a field. You're in there. You can see the edge just a few hundred yards away and suddenly you're stuck. You can get dragged by ice-floes over reefs. In the old days of sail-boats it was the ice that drove you back from Antarctica. They didn't have engines to assist them through it. That was possibly one of the reasons why it took the Antarctic continent such a long time to be discovered. You just couldn't get close enough.'

'Will we see any whales?' I asked from my position half-way down on the starboard side.

'Two or three sightings and you'll be lucky. And a sighting might be just seeing a whale blowing on the horizon.'

I longed to see a whale, even just blowing on the horizon. I think it's what I wanted most in life just at that moment.

Colin told us that when he and Steve and the others came down in 1934 and 1935 on the British Graham Land Expedition they saw lots of whales: 'They'd be all around the *Penola*.'

Knowing a man who's seen the sea full of whales means something. You can tell your children and grandchildren about that.

'I hope we *do* see some whales', I said. The idea had an almost mythological quality. In the event, I was lucky. We all were.

Steve was on the whole a more silent man than his fellow explorer, Colin. But when he spoke he was always well worth listening to. He spoke now about Shackleton and about Shackleton's incredible voyage in an open boat from Elephant Island to South Georgia.

'Worsley', Steve recalled in a low staccato manner, 'was Master of the *Endurance* – brilliant navigator. Managed to get a shot at the sun no matter how much that little open boat was rolling. The Falklands were only six hundred miles away. South Georgia was eight hundred miles. But if they had gone to the Falklands, they'd have been going against the prevailing westerlies. Of course, if they had missed South Georgia, they would have had to go on round the world. There was no other land. Once they reached South Georgia, Shackleton had to land on the western side and climb over the mountains to find help. If they had gone round to the other side, the Grytviken side, they would never have been able to put in to land, since the sea would have been against them.'

He went on to recount how Shackleton put a rescue party together in South Georgia and went back to pick up his men who were still stranded.

'I was having dinner in the Café de Paris in London once with Worsley,' he continued. 'He had brought back the ship's bell from the wreckage of the *Endurance* and he insisted on ringing it whenever he wanted the waiter. Finally the manager of the restaurant came up to him and said, "It may be eight bells, sir, but all's not well."'

We ate our way determinedly through that first dinner. The prophylactic Dramamine turned out to be an unnecessary precaution. The sea stayed calm. We passed the gloomy sombre shape of Dawson's Island, the place where so somebody says – the Chileans keep their political prisoners. Even in quiet seas it looks an effective Alcatraz. What must it be like in a storm?

Inevitably talk turns to the weather. At sea, weather is everything. Chris Elliott says that the official Chilean description of the Punta Arenas/Tierra del Fuego area is 'a place of intensive aeolian movement' in other words very windy. Jerry Burgan, the First Mate, who has a cheerful uncomplicated view of life and a nice sense of humour, explains that United States radio gives comprehensive ice reports but the ship is not apparently on the right frequency to receive them. However, he says, BAS bases like Rothera which have their own planes may make aerial surveys of the ice. They also receive satellite data from Cambridge.

'Both the *Biscoe* and the *Bransfield*, as well as two of the four bases, are able to receive instantaneous facsimile transmission from Cambridge.'

Mention of Cambridge – home to so many of those on board – reminds Anne Todd of the time Francis Pym, when he was Foreign Secretary, visited

Cambridge and BAS headquarters. 'A sniffer dog came in and attacked the stuffed king penguin which stands in the entry hall. The dog did considerable damage to a flipper.'

3

Arriving in Antarctica

As we came out of the Magellan Straits there were still mountains on either side, capped with snow, but I could see open water ahead. A greyish sun broke through the clouds from time to time to shine silver on the waves. The petrels followed behind as always, keeping pace with the ship, soaring, swooping, giving occasional beats of their wings, but for the most part just riding the wind.

At around 10 a.m. passengers were asked to assemble in the Fids room for a briefing by the Captain and the First Mate, Jerry Burgan. People who work for the British Antarctic Survey in the Antarctic are called Fids – the name goes back to the time when BAS was called the Falkland Islands Dependency Survey, British Antarctic Territory being then – as it is now – a dependency of the Falkland Islands.

The Fids room is on the lower deck. There is less air but, by the same token, the motion of the ship is also less since we are nearer the centre of gravity. We all looked queasy – it was our first morning in the open sea – but we tried determinedly to keep our minds on what the Captain and First Mate were saying. No smoking on deck, we were told, because we are loaded with fuel. No going up to the bridge when the ship is manoeuvring. Please sign for drinks. Boat drill at 11 a.m. Any questions?

By the same time we finished in the Fids room, the alarm was sounding. I stumbled into the cabin which I shared with Adrian to put on the waterproof anorak and trousers which had been air-freighted out from England and then made my way to the boat deck. Each member of the crew, each passenger, knew which boat he had been assigned to – mine was boat number 4 on the port side. As we climbed up the companion-way to the boat deck, one of the crew handed us each a life-jacket. It is bright orange and stamped in black ink with the words PERSONAL FLOTATION DEVICE.

'How long actually could you stay alive in the water?' I asked the First Mate when he came by to check that we were all present and correct and that our life-jackets were properly fitted.

'Oh, about thirty minutes,' he replied cheerfully, 'if you're lucky.'

Conditions worsened steadily during the day. Perhaps I would have felt worse if I hadn't taken a pill, but it is hard to imagine.

'Keep your eye on the horizon.' Charlie Cutsforth, Chief Petty Officer from the engine room and a veteran of at least a score of Antarctic voyages, came on deck in his white grease-stained boiler suit and proffered some friendly advice. It is easier said than done, for the horizon is never where you think it is.

'Yes, she does roll a bit, doesn't she?' Charlie chuckles, swaying gently, almost musically, with the motion of the ship while I seem to be flying from one railing to the other, pausing only long enough to vomit over the side. 'In fact, I'd say it's one of the worst vessels I've known for rolling.'

He is an engineer so he explains the problems scientifically. 'It's a question of the ratio of beam to length. The *Biscoe* is a very broad ship for its length. I've been on eighty ships in my time and this is the worst for rolling, bar one.'

I didn't ask him about the one. I was learning the secret – don't move, don't talk, don't eat. Just try to get through one minute to the next. I found a chair in the 'wet' lab, an area near the after-deck used normally by the scientists from the Offshore Biological Programme – OBP. Because the scientists had done a winter rather than a summer Antarctic programme this year, the 'wet' lab was not in use. There was a fine view of the horizon from every angle – and of some large metal sinks which I presume are normally used for washing marine samples and so forth. The mere sight of them induced another round of nausea. When I recovered I tied the chair to the basin and myself to the chair. The horizon came and went . . . but on the whole I stayed with it. After about sixty hours it was time for bed.

If anything, the motion of the ship is worse at night. You can't tie yourself to a chair. What you do is lie on your stomach and thrust your toes deep down between the mattress and the tail-board of the bunk. Thus anchored, you roll with the ship in a vigorous see-saw movement, one moment head-up, the next head-down.

The problem comes when you drop off to sleep. The grip of the toes is then relaxed; perhaps you turn on your side or back – and the next thing you know you have been shot head first down a chute before sliding back again to hit the base-board with your feet.

Adrian Henderson, the doctor, told me the next day that on occasion, when the ship is rolling violently, he has had to treat people for sheet-burn. 'The friction of the bedclothes in the course of a rough night as you're propelled up and down in the bunk can cause quite severe injuries.'

I can understand now why the navy went in for hammocks. Neat, cheap devices easily stowed. Above all they stay horizontal when the world is tilting topsy-turvy. It's a small matter of physics.

We survived. I survived. I staggered up on deck before breakfast to see that the giant petrels had left us. I guess they'd turned back having seen us well on our way across the Drake Passage. Some smaller birds which I had not yet identified (later I learnt that they are Wilson's petrels) had taken their place.

In the wardroom Jerry Burgan, the First Mate, said he had seen a minke whale during the night.

'It stayed with the ship about five or ten minutes,' Jerry informed us, 'blowing alongside. There was a time when we carried a whale book. We'd write down what we saw. We don't really bother now because the whale sightings are so few.'

Towards the end of the afternoon I went up to the bridge of the *John Biscoe* as we headed south. Jerry showed me round, explaining the various instruments – compasses, radar, satellite navigation systems. The place had a modern up-to-date look about it.

'There are windscreen wipers if you need them.' He flipped a switch to show me. Giant sweepers moved across the transparent shield in front of us.

On the starboard side of the bridge there was a table on which navigation charts were spread. Our course, actual and projected, is plotted hour by hour, pencil lines being drawn on a map with distances and bearings shown.

'We should be crossing the Antarctic convergence tomorrow,' said Jerry. 'That's the place where the cold water coming up from the Antarctic meets the warmer water from the South Atlantic. You see an extraordinary change, a great abundance suddenly of bird life.'

One of the Fids, taking his turn at watch, shouted that he could see a whale blowing ahead – I looked where he pointed and for the first time in my life saw a distant spout of water. It is a thrilling moment. The look-out says he saw another whale that morning. I rather wish they still kept up the book. It would be one way of recording information, however imperfect, about the presence of the world's greatest mammal in the South Atlantic.

I looked down from the bridge to the bows of the ship. The seas were a good deal calmer than yesterday, though there was still a fair amount of swell with waves breaking over the foredeck. There is something profoundly exciting about, literally, plunging our way south – as far south as I have ever been. No sign or hint of land anywhere.

Next day was Sunday. Appropriately, the sun was shining and the sea much calmer. I was no longer glued to my chair in the 'wet' lab with my eyes fixed on the horizon, but was at last able to take an intelligent interest in my surroundings, and in particular in the impressive array of equipment – echo-sounders, water analysers, computers, records and print-outs which are the basic tools of the trade for the scientists who work on the OBP.

Later on in the voyage Martin White – head of OBP – would join the *Biscoe* on its way home from Antarctica after almost twelve continuous months down south. Martin would explain in great detail the purpose and complexity of OBP and in particular its crucial role in assessing populations of krill, that small crustacean at the base of the Antarctic food chain on which so much of the biological productivity of the southern oceans seems to depend. For the time being I had to be content with a whistle-stop tour of the facilities, during the course of which one salient fact emerged: namely, the disappearance of the krill during the 1983 Antarctic winter. The krill population, it seems, simply wasn't where it was expected to be. The OBP scientists sampled and echo-sounded in vain. The dearth of small crustaceans was impressive. The question was: what had happened to them?

I was reminded of how Holden Caulfield in J. D. Salinger's *Catcher in the Rye* asks what happens to the ducks in Central Park when the pond freezes over in winter. The disappearance of the krill seemed to pose a problem of a similar order.

'So where did they go, do you think?' I asked Norman Thomas, the ship's electrician, our guide on this first visit to the *Biscoe*'s scientific quarters. 'Have the Russians hoovered them all up?'

Norman is a cautious Glaswegian, given to thinking before speaking. 'I don't think anyone really knows,' he replied. 'Certainly the Russians and East Europeans have been fishing in Antarctic waters but that couldn't explain the absence of krill. Not by itself, I mean.'

It was a day spent mainly watching the sea – and reading. The ship has a good library of Antarctic books and I ran through volume after volume at a rapid rate. Colin and Steve were pleased to see that the *Biscoe* had a copy of *Southern Lights*, John Rymill's account of the British Graham Land Expedition in which they both served. I had also been reading Vivian Fuchs's story of the work of the British Antarctic Survey since its inception. *Of Ice and Men* is an absorbing account of an enterprise that has grown from small beginnings (the secret naval operation, Tabarin, designed mainly to forestall the Argentines, was the post-war precursor of the Falkland Islands Dependency Survey) into the major and permanent Antarctic presence that is BAS today. Now that the sea was calmer, I found it easier to concentrate on the written word. Reading about Antarctica is probably the next best thing to visiting it. Fortunately, I am going to be able to do both.

After dinner I went out on deck again. It was a particularly beautiful and calm evening. Some little white or greyish-white birds, prions I was told, dashed about in the wake of the ship, and the sun lay low on the horizon. Once we are south of the Antarctic Circle there will be sun twenty-four hours a day because of the way the earth is tilted on its axis.

At dinner we talked about icebergs. There was a time when scientists met in agreeable environments like Boulder, Colorado, and discussed serious scientific papers about how to bring fresh water to drought-ridden places like Saudi Arabia. One proposal, which gained a good deal of currency at the time, was to tow icebergs from the southern oceans to the world's arid lands. The scientists had a field-day calculating the amounts of energy that would be consumed in the tow – assuming a way could be found to overcome the technical problems involved; also how fast the iceberg would melt *en route*. I learned that there are all kinds of icebergs, tabular bergs, glacial bergs, bergs with holes in them, blue bergs, even red bergs – depending on the algal composition of the water. Icebergs are essential elements in the scenery of the Antarctic. You soon become quite a connoisseur of the different shapes and sizes. I looked forward to seeing my first iceberg.

Before the meal ended Dallas – our radio-operator – came down with a message for the Captain. She said the BAS station of Faraday on the Antarctic Peninsula had been on the air. They have fast ice down there so we'll have difficulty putting in. Chris took it calmly.

'We'll send a Zodiac in with the mail and call in ourselves on our way back when the ice may have cleared. We can make a wide swing round the west end of Adelaide Island to get to Rothera.'

'What happens', I asked, 'if you can't get in at all?'

'Oh, they just have to wait another year,' Chris replied with a smile.

In the Antarctic, more than most other places, the 'window of opportunity' is narrow.

Adrian Berry says that to him this trip to Antarctica is much the same as going to outer space. Adrian has written two novels set in outer space – I have read and enjoyed them both and am prepared to believe that he knows whereof he speaks. He says the sea we have been steaming across these last several days could be infinity; the birds we have seen could be visiting asteroids. I, in turn, produce a quotation from one of the books I've been reading on the way down. It comes from the opening pages of Admiral Richard Byrd's story of his journey to the Pole: *Discovery*.

'Of all the continents,' writes Byrd, 'Antarctica is the fairest, white and unspoilt, spacious and austere, fashioned in the clean, antiseptic quarries of an ice age.'

Munro Sievewright has a more practical view. He talks about the unique positioning of the poles, in particular the South Pole, for geophysical work. To a layman like myself he patiently explains the workings of the solar current, those streams of charged particles which reach the earth after electrical activity on the sun, to be deflected around the poles, thus setting up disturbances in the ionosphere.

'Research has to be cost-effective,' Munro reminded us all just in case we were in danger of forgetting. 'The Antarctic is an excellent place for geophysical research, as you'll see when we get to Faraday . . . '

I was up on deck early. This is the day of our first landfall in Antarctica and not a moment of it is to be missed. The birds seemed to sense that this was a special occasion because they were out in force. Cape pigeons, otherwise known as pintado petrels – white with black markings on the wings – skimmed across the surface of the water. Ernest Shackleton, writing in *South* (another of the books I had read on the way down) says about Cape pigeons: 'These little black and white birds have an air of friendliness that is not possessed by the great circling Albatross.'

I could see what Shackleton meant when, further astern, sweeping in wide arcs into the wind, then rising and banking to turn, I saw a pair of black-browed albatross, a species which we would later observe in all its abundance as we beat our way up from the South Orkneys to Bird Island. And the prions, of course, were there too – smaller and quicker than the others and harder to see as they darted in and out of the waves.

We are all up on the bridge or the monkey-deck. Binoculars bring the horizon nearer. At 1.26 p.m., far away on the port bow, we see the first iceberg, gleaming white and majestic in the sun and quite unencumbered by any smaller acolytes. At about the same time two or three whales blow to starboard, spouts of water shooting into the air, deep calling to deep. You look with binoculars at the spray; it is there one second, gone the next. You keep the glass trained on the ocean, hoping to catch the next burst as it happens. Too far away to photograph, too far away to hear the noise of the water-pipes, you know none the less that somewhere out there the great beasts are moving through the water.

The radar on the bridge is picking up the coastline ahead of us now, but still there is nothing in sight. The sea is dead calm; the sun strong; a small party of birds has congregated on the water ahead of the ship – half a dozen albatross, a score of Cape pigeons, joined later by one or two southern fulmars.

Around three o'clock in the afternoon, we were near enough to land for the barrier of ice ahead of us to be clearly distinguished. I shall never forget those few hours as the *Biscoe* drew steadily nearer to the Antarctic Continent. That barrier of ice began as a thin line on the horizon, like some ridge in a plaster of Paris map. As the afternoon passed, it grew and grew until it seemed that we were approaching great towering cliffs of ice.

'That's Anvers Island,' said Jerry, 'still about twenty miles ahead of us, I'd say. See the peak rising up behind the ice-barrier? That's Mount Fosse – it's over nine thousand feet high. There aren't many places in the world where ice-covered mountains rise sheer out of the water as they do here.'

I was standing next to Anne Todd on the bridge, and asked her, banally, how she felt at this first glimpse of land. She was overcome with emotion. Finally she said, 'I think it's a dream; I think I shall wake up in a moment and find myself back in Cambridge.'

The icebergs, after that first solitary sentinel, came thick and fast. As we neared land we passed increasing numbers of them. Adrian, whose enthusiasm is always infectious, stepped below for half an hour to dash off a piece for the thousands, possibly millions, of *Daily Telegraph* readers anxious for news of his whereabouts. He began by quoting Coleridge's 'Ancient Mariner': 'We were the first that ever burst Into that silent sea.' It is not exactly the truth, certainly not the whole truth, but we know what he means. He went on to talk about 'crusader castles floating past' and 'palaces of ice'. It is good heady stuff and Dallas, our loyal radio-operator, took it from him with a smile to send off at once from her 'shack' on the upper deck. The article duly appeared the following morning on breakfast tables up and down the country. It was all a far cry from the days when explorers raced hundreds of miles to the nearest telegraph office to be the first to report the news of their exploits. Winning the race was one thing. Communicating the fact that you had won was another thing altogether. The truly successful polar explorers managed to do both.

I spent the afternoon on the monkey-deck before going down to the wardroom somewhat reluctantly for dinner. Just as a matter of record our dinner menu tonight – the night of our landfall in Antarctica – began with water-melon and stuffed peppers, followed by braised beefsteak, onions, Maquis potatoes, dressed cabbage and butter beans; it ended with strawberries and ice-cream, cheese and biscuits, tea or coffee. As we sat at the table, icebergs in all their varied shapes and sizes and colours sailed past the windows. One unexpected occupational hazard – apart from over-eating – was that my neck became sore because I had been turning it constantly from side to side to take in the full wonders of the scenery, and the skin had been chafed by the collar of the sturdy BAS shirt issued to me in Cambridge.

Chris told me that in the old days, when the BAS station was on Adelaide Island, they used to call it Iceberg Alley.

'I'm sorry I can't produce some thick pack-ice for you and have the ship creaking and groaning its way through. You have to wait till the end of the summer. Do you have the time?'

The last thing any Captain wants to do is have his vessel trapped by ice. It may make a striking photograph, but if you're trying to stick to a tight schedule which has been worked out months in advance it's a positive disaster.

'We stopped at Palmer once,' Chris said. 'That's the US base on Adelaide Island. There's a good anchorage there. But we had no sooner sat down to dinner than an iceberg loomed up behind the ship almost blocking us in, so we had to move off again very quickly.'

By 8 p.m. we were slowing down and nosing our way through the icebergs along what is known as French Channel. This is not a passage between islands. It is a passage between reefs and obviously great care has to be taken. A bottle of wine was brought up to the monkey-deck and half a dozen of us were celebrating our arrival in Antarctica. As we raised our glasses we passed an iceberg with a great big hole in it, and we could see through the hole to the sea and the ice-cliffs of the continent beyond.

According to Munro: 'These bergs we are seeing don't come from the shelf ice. They probably come from glacier ice and have calved locally. The big tabular or flat-topped bergs are the ones which have come from the shelf ice. You have icebergs a hundred miles or so long. Some of them have been tracked by satellites for years floating around the world. The blue compressed ice you can see can be millions of years old. You've got shelves which can be five or six hundred feet thick.'

One of the crew added that he once sailed alongside an iceberg which they reckoned was 400 miles long. They never knew what became of it.

Just before 9 p.m. I saw my first penguin on an ice-floe. It tottered into the water as the ship came close and we all cheered.

Faraday station is on Gerlíndez Island, one of the Argentine group. (Gerlíndez was one of the French explorer Charcot's people. Colin tells us that, when still a student at Cambridge, he went to Greenland with Charcot.) The *Biscoe* – flag flying – dropped anchor amongst the icebergs out in the bay. Gemini – with the mail on board and some supplies which can't wait for our return from Rothera to be delivered – is hoisted out over the starboard after-deck. The First Mate, Jerry, gets in with a couple of the crew and they are lowered into the water. Seconds later the engine of the Gemini has started and the rubber boat nips smartly in and out of the bergs to cover the mile or so which separates the *Biscoe* from the shore.

Standing next to me, as I watched the Gemini make its quick shuttle between ship and shore, is a pilot, Santiago Cervantes. He is on his way south to Rothera under a three-year BAS contract. He tells me that he has thrown up his job in Scotland to come down here. It's something he has wanted to do for a long time.

'Is flying down here very different from flying elsewhere?'

'It certainly is. One of the techniques, for example, is that you trail the plane's skis in the snow when you come in to land, checking for crevasses. It's a trial go-round. If you don't like it, you don't land.'

'Do you land on water as well?'

'No,' Cervantes replies. 'They used to use floats in the old days – with the British Graham Land Expedition, for example – but they don't any more. It's too dangerous. The smallest piece of ice can do damage to an airplane on take-off. Even when they were using flying boats on the Solent, they always had to sweep the water.'

Two days later we would fly out from Rothera in a ski-equipped Twin Otter and I would have a chance to appreciate at first hand something of what Cervantes was describing.

At about 11 p.m. I went up on deck again. The sun had been hanging in the sky, low and orange, for the last half an hour. The icebergs were lined up like the fleet at Spithead, grey and black shapes in the dying light. The only sound in the stillness was the noise of the ship's engines and the wake that rippled and curved behind us as we continued to make our way south. Thirty feet away from us, on the starboard bow, we glimpsed the back of a whale – too briefly to be able to say for sure what kind of whale. A minke whale, probably, or a humpback. And then, stretched out on an ice-floe and totally undisturbed by the passage of the *Biscoe*, I observed a crab-eater seal. Though we would see in the course of our voyage hundreds or even thousands of seals, this first sighting for me was especially thrilling. During my time in the European Parliament I was deeply involved with the (successful) attempt to achieve an EEC-wide ban on the import of harp and hooded seal products – a move which dealt a severe and possibly fatal blow to the annual Canadian seal-hunt. I even went up to the Magdalen Islands in the Gulf of St Lawrence at the time when the harp seals were returning from the Arctic to their breeding grounds and saw the magnificent spectacle of thousands of harp seals spread out on the ice with their pups beside them. The harp and hooded seal are kith and kin to crab-eaters and leopards – all of them members of the family of earless seals, known to scientists as *phocidae* – so I experienced, to put it mildly, a deep personal satisfaction at seeing this rather pretty fellow basking on the ice-floe in the last slanting red rays of the sun.

By ten o'clock next day we were running along Adelaide Island ten miles out to sea. We could see the mountains rise in the middle of the island and the great wide glacier swooping down to the water's edge. The pressure of the ice building up behind pushes the glacier towards the coast and causes the icebergs to 'calve'. They call the sheet of ice which leads from the mountains to the sea the piedmont. Stan Jolly, the Chief Engineer, taking a break from his duties, comes to stand beside me on deck:

'It's an amazing sight when the icebergs break off from the piedmont,' he tells me. 'They make a terrific noise. My wife asks me why I keep coming down here. There's nothing but ice, she says. I say, ah, but it's ice in peculiar forms. You have to see it to understand it. You can't describe it.'

Steve comes to join us. He talks about mapping. In those early years of Antarctic exploration, mapping and survey played a crucial role. Often, indeed, it was the principal objective of the expedition.

'How much could you have done from satellite photographs?' I asked, not meaning to imply that I think the painstaking work in the early days – measuring and estimating and reporting – was so much wasted effort, but still it would be interesting to know just how crucial all that plodding around was. If fifty years later the whole of Antarctica could be efficiently mapped as a result of a couple of satellite passes, would it have mattered much if that stream of expeditions – Steve Stephenson's included – had *not* set off for Antarctica in the earlier years of the century?

Steve takes the question in good part. 'Much of the mapping could probably have been done using the satellite data. But some of the more detailed charting and verification on the ground, the ground control if you like, certainly *couldn't* have been done.'

I stayed up on deck for a time, then went down to talk to some of the Fids in the Fiddery – that's the equivalent of the wardroom as far as BAS non-crew personnel on board are concerned. (The crew, who are also BAS employees, have their own quarters, which include a bar with regulation dartboard and pin-ups.)

Four of the Fids came on board at Faraday for the short trip on the *Biscoe* down to Rothera. For them it will mean a break in what is often a somewhat monotonous Antarctic existence. Also, four extra pairs of hands will be welcome at Rothera when the unloading starts. We have a lot of cargo to discharge and time, as always, is short.

The Fids, who are recruited back in England, come down here for two winters and two summers, so they're often away over two years. Some of them even come back for a second tour later on. They're young men, in their prime of life. As the *Biscoe* sailed from base to base in the Antarctic, I came to realize that the people who live and work here, who hold – as it were – certain truths to be self-evident and, most particularly, that wilderness has a special value, are in themselves an important part of the 'message of Antarctica'. These young men, when their tour of duty is over, may leave the employ of BAS and go out into the wider world – if that's the right expression. (Sometimes when you're standing on deck looking at the vast seas dotted with icebergs, it's hard to imagine a wider world.) At all events, they do something different, but they carry with them for ever the memory of these years spent down south. They join the club of men who have had a different vision of the way things are. And some of them perhaps may form part of a constituency whose voice can, I believe, be relied upon to speak up in Antarctica's defence when the need arises.

At Rothera the BAS personnel are engaged mainly on earth sciences; at Faraday, on the geophysical programme. At Signy in the South Orkneys and at Bird Island, off South Georgia, the emphasis is on biological work. By the time the *Biscoe*'s tour was over, I would have gained a very fair impression of the full range of BAS scientific activities and of the dedication of these young men who 'spearhead' its different programmes.

Back on the bridge an hour or so later I took the binoculars out to look at an iceberg a few miles away; it was probably about ten miles long and two miles wide. There was another smaller berg somewhere ahead of us, flat enough on top to land an aircraft. Indeed that feat is not unknown. Nearer at hand, perhaps a quarter of a mile away on the starboard bow, we passed another medium-sized berg. The sea was rougher than the day before and I watched the waves crashing against the deep blue ice, eating away the underside of the berg to create a pronounced overhang, almost like ice-cream spilling over a cone or the beginnings of a mushroom cloud. Coleridge came to mind again. In Kubla Khan he talks about 'caves of ice' – and I could see now what he meant.

Looking at the top of the berg, I noted the layering which marks each successive year's snowfall. Further down, of course, the ice is compacted into a solid mass under the sheer weight of the superstructure.

Steve looks at it with a professional eye. 'That one's going to go soon,' he says – by which he means the berg is going to disintegrate. And he adds: 'Watch out you don't get in the way when they break up. They set off a terrible tidal wave.' That's something I'm glad to know.

At lunch, while we were steering a course parallel to Adelaide Island, we talked about dogs, where to get them, how to use them. 'West Greenland', says Steve, 'is a much better bet than East Greenland. They're a thin weakly lot in East Greenland. Getting good dogs gives you a head start. That was Amundsen's great strength.'

Talk of Amundsen inevitably leads to talk of Scott. In the wardroom there is a copy of a publicity brochure put out by two young men who hope to manhaul a sledge to the Pole following Scott's exact route. The brochure, like any company prospectus, is full of competent realistic detail. The party's sleeping bags, for example, will be much lighter than Scott's; diet will be 'scientifically balanced', not a hit-and-miss affair which led to serious vitamin shortages in earlier days; navigation, as for Scott, will be by the classic methods of sun, star and compass.

The general sentiment among those who sit around the table is one of mild disapproval. People who work for and with BAS are certainly not against heroism. Indeed BAS would not exist had it not been for the heroic efforts of the early pioneers. But on the whole BAS people are against heroism for heroism's sake. There is a strong, though understated, implication in the conversation that 'manhauling' to the Pole was a fairly barmy idea even when Scott did it, though he had every excuse in that his motorized sledges didn't work and his ponies died on him (though he could of course have gone for 'dogs and more dogs' like Amundsen, but that is another story). In their defence, I should point out that the two young men have declared their intention of using any publicity attracted by their exploits to draw attention to the conservation issues in Antarctica.

If talking about Amundsen leads to talking about Scott, talking about Scott leads to talking about Oates.

'A very interesting man,' says Steve. 'With his background in the cavalry, he had a real eye for horses. Did you know there's a new biography out about Captain Oates?'

I wonder as we sit there whether in fact Oates actually spoke that famous line in precisely the words that Scott attributed to him: 'I am just going outside and may be some time.' Scott certainly had a gift for a telling phrase. It is quite possible, I suppose, that the gallant Captain said something altogether less felicitous which was then transformed by the magic of Scott's pen and the mysterious alchemy of death with honour.

Out on the deck Ray, one of the three stewards who take it in turns to serve the wardroom, has rigged up a record-player and a loudspeaker. Some Fids gather to sun themselves and listen to the music. It is a strange juxtaposition – the clear, completely cloudless sky, the white cliffs of Antarctica gleaming in the distance, this vast empty land whose only true inhabitants are the birds and the whales, the seals and the penguins, and then, suddenly bearing down from northern latitudes, comes a ship of fools, some of them stripped to the waist in the surprising warmth of the sun, listening to Mike Oldfield and Bruce Springsteen turned up full blast.

Just after 4 p.m. we turned 20° to port. We had been steaming for most of the day more or less south along Adelaide Island. Now we are tucking in behind it. It turns out that we are not going to go all the way to Rothera this evening; we are going to anchor somewhere and go on in early tomorrow morning.

As we change course a skua – a large browny-black bird, a kind of Antarctic crow which is mainly a scavenger, preying on other birds' eggs and any carrion it can find – wheels overhead. On land I would learn to watch out for skuas. They have a nasty habit of making kamikaze attacks on unsuspecting visitors, dive-bombing from a distance with loud screeching calls and occasionally slashing an uncovered head with their sharpened claws.

Rounding Adelaide Island you can see – on the other side of Marguerite Bay – the mountains of Alexander Island, named by the Russian explorer Thaddeus Bellingshausen in honour of the Tsar. BAS used to have a base on Adelaide Island before they moved to Rothera. Munro tells me that the Chileans are now going to take it over.

'This is helpful,' he says. 'It means that Chileans won't be using our airstrip at Rothera. They fly down from their base at Rodolfo Marsh and this area is a good staging-point for them. They were doing a certain amount of damage to the ski-way. You have to be terribly careful, you know. If you let things fall on the ski-way, the snow ablates and you get snow-melt holes and so forth which can cause problems. So everyone is quite happy with the idea of the Chileans using our old base. The agreement hasn't been formalized yet, but that's the reality.'

I ask whether the Chileans are doing serious scientific work and Munro replies diplomatically that 'they're probably doing good meteorology at Rodolfo Marsh'.

Towards evening, we slowed right down because of ice-floes ahead. I saw my first bunch of a dozen penguins standing on the spur-arm of one of the icebergs. I could hear their squawking as the *Biscoe* went past at a distance of, I suppose, eighty yards. In fact, as I looked around, I could see groups of penguins on several of the ice-floes, standing together stiff and upright, black and white on white. One of the Fids said they were Adélies and I felt sure he was right. I was going to have to bone up on penguins.

The extraordinary thing is that when you look closely at the water you can see that this too is literally teeming with penguins. Every few seconds a bird lunges forward through the sea, almost like a dolphin leaping. Some penguins – swimming alongside with this butterfly stroke or 'porpoising' motion – almost manage to keep pace with the ship. I can hardly believe what I'm seeing.

At dinner the look-out on the bridge uses the intercom to tell the ward-room: 'Whales four points to starboard.' So we all rush up to the bridge but, unfortunately, see only a distant glimpse of whales breaking the surface.

Stan, the Chief Engineer, tells us how last season when they were coming down from Rio, they were all on deck doing boat-drill 'and there was a hump-back whale proceeding calmly, sedately about its business. Down, up, blow: down, up, blow. Whales are a symbol if you like,' says Stan. 'If we can keep them alive, then maybe the world isn't so bad after all.' He adds: 'If you're close enough, you can hear the whoosh as they blow.'

After dinner we dropped anchor in Jennie Bay. This would be our haven for the next twelve hours, provided no icebergs loomed up against the ship in the course of the night. Now that the ship's engines had been turned off the silence was, as Stan put it, 'deafening'.

'When you get to the base,' says Stan, 'you ought to go and walk. Walk for miles beyond the base. Sit down. It's the only place in the world where you'll be able to hear your own heartbeat. I was walking in South Georgia once, in Grytviken, in the mountains behind the base. I heard steps behind me – I turned round, but there was nobody there. It was the echo of my own footsteps.'

Precisely because of the silence the sounds that there are in Antarctica – the call of the birds, the bark of the seals – can seem extraordinarily loud and distinct. Because we live our lives surrounded by so much background noise, other sounds are lost or blurred. Here there is no blurring. In its way, pure silence is as intoxicating as pure oxygen.

I turned in at last, passing by the pantry outside the wardroom for a do-it-yourself midnight snack, like any truant schoolboy. There is a notice pinned up – for the steward's information – entitled 'Officers' Steak List'. It shows the preferences of captain and brother officers. Chris Elliott, I note, likes his steak medium-rare. It seems a good note on which to end the day.

Jennie Island (named after someone's wife) is a small mountain, its sides rising sheer and dramatic from the sea, which guards the entrance to Rothera Bay. It provided us with shelter for the night. Around four o'clock in the morning, another glorious calm sunny morning, we slipped our anchor and entered the short channel which led into the bay. It was the New World Symphony all over again: brilliant sunshine, the red hull of the *Biscoe* moving majestically through the water and on the far distant shore we know the welcoming party will be waiting.

The Captain is always on the bridge in person when his ship is entering or leaving harbour. If something goes wrong, it's no excuse for him to say he wasn't around at the time. Chris scans the channel ahead and the ice-floes which dot our path. 'Often we don't have good information on the charts, even though a particular stretch of water may have been travelled quite frequently.'

Charting – and reporting the findings to the Admiralty's hydrographic division in Taunton – is still an important task for ships like the *Biscoe* and the *Endurance* which find themselves frequently in Antarctic waters. Echo-sounders and satellite navigation systems have made the job easier than it used to be in the old days but the essential principles and techniques remain the same as they have for centuries.

Steve has pasted up a large-scale map of Antarctica on an ordnance survey sheet of London. He takes it out of his pocket and shows me precisely where we are going. For Steve and Colin, this is a high point, the search for lost time at last rewarded. Above all they hope that the weather will be clear enough for them to be able to fly down from Rothera to the very place on King George VI Sound (named by the British Graham Land Expedition) where they and their colleagues had their camp fifty years before.

The ship scrunches against the smaller chunks of ice as it crosses the bay. We see a group of crab-eater seals on a floe and then a dark shape in the water, possibly a leopard seal.

Colin says: 'Leopard seals are solitary wanderers. You can see them going after a penguin, catching and almost shaking it out of its skin.' Two more crab-eaters on a floe, one lying on its back sunning itself. Two skuas in a hurry come out to inspect us, flapping overhead and then taking up their position astern. We can see the wireless mast of Rothera base now, but we can't see the huts yet because they are still round the point.

Shortly before six a.m. the ship moved very slowly, very quietly on the last slide into Rothera. The water was dead flat and quite calm. We could now see the base huts quite clearly. The main living accommodation was a two-storey hut on the right as you looked at the shoreline; on the left there was a one-storey building which housed supplies and equipment and workshops. Two large tractors which would help in the unloading were already waiting for us by the water's edge; over to the left, the land rose evenly. This was the ski-way leading up to the airstrip about four kilometres away on the glacier.

I wonder, as we come in, what we must look like to the party gathered on shore waiting for us. These bases are about as remote as any place on earth. For six months of the year, since the sun doesn't appear over the horizon, they're in complete darkness. During the summer, daylight returns but contact with the outside world is at best sporadic. There are occasional visits by the BAS supply and research vessels – the *Bransfield* and the *Biscoe* – and possibly by tourist vessels such as the *Lindblad Explorer* which pass by and decide to land a shore party or two to visit the bases. (Such visits, I discovered, are viewed rather ambivalently. Any break in the monotony is to be welcomed; on the other hand tourist visits can disrupt the scientific work of the base besides risking damage to the environment.) Apart from the ships, there are wireless and telegraphic communications – each Fid is allowed to send and to receive a strictly limited number of words each month. But essentially this is isolation of the most total kind.

We lower the ship's launch, a solid competent-looking craft which now chugs over to the shore with two lighter cables to which the heavy stern lines are attached. The *Biscoe* winches itself in until it is about one hundred yards from the shore, a small reception party watching our arrival. There is a rattle of chains as we drop anchor. Adrian and I, immediately and hopefully, boarded the launch as it lay alongside the foredeck with its engine bellowing poisonous fumes into the unpolluted air. We then had to wait a good half-hour while cargo of various kinds was loaded on board to make the short trip to the shore.

Even when conditions are perfect – and they're not perfect today – the *Biscoe* can't go right in to shore. There is no jetty; so discharging cargo is necessarily a laborious job, involving scores of round trips. The bulky items, in particular the drums of aviation fuel, are loaded on to the scow, a vessel which looks like an oversize builders' skip which is in turn towed by the launch.

I asked Jerry Burgan whether the barrels of fuel couldn't simply be pushed over the side and guided in the direction of the shore where the base's mechanical lifter could fish them out of the water. Since oil is lighter than water, surely the barrels would float? Such a system, I suggested, would avoid some of the laborious manhandling.

Jerry replied that he too had thought of that idea and indeed once – when they were visiting a base in Deception Island – they had actually tried it. It hadn't worked. The drums had all been bobbing about in the water when the wind got up and the oil was blown about in all directions. It had been the devil's own job, Jerry said, to fish the drums out again and even then they hadn't recovered them all.

At last we were ready. Carys Williams and Miriam Booth stepped on board the launch to join us – they had wisely waited until departure was imminent. The engine note changed as we pulled away from the *Biscoe*'s side to head for the shore all of two hundred yards away.

4

Rothera

When Neil Armstrong, back in 1969, became the first human being to set foot on the surface of the moon, he spoke about a small leap for man being a giant leap for mankind. I felt a bit like that when the scow bumped up against the rock at the water's edge and, one by one, we leapt across the gap. A line from Caesar's *Gallic War* came back to me, probably the first Latin I ever learned: *Desilite, inquit, milites!* This is what Caesar's captain says to his men as they approach Britain's rocky coast: Jump down, soldiers! For Britain read Antarctica. For soldiers read BAS's assorted guests. And for the subject of the sentence, the man who is doing the ordering, read John Hall, a lithe fair-haired scientist who, as Base Commander at Rothera, was waiting on the shoreline in his orange Antarctic clothing to receive the emissaries of the *Biscoe* on her annual visit to his domain.

We would talk to him at length later. For the moment John Hall was occupied with the unloading operation. The base was equipped with a couple of Muskeg forklift tractors and these were now busy removing and storing the supplies as fast as the scow brought them over. In addition to oil and other supplies, the *Biscoe* was delivering several new skidoos to be added to the thirty or so which the base already held. We watched while the crates containing the skidoos were unloaded from the scow and then we followed Munro up to the base itself.

Because most of the Rothera hands were involved with what was happening at the water's edge, Munro showed us round. We saw the bunks (the men sleep two and sometimes four to a room); the library, well stocked with novels but also with a good selection of Antarctic literature (books of every sort are a necessity during the long dark Antarctic winters); the desalination plant, particularly important in the summer when you can't get enough fresh water from snow-melt; the electricity generating units. Upstairs was a large, light, airy room amply equipped with fire extinguishers.

'In this ultra-dry Antarctic environment,' Munro tells us, 'fire is a very real danger. Everybody has to have fire training.' It's not hard to understand the fear of fire. Much of the base is constructed from combustible material. A fire, once it starts, can be very difficult to control. You can't ring for the fire engines. If your hut burns down, you can't take shelter with your next-door neighbour. All BAS bases are equipped with emergency huts set apart from the main buildings, stocked with emergency supplies to last a limited period of time – hopefully until help arrives. But fire precautions, carefully thought out and stringently applied, are the best guarantee of safety.

There are other dos and don'ts on an Antarctic base. I noticed a list pinned up on a board as we came into the main hut, signed by John Hall, Base Commander.

'Don't litter the ski-ramp'. This, as I already know, is not just an injunction based on aesthetic considerations. It's a matter of keeping the planes flying. If you can't get up the ski-ramp because the snow has melted because people have been dropping litter on it, you can't fly the planes from Rothera; if you can't fly the planes, you can't put the field parties in place and support them as necessary, so you may as well all pack up and go home.

'Don't walk into the nature reserve'. Down towards the point there are areas where scientists have been conducting long-term observations – for example on skua populations, lichen growths, etc. In the Antarctic, as much as anywhere else, there is always a danger that the very presence of scientists will skew the experiments, even when they are taking the greatest of care. The last thing you need is to have random tourism, however well meaning, add to that danger.

'Don't borrow the skidoos'. Skidoos are as vital today as dogs were forty years ago. They have to be kept one hundred per cent fit. They have to be reliable. You have to know when you head out for the next depot of fuel and supplies, fifty or one hundred miles away, that the machine you are riding on is going to bring you safely to your destination. That's not going to happen if people on the base treat skidoos as casually as Oxford undergraduates treat bicycles leaning against a college wall.

Any society needs its list of dos and don'ts. In a place like Rothera where scientists live (sometimes literally) on top of each other, rules – unwritten as well as written – are the necessary lubrication of coexistence. When we were there, there were thirteen scientists at the base. But at the beginning and end of the season that population can rise to over fifty as the field parties either prepare to set out or return to base at the end of a trip. As we walked around, Munro tried to give us a preliminary insight into the work which is being controlled and directed from Rothera.

'About 1,000 miles from here' – pointing the place out on a map which is pinned to the wall in the radio room – 'BAS has a joint project with the Americans – there are twelve Britons and four Americans. That's getting right up towards the Pole. Here at 67° South, we're 1,380 miles from the Pole. It's sixty miles for every minute of latitude.'

The radio-operator was talking to the Twin Otter aircraft which had taken off from the ski-way earlier in the day carrying Colin, Steve, Anne Todd and Rowena Harris on a flight down to Fossil Bluff. This is a Red Letter Day for Steve and Colin since it's almost the fiftieth anniversary to the day of their first visit to that area with the British Graham Land Expedition.

I hear the pilot say over the RT that there's cloud over King George VI Sound and he's not sure whether he will be able to go in under it to land at the BAS Fossil Bluff outpost.

'And if he doesn't?' I ask.

'He'll turn round and come back,' Munro says. 'Or else he'll put down somewhere else.' With skis, of course, and a plentiful supply of glaciers, landing-places are not so hard to find.

The radio operator flips a switch and some 'pop' music blares out. 'Radio Rothera,' he tells us proudly. 'Our own way of keeping in touch. It can be picked up over a fifty-mile radius.'

He flips the switch again and we hear the pilot of the Otter say that the weather's 'a bit manky but we're going in anyway'.

'Colin and Steve will be pleased.' Munro turns back to the map. 'There's another party doing aeromagnetic work here at Martin Hill.' He points to an area about 600 miles south of Rothera. 'And then we've got four geologists in the Thiel Mountains, working on nunataks.'

'What are nunataks?'

'Isolated rocky outcrops. You'll be seeing some later.'

As we stand there in front of the map, he briefly explains the Gondwanaland theory: how Antarctica, still joined to Australia, floated away when the great super-continent that was Gondwana broke up; how Australia in turn split off and Antarctica came to rest in its polar position. 'Actually, Antarctica is made up of two plates. The reason the geology is so interesting here -- the nunataks and so forth – is that where we are is where the plates came together, fusing and throwing up the mountains.'

This is my first exposure to the Gondwana theory. Suddenly geology comes to life.

Munro continues with his snapshot survey of the work being carried out from Rothera.

'We've some people over here,' he points at the Weddell Sea. 'They're doing work on the ice-shelf. They're using highly sensitive chill meters to find out how the ice feeds into the ice-shelf.' He explains that this particular party will be travelling some 1,500 miles by skidoo on the Ronne ice-shelf, a major feat in itself.

'They have satellite surveyors with them on their sledges. You use them in much the same way as a ship uses its own satellite navigation system. You can achieve pinpoint accuracy and when I say 'pinpoint' I mean within yards.

'They are trying to find out where the ice-shelf rests on the sea; where it rests on the bedrock. They'll be taking radio echo-soundings to find out the thickness of the ice and its internal structures. They'll be using depots put in by air. The Americans from Siple station helped us put some of the depots in.'

Munro's last remark seems to me to be a marvellous illustration of practical peaceful collaboration between nations in Antarctica. Whatever heads of state or government may be saying to each other in the context of their bilateral relationships, down here there are a dozen examples each week of genuine international cooperation. Chilean planes flying south may refuel at Rothera; British planes going over to the easternmost British base at Halley on the Weddell Sea ice-shelf may put in at the Russian base at Druzhnaya. An informal accounting system keeps a rough record of who owes whom how many barrels of fuel – and the system seems to work.

Munro finished his résumé by referring to two parties of geologists and geomorphologists on Alexander Island – one of which we would meet later – as well as a party of glaciologists working at the northern end of King George VI Sound.

'They'll be using current meters to find out what the ice-flows are at the bottom of the ice-sheet. If you didn't get melt at the bottom of the ice-sheet, you would have a constant accumulation on the ice-shelf as new ice is coming in. Since you don't get that constant accumulation, there must be melt at the bottom. What kind of melt is it? How fast does it take place?'

We stand back to look at the map as a whole. It is clear to me that BAS's operation extends much further afield than the Antarctic Peninsula, further indeed than the British sector.

'Of course,' says Munro, 'we are free under the terms of the Treaty to conduct our research anywhere we please – and we do. How far we go, and the kind of research we undertake, is bound to be influenced by logistics. There's been a change in the system of work. In the old days scientists used to come down to winter here and do their work in the summer months. Now we tend to fly them down for the summer season and pull them back when it's over. It makes for a more efficient use of scientific time. So much of the analysis now takes place with highly complicated machinery back in England that it doesn't make sense to let scientists sit around doing nothing for several months each winter and possibly getting frustrated in the process. So we ship them into Damoy – that's a small hut up north of Faraday which we will be visiting later and then we fly up there from Rothera to bring them down. It saves waiting for the ice to clear down here. Once they're at Rothera, they'll be taken on to Martin Hill or wherever they need to be.'

Our talk continues as we go downstairs again and out to the neighbouring hut to look at the generator. Actually there are three generators. Two will be in action most of the time, one is kept as a back-up to be brought into action when the others are being serviced or repaired. (All the mechanical work has of course to be performed by base personnel – you can't ring up the electricity company and ask them to drop by to sort out the problem.) Beyond the generating shed is the repair shop – available for work of all kinds, such as keeping the Nansen sledges (named after Amundsen's famous precursor) in good condition. We also go to look at the stores – stores piled into every nook and cranny. One attic which we visit is stuffed full of Bovril jars, and boxes of Mars Bars and Kelloggs Cornflakes, Huntley and Palmer biscuits, Heinz tomato ketchup. All the household names are there. The place is a snapshot of what people – or at least some people – are eating in Britain in the 1980s and if for any reason culinary habits here change (or Britain goes down the drain) the supplies in that attic – because there seem to be enough to last an age – will surely bear witness to the way things were, just as the supplies still to be seen in Scott's hut on the Ross ice-shelf indicate the tastes of *his* time.

In reality, of course, those supplies, however seemingly copious, are finite and exhaustible. Each last tin and carton is imported from Britain. The quantity and variety of the provisions are worked out down to the last pack of dried milk. They have to meet the normal needs of the base; there has to be a reserve in case of emergencies – a delay in the arrival of the supply ships for example. Yet stocks cost money and take up space – neither is in unlimited supply. Back in Cambridge there are men with quartermaster's training who know how to calculate these things nicely.

The one exception to the otherwise all-British catering was the wine we had with our lunch on the base that first day. It is a respectable Beaujolais which slips down nicely with tinned ham, tinned salmon and home-made bread which we ate in the mess upstairs. (It's hard to imagine how bread could be anything except home-made when you come to think about it.) There was also a rather fine goulash with noodles. I congratulated the cook (he's called Peter Forman and I know he's the cook because he's wearing cook's trousers) and asked him how he likes the life. He tells me he has been here sixteen months with fourteen months to go and he's 'having a marvellous time'.

'Where did you learn to cook?'

'I didn't. I just make it up as I go along. They don't complain.'

Talk about food leads to talk about sewage. 'We've got chemical toilets,' says Peter Forman. 'If you've got five minutes to spare on your way out, you can empty them.' I suppose I asked for that.

Morale is always high on the bases the day a ship arrives. Mail is piled on the table in the mess waiting for the Fids to collect it as they come into lunch. The men on the shore greet friends from the *Biscoe*. Some of the Fids will have done more than one season and the *Biscoe*, like the *Bransfield*, has been a regular visitor for years. We bring news; we also *are* news. The *Biscoe*'s January arrival will feature in letters home and in the base's monthly round-up of news which is telexed to Cambridge as well as being copied to other British bases in Antarctica. (There's a copy of the latest, the December, round-up pinned up in the mess. It's chattily written, beginning with a reference to a Chilean helicopter clattering noisily overhead as the month began, then going on to tell of the various happenings at Rothera, about the ice being 'pretty thick' and 'ships having difficulty getting beyond Penguin Point'.)

After lunch five of us – Adrian Berry, Carys, Miriam, Munro and myself – set off in a Tucker snowcat up the ramp to the ski-way which leads up to the glacier. It's a smooth easy ride; the snowcat has automatic transmission so there's no loss of momentum as you change gear. And it's a brilliantly sunny afternoon. I still find it hard to imagine that I'm in Antarctica. As we climb away, I can see the seals still on the ice-floe where they were when we came in this morning. The way to the airstrip on the glacier is marked with flags. We keep between the flags because there are crevasses all round and even a snowcat could go in.

The glare is strong, so we are all wearing sun-glasses or goggles. Looking through his at the surrounding scenery, Adrian exclaims: 'What a place! Put in some ski-lifts, *téléfériques* and *télécabines* and it would be just like the Alps. Of course, you'd have to de-avalanche it!'

Our arrival at the glacier airstrip coincided exactly with the return of the Twin Otter which had taken the party to Fossil Bluff earlier in the day. The plane, a striking red which contrasts with the dazzling whiteness of the surroundings, appears from behind a mountain and lands on its skis in front of us. It's the first time I've seen a plane land on skis (so many 'firsts' on this trip), and it seems to be a particularly efficient mode of travel in Antarctica. It means you can put down more or less anywhere you can find a flat crevasse-free surface. On both sides of the fuselage the words British Antarctic Survey are painted in large black letters.

As we walk across the snow to board the aircraft the others disembark. Colin and Steve are clearly thrilled with their flight down to King George vi Sound, following in their own footsteps as it were. Rowena Harris and Anne Todd seem hardly less impressed. Now it is our turn. For the pilot, two journeys on the trot to Fossil Bluff means a long day's flying.

There are five seats in the body of the plane. In passenger service, the Twin Otter can carry twenty, but for work down here in Antarctica space is needed for cargo as well. Today we have three drums of fuel on board, a canvas tent, some wires and cable.

We took off at 2.55 p.m. Seconds later we were over the base and the bay where the *John Biscoe* lay at anchor looking like a visitor from another planet. The friendly seals were still basking in the sun. Twenty minutes into the flight, we were over pack-ice, not fast-ice, nothing solid enough to deter a determined vessel, more like a gentle hint of what to expect as the season grows old.

Twenty minutes later we flew fairly low over the Argentine base San Martín, which consisted of two or three large red-painted huts. The Argentines apparently have a considerable presence in Antarctica with a dozen bases dotted about the 'Argentine sector'. I am told that, compared with bas, the

Argentine Antarctic operation is an expensive affair. Most of their bases are manned by soldiers who, under the terms of the Antarctic Treaty, must be unarmed, though whether they actually absolutely are is a moot point. Be that as it may, even unarmed soldiers have to be housed and fed and, above all, paid. The average Argentine conscript who is posted to Antarctica as part of the demonstration of 'effective occupation' is probably being paid twice or three times the normal rate, while each year's service in Antarctica counts double as far as his pension or discharge is concerned.

From the air there was nothing much to be seen; no sign of life or movement. Apparently, if you land at the base, you see a sign saying 'Bienvenido a Argentina' – Welcome to Argentina. We didn't land because we still had a lot of ground to cover: anyway, in the circumstances it didn't seem especially politic. A few minutes later we flew over Stonington, a former British base (Vivian Fuchs was here) now abandoned. Again I could see the huts clearly from the air.

Out over the starboard wing I note that the pack-ice now forms an uninterrupted sheet stretching out as far as the eye can see, which is quite a few miles. I'm reminded of the first time I ever saw pack-ice at close range (as opposed to from stratocruiser height). It was early in 1982 during that visit I made to the Magdalen Islands in the Gulf of St Lawrence to visit the nurseries of the harp seal. Ice, wherever it is, says something to the soul. Poetics aside, Antarctica as a continent is much enhanced by ice. The seas freeze for hundreds of miles around its coasts in winter, effectively doubling its size. As we fly over the Terra Firma Islands (so named by Steve and Colin – I would learn why later), Munro casts a professional eye down on the white desert below.

'It looks solid,' he says, 'but some of that stuff can be awfully rotten. A ship would probably be able to get through it even though it might not be able to steam continuously.'

Looking down from around 8,000 feet it seems strange to me, almost distasteful, that institutions have to be created, and mechanisms devised, to ensure that such beauty remains. How much better it would be, I reflect, if man could stay out of it altogether. If any comfort is to be found, it lies in the fact that there could – as far as environmental protection is concerned – certainly be less effective institutions and mechanisms than those of the Antarctic Treaty. As Hilaire Belloc put it, sometimes it is best to 'hold on to nurse, for fear of finding something worse'.

Our pilot is Gary Studd, a bronzed, bearded man who has been down here for seven seasons. He wears jeans and a denim jacket, and turns round in his seat in the cockpit to address the passengers. 'There's a cloud problem,' he says. 'We've got cloud over King George VI Sound. The question is: can we nip in beneath it to land at the Fossil Bluff base?'

Looking out of the windows of the Twin Otter I could see what he meant.

We were flying more or less south between two lines of peaks. The mountains of Alexander Island were to our east and the mainland to the west. The Sound was directly below us, covered by a thick white layer of vapour extending at least half-way up the line of mountains on either side, though the peaks themselves – on a level with the plane – had burst through into the sun.

'That's Mount Guernsey and Mount Edgel,' the pilot tells us, while he makes up his mind what to do. Finally he says, 'I think we'll go on down.'

We dropped down below the tops of the mountains into the white stuff. Suddenly there was nothing to be seen except a dense fog. The pilot, we imagine, was looking for a layer of visibility between the base of the cloud and the ice of the Sound. He found it. I realized it was not white fog I was staring at below, but white ice and a pile of fuel drums with a Union Jack stuck on top of them. Our skis touched the ground, or rather the ice, of Fossil Bluff base. At 71° 20′ South it was – and remains – my own personal 'farthest south'.

They had heard the plane coming. As we taxied to halt beside the fuel drums and the flag (this is as far south as the Union Jack flies), a small tractor pulling a sledge came towards us through the mist. Barry Finch, one of the two-man team at the base, was driving the tractor to welcome his second party of visitors in the course of a single day. In spite of that he seemed glad to see us.

We draped ourselves across the sledge while Barry turned the tractor round and headed back to the base hut.

Fossil Bluff base is essentially a support base. BAS puts a two-man team in during the summer to stay there a month or five weeks at a time. Their job is to provide logistical assistance for planes and personnel flying further south, to Martin Hill for example, or even the South Pole. The hut, which normally accommodates two, can take ten or twelve people at a squeeze – sometimes planes may fly into the base and then, because of bad weather for example, be unable to continue. The base provides a refuge from the storm.

And a comfortable refuge at that. The tractor, after a journey of about half a mile, deposited us in front of the hut. 'Come on in,' says Barry. 'Dick's got some tea ready.'

Dick Barber is the other half of the two-man team. He had baked some scones in the coal-fired Rayburn, and produces jam, butter, tea and coffee in honour of our visit. There is a generator so we have electric light as well. We sit down on the bunks and help ourselves.

'Five Germans flew in the other day with Dorniers,' says Barry. 'They looked around and took photographs of the flag. They were very interested in the flag.'

Dick Barber in turn explains the geology of the place. 'King George VI Sound is 200 feet of ice down to sea level. Then you've got another layer of ice which could be up to 600 feet thick before you hit the water at the bottom. There's no doubt that this *is* a sound because it's been shown that water moves from one end to the other. There are glaciers coming into the Sound at all sides. It would soon fill up with ice if there wasn't water at the bottom.'

While on the subject of geology, Barber shows us his collection of fossils. 'The place is called Fossil Bluff because of the number of fossils that have been found here, beginning with Launcelot Fleming, the geologist on the British Graham Land Expedition. You've even got some mammalian fossils in Antarctica similar to the kind of fossils that are found in the Andes. That's another piece of evidence for the Gondwanaland theory.'

After tea I climbed up the scree slope behind the hut. This is where the first fossils were found over fifty years ago, long before anyone had heard of Gondwanaland. It's not hard to imagine, in this land where terrestrial life-forms are limited in the extreme – mosses, lichen, bacteria, the occasional cold-enduring mite – how exciting it must have been to have found proof of other higher orders of fauna and flora.

After our visit, instead of taking the tractor and sledge back to the airstrip from the hut, I decided to walk. It was about time I walked somewhere in Antarctica. Scott after all walked all the way to the Pole and back and there were no hot buttered scones waiting for him at the other end. So, doing my bit to live up to the 'heroic' era, I trudged alongside the vehicle as it pulled the rest of the party back to the plane.

'How did the tractor get here anyway?' I shout.

'Years ago,' Barry Finch, who once more is driving, shouts back. 'They drove it down over the ice from Adelaide Island. Took them several weeks. Camped on the ice *en route*.'

The tractor, from the look of it, has done yeoman service over the years. I rather doubt whether at the end of its useful life anyone will drive it back the way it came. It will more likely end up on the rocks behind the hut, a different kind of fossil.

We flew back on the reverse heading taking off through the low cloud and rising into the sunny peak-filled air above. We had been going for about forty minutes when, on the glacier below, we saw tracks which were not made by penguins or crab-eater seals. They are ski-tracks, no doubt about it.

'They could have been made a week ago,' our pilot pokes his head into the cabin to tell us. 'We'll go down anyway and take a look.'

We do a trial circuit, trailing the plane's skis lightly along the surface of the glacier to check for crevasses or collapsed snow bridges, then – on the second go – we land on the glacier. It turns out that we have timed our arrival perfectly for, careering at high speed down the slope towards us as we disembark from our plane, come two bright yellow skidoos and two sunburnt scientists.

'We've brought your mail,' says Gary Studd. 'We took it along just in case we met you. We were lucky to see your tracks from the air. Lucky you were in the vicinity.'

Mike Sharp gets off the lead skidoo. He is tall, with a peeling nose. He's wearing long john underpants because he finds them comfortable to work in and he doesn't expect to be literally dropped in on out of the blue, least of all by *entre autres* two females, namely Carys and Miriam. But the long johns are quite decent and this is Antarctica and anyway, who cares?

He takes his letters gladly. He and his colleague have been sixty-five days in the field already with another twenty or so to go. It's good to have news.

'Air-mail delivery, huh?' He stuffs the letters in the pocket of his pants, to be saved up for reading later during the long evenings ahead.

He tells me, when I introduce myself, that after this stint is finished he'll have done 365 days altogether in the field. And this really is the field. Apart from radio contact with the base at Rothera, they have only themselves for company.

Mike is a mountaineer by training and profession. His job on the two-man team is to make sure that his geologist colleague can do his work safely and effectively. He points out the features of the skidoo to me.

'The two skidoos, as you can see, are roped together and the driver is in turn tied on to the skidoo with a further fifteen feet of rope. If the skidoo goes into a crevasse and the driver is thrown off, he'll fall fifteen feet but it's quite a comfortable fall since the ropes have 60% "give" built into them. The skidoo's engine is automatically turned off because the driver's roped to a switch which throws the engine if he falls.'

He tells me how, when he was doing some demonstration work not long ago, he actually fell into a crevasse. 'I was probing a bridge and the bridge went. I had to climb back up the rope. When I reached the top, they had to pull me over because there was an overhang. I had a high for several days after that. A real buzz. It was the first time I had ever been in a crevasse. Normally, if you can't see the crevasse, the bridge ought to be strong enough to take you, though of course you have to probe. We're tied together all the time, no matter what. Visibility is important. Today there's good contrast because there's bright sunlight. When you have cloud and there's no sun, you can't tell which way you are going except by the angle of the sledge.'

He adds that skiing has been good today. No problem with crevasses. In any case you can learn where to anticipate them. 'Crevasses occur mainly when the snow is stressed, for example where the glacier is moving over rocks or humps.'

I look at the man with interest as he stands there, tall and fit, talking about his way of life. I can't help wondering whether I would get a 'buzz', a real 'high' from dangling at the end of a rope down a crevasse. I suppose it would depend on whether you thought you were going to be pulled out of it or not. When you're travelling around Antarctica, you can't help hearing stories of people who fall down crevasses and don't get pulled out of them. Not so much of a 'buzz' then, I imagine – but I could be wrong. Perhaps it's like drowning. Some of those who have suffered near-fatal accidents are reported to have enjoyed the experience.

His colleague, Steve Harris, is – as Mike explained – the geologist. Shorter than Mike. Chunkier. Just as brown. Just as bearded. He tells me he's come from the University of Aberdeen and he is 'thrilled to have a job out here'.

'Our basic project is to find the origins of deformed rock. Are they igneous or sedimentary deformed rocks?' He pauses; I wait for him to continue. I expect him to say 'sedimentary, my dear Watson', but he doesn't. Instead he says, 'Banded rocks tell you about the structure of the earth at the time of their formation. Our project is to analyse the rocks of the peninsula and find out their origins, their geological history.'

There's something slightly unreal about the experience. Here I am, a classicist by training who chickened out after Mods so ended up with a BA (Hons) in English, standing on a glacier about six thousand feet up in Antarctica having my first and – as it turns out – only lecture in geology from a young man who, standing confidently beside his crowded skidoo, sees nothing incongruous or unusual about the situation.

I may not have got all the technical detail right, but this is what I think Steve said: 'Lesser Antarctica is much younger than the rest of Antarctica. It's very similar to the Andes. Greater Antarctica on the other hand has much older rocks, over two thousand million years old, whereas here we're talking about a system less than six hundred million years old.'

As he talks I look around at the mountains jutting out from the glacier. It's hard to imagine two thousand million years. Hard to imagine six hundred million years for that matter. But to a man like Steve Harris the difference can be all-important.

'Basically the rocks have been formed by the ocean crust being ducted beneath the margin. The plutonic rocks, such as granite, are deeper down. The volcanic rocks are where the magma has reached the surface. The exciting thing would be to find continental crust here, as in Greater Antarctica. Not just oceanic crust.'

Looking back, that random encounter on the glacier with those two men was probably one of the most moving moments of the whole trip. If you can't get a sense of perspective there, when you are surrounded by time, solidified geological time and not much else besides, where can you get such a sense?

We had to go. You don't fly by night in Antarctica, at least not in the British sector. There's no flare-path at Rothera, no call for one. We took off from the glacier, banked, turned and came back low over the skidoo party. Mike and Steve looked up at us and waved as we passed. We were probably the last human beings they would see until they came back to the base at Rothera at the end of the season.

This is the sharp end, I reflected, of the Antarctic operation. Keeping a man or two men in the field is rather like getting someone to the summit of Everest. Like the mountain itself, you need a pyramid-shaped support structure. That man at the top requires a whole team at base camp and the team at base camp is itself probably the reflection of a much larger logistical operation back in the home country. So it is with a skidoo party on an Antarctic glacier. Base camp in this case means Rothera, while the overall planning and logistical support – ships, supplies, telexes, transfer payments or whatever – is provided from BAS headquarters in Cambridge.

Another way of looking at it is to think of the space programme. Here the name of the game is to put up the maximum payload for each unit of effort, whether financial or material.

It was half-past eight when we finally came back to base – a fine clear evening with the sun still streaming over the mountains. Gary Studd turned off the Otter's two Pratt – Whitney engines and we climbed back into the snowcat which had come up to the airstrip to pick us up.

Munro points out the hatch in the roof of the driver's cabin. 'You need that,' he says, 'in case you sink through the sea-ice and can't open the door.'

When the base came into sight below us, I jumped out and ran behind the tractor in my snow-boots. Antarctica seems such a rugged environment yet, paradoxically, the opportunities for taking exercise are often limited especially when, as we were, one is trying to cram as much as possible into a short visit.

We had a quick meal in the mess when we got back. I talked to a meteorologist called Peter Stark. 'Antarctic weather', he tells me, 'is the engine that drives the whole world's weather. Meteorological data from Rothera, from other Antarctic stations and from many ships in the area, is sent up to Faraday and from there it goes to Washington or to Bracknell – that's the UK weather centre – who use it in their world reports. Washington and Bracknell use different models and they might arrive at different weather forecasts and predictions. It's all a matter of applied fluid dynamics.

'These weather stations down here in Antarctica are crucial. There's so little else down here. It's not as though you're anywhere near the civilized world, as you are in the Arctic. I mean Russian mainland territory pushes right up north into the 80s. You've got the Norwegians up in Spitzbergen. Both Russians and Norwegians have weather stations in the Arctic – so do the US and Canada of course. But down here you've got no routine stations at all. South Georgia and Kerguelen island – Kerguelen is owned by the French – are about all you've got in the 60s. If you go up to New Zealand or South Africa, you're talking about 40° South which is a long way away from the Pole. So these Antarctic stations are vital.'

He tells me that the UK meteorological office provides a grant for some of the work at Halley station, over to the east. 'They're sending balloons up twenty to thirty kilometres till they hit the lower stratosphere. Those balloons are transmitting data back to the surface all the time until they burst.'

We came back to the ship on the last shuttle. The bow of the little rubber boat lifts out of the water as we zip smartly between the ice-floes towards the red bulk of the *Biscoe*. The others are still sitting round the table in the wardroom, Colin and Steve being very much the centre of attention. After all, it's their day. They are the heroes of the hour. Fifty years earlier they showed the way, worked out the systems for tents and sledges, the way to handle the dogs. Today they have been looking at old landmarks, reviving old memories.

'How come', I asked when it is my turn to pay homage, 'that you named it King George vi Sound?'

Colin smiled. 'We actually wanted to name it for Edward viii. He was king at the time and since we'd been without news for three weeks, we had no reason to suppose anything different. And then we heard on the radio: 'There will be an important announcement tomorrow night', and of course that was the announcement about the Abdication.'

'We were most interested', intervened Steve in his deadpan way, 'to know about the other party. We had heard that she was *petite* and pretty. Anyway, the committee got to work back home. Launcelot Fleming got on to it and the name was quickly changed from King Edward viii Sound to King George vi Sound.'

The talk moved on, as the two men recalled the details of their time in the Antarctic. 'It took us ten weeks to get from the Debenhams to Bluff Cove. Mind you,' said Steve, 'we spent nine days lying up against a foul wind.'

There is a Stephenson mountain and a Bertram glacier. There is also a Todd glacier. Anne says she had almost forgotten that a glacier had been named after her, until she saw it from the air. 'The Royal Geographical Society', she explains, 'used to have a rule that explorers can't name features after themselves. But they discovered that the Americans had started naming peaks and glaciers after cooks and bottlewashers and heaven knows what, so they thought they ought to get a few names on the map.'

'That's why Colin and I feature,' Steve chips in. And he adds wrily: 'The Danes have a rule that nobody can have a feature named after him until his death. It has to be posthumous. I've got a mountain coming up in Greenland but I suppose it will have to wait.'

As the evening wears on the brandy and liqueurs are passed around. 'We had a cat which the Dean of the cathedral at Port Stanley gave us. We called it Lummo after the Dean who was called Lumsdale. The cat stayed with us during the expedition,' says Steve, 'and after that we took it back to England. I think it was probably the first cat to have been in Antarctica. After it had been through quarantine it went to live with Brian Roberts in Cambridge. When it died, Brian Roberts wrote a Fourth Leader in *The Times* about it. Brian Roberts', he explains, 'used to do the job John Heap does now, except he was at the Scott Polar Research Institute as well.'

The following morning, while we were waiting for the launch to take us over to the base, a smallish iceberg came over and nudged itself up against the bow of the ship, pushing it over so that the stern-lines running from the *Biscoe* to the shore were stretched tight. This is the kind of little incident the Captain has to be constantly on the look-out for. You don't argue with icebergs; if they look as though they mean business, you move out of the way. In this particular case the berg wandered on; the tension came off the stern-ropes and the launch, the alarm over, was ready for the excursion.

It was a dull day – 'manky' I had learnt to call it, as opposed to 'dingle' (which meant fine). The sky was heavily overcast and there was no flying. We found Gary Studd, our pilot from yesterday, in the mess-room. Over a beer he talks about crises he has had flying in Antarctica.

'Well,' he laughs, 'one time both engines stopped, first one engine, then the other about five minutes later. The fuel was frozen. In fact, eight filters were frozen. There was probably water in the fuel. We'd been using some Argentine stuff we picked up from one of their bases. Normally aviation fuel freezes at -56 degrees Centigrade. But water in it would have separated out and blocked the carburettor and the filters and so on.'

'What's the glide ratio of the Otter?' I ask.

Gary Studd laughs. 'I suppose I ought to know. It took me only four minutes to come down from 8,000 feet!'

Later Adrian Berry and I had a talk with John Hall, the Base Commander. We sat in the little library. Looking round the shelves while waiting for Hall to come in from outside, I couldn't help thinking that in this instance books do indeed furnish, not just a room, but a base. Few things can be more important to a base than its library. A plentiful supply of reading matter during the Antarctic winter can go a long way towards taking the edge off the boredom and the monotony. Several thousand miles away in Cambridge there is a library 'supremo' – someone who knows exactly which books are to be found at each of BAS's five Antarctic bases and who will see to it that stocks are replenished or changed at regular intervals. Of course, in addition to the lighter material, whether fact or fiction, each place will have its own Antarctic section containing the classic works of Antarctic science or exploration. There was a banjo leaning against one of the bookcases. In addition to providing a place where a man may sit and read, the library can be a retreat for independent souls who want to do their own thing. For all its emptiness, Antarctica can sometimes be a very crowded environment.

John Hall, when he arrived, had changed into jeans and T-shirt (he had left a colleague to supervise the unloading). He sat down in an armchair opposite us, strikingly handsome with his sun-bronzed face and strong features. He radiated enthusiasm and commitment. It was clear that he had come to Antarctica because he wanted to be here.

'I was two years at South Georgia as Base Commander before I came to

Rothera. Before that I was a high school teacher back in England.' He had been married and a National Park Ranger; then he had 'got unmarried'.

'As a child I had read the books about Antarctica, seen the pictures of the big snowcats, the snow-blowers. That was very much the time when the Americans were leading the way. In fact what I like is the kind of work we're doing here; work of the sort Colin and Steve pioneered, their kind of travel. We're still using the pyramid tents which they used. Sledging methods have changed, of course. We have skidoos, not dogs; but here on the Peninsula there's a great deal of similarity.'

It was clear as we talked that Hall had 'got the bug'. He was there for love, not money.

'I get a big buzz when I see a whale. I get a buzz when I sit on the steps out here and look out across the bay. Or from planning and executing the field programmes. And an even bigger buzz from actually succeeding. This is still an exciting environment.'

There were fifty or sixty skidoos altogether, counting the ones we had just brought with us. Hall, as Base Commander, was responsible for keeping in touch with all the different field parties.

'The skidoos normally go out on a two-man basis. Two skidoos, two men. One of them is a GA – a general assistant – who will have some mountain experience, including polar experience. The other will be the geologist. When they're out in the 'bundu', we try to put an experienced GA alongside any newcomer. That's another reason why the BAS system of doing two and a half years in the field is a good idea. You can get an overlap between incoming and outgoing personnel.'

Adrian Berry, with his optimistic technological view of life, is especially interested in the skidoos. 'How many miles can they do to the gallon?' he asks.

'About five,' Hall replies. 'You're pulling a heavy sledge with a two-stroke engine which is one of the reasons why fuel consumption is high. You can pull about 1,000 pounds with a skidoo. Of course that will have to include the jerry-cans of fuel on the sledge between depots. Normally you work from depot to depot. We will put the depots in by air. You've got to fix the positions with considerable accuracy. One may think a depot should stick out like a sore thumb but they're easy to miss. We're going to try leaving VHF homing devices switched on in the depots, working on the basis of solar panels.'

He talked about the party which was sledging those 1,500 miles back towards the Antarctic Peninsula from the Ronne ice-shelf. 'We will try to have daily contact with this and the other teams. If we don't get them on an evening call, then they switch to their second frequency and try again next morning. I'll begin to get worried if a couple of days have elapsed without contact, especially if they're in difficult country.'

He said the Russians had been helpful to BAS's Weddell Sea operations. 'They were coming in by ship to their base at Druzhnaya. We told them we wanted to leave some fuel for our Weddell Sea party so they sent a helicopter ahead of the ship to meet us. Down here the Russians are very willing to cooperate.'

Adrian wanted to know how cost-effective the British Antarctic programme was. Was it for example much more cost-effective than the Americans'? The previous day we had seen the two-man skidoo party up on the glacier. Was it true that the Americans would have put in a whole line of depots before letting those two people off together?

A base commander has to be something of a diplomat as well as a natural leader. John Hall said he wasn't too familiar with the details of the American Antarctic operation, but they were working on a joint project with the US at the moment and it was going well.

'The Americans with their C130s are putting in the fuel, BAS is putting in most of the science. There's no way', he said, 'BAS could have undertaken the logistics for the kind of operation we're working on at the moment. Yesterday you flew down to Fossil Bluff. Well, it costs a drum of fuel simply to put a drum of fuel in there.'

That brought us on to the subject of planes. There were plans to build a hard runway at Rothera. It would start on the foreshore where they were unloading the supplies and run obliquely across the headland on which the base was situated, to the bay on the other side. It would be about 720 metres long. Plenty for a fully-loaded Twin Otter though not enough for a C130 which needs 800 metres.

'We'd feel more secure about flying if we had a hard runway near the base. We'd still have to fly visual but we could put in some navaids – navigation aids. Also having the planes down here means we could look after them a bit more. We lost two planes two years ago in a blizzard up there. They were brought down the ski-way on tractors, taken to pieces, loaded on to the scow when the *Bransfield* came in and transported back to England. One of the planes, that's the one you were flying in yesterday, was totally rebuilt in England. The other one's not worth repairing. Well, those Otters cost £1 million each now, so there's an economic aspect to it as well as a safety aspect. In terms of actual flying time, building a runway probably wouldn't make much difference, though it might possibly permit more take-offs. The clouds are often at about 1,000 feet. You could be in dense cloud up on the glacier but the base could be clear.'

'How much will the runway cost?' I asked.

'About £2.8 million on present costings,' Hall replied, and he went on to explain that because of some problem to do with external contractors and the need for special Treasury permission, the project had been shelved for the time being.

'How much of an impact would it make on the environment?'

'You'd have to grade the runway. There would have to be some blasting and drilling.' In Hall's view, the plan to build an airstrip at Rothera clearly would have few of the environmental consequences that were being predicted for the airfield to be built by the French near their base in Adélie Land where whole penguin colonies were threatened with disturbance or destruction.

Hall understood the concern that people felt about the construction of airstrips and similar projects in Antarctica. But the BAS Twin Otters, in his view, clearly came into the category of 'appropriate technology', an extension, almost, of Antarctic bird life. After all, they too moved with the seasons.

'As you know, the Otters fly out here all the way from England. They go round the Arctic, down through North and South America with their skis on all the way. Last year we were trying to find out where our planes had got to; we made contact with some station in the Bahamas or thereabouts and asked if they had by any chance seen the Twin Otters and the radio-operator up there said, 'Oh, yes, man, you mean de planes with de planks on de wheels?'

The window of the library looked out on to the foreshore. We could see the scow laden with oil-drums, moving between ship and shore. At the water's edge the mechanical lifter would be waiting to transfer the drums to the tractor-trailer. No matter how pressing their other tasks, when the *Biscoe* or the *Bransfield* shows up the base personnel rally round to help. An extra day spent unloading at Rothera means you arrive at the next base a day later and this can have a knock-on effect all the way down the line. Quite apart from the need to respect the Antarctic seasons and take advantage of the periods in summer when the seas are relatively free of ice, delay down here means eventual delay in returning to England. The Captain has his crew to think of, amongst other things. When they've already been away from home six months or more, he is understandably anxious to make sure that the voyage is not unnecessarily prolonged.

Hall cast a professional eye over the activities outside, gauging – I suppose – from progress already made just how much longer unloading was going to take. He was obviously proud of his team.

'Fifty-six people work out of the base in the summer; in the winter we're down to fourteen. A cook, wireless-operator, carpenter, builder, diesel mechanic, electrician, two tractor operators, a doctor, five GAs. The GAs will be preparing equipment for the coming field season: repairing the tents, checking the sledge, tow-ropes, the climbing equipment; taking the primuses down and cleaning them out. The tractor mechanics will work on the big vehicles but they'll also strip the skidoos down to their crank-cases. Also winter is when you take the fuel-drums up the ski-way. The surface is harder then, but it still takes about four days to get the fuel up there. And there are always the dogs to look after.'

We had already seen the dogs spanned out 150 yards away from the huts, just before the beginning of the ski-way. They had greeted us with enthusiasm, though not perhaps with as much enthusiasm as they greeted the occasional penguin which unwisely waddled within range.

'You're seeing the dogs at a bad time,' Hall said. 'They're on the spans now. We use them for training in the winter. At Stonington' – that was the now abandoned British base we had flown over the previous day – 'all the field sciences were done with the aid of dogs. When you're travelling with dogs you're close to your environment. Things take longer. That slows you down. It makes you more tranquil, more careful. Let's say it's a cold evening and you've got half an hour to go. You come to a badly crevassed area, the kind of place where you ought to get off and probe. When you're using dogs that's exactly what you do because – as I say – they slow you down. But if you're in a skidoo you might say, "What the hell, I'll just smash on." We use the dogs for training, therefore – and for recreation. We don't let them inside the house of course unless they're puppies.'

From time to time we can hear a yapping outside as the dogs registered their interest in the current unloading activities. I could well understand how dogs, even today, have a role in Antarctic life. Quite apart from their training value which Hall had described, there was the psychological dimension. Looking after the dogs in the long winter months, taking them out on the ice, showing them affection and, in turn, receiving their gratitude – all this added an extra and agreeable dimension to what, on any assessment, is a fairly harsh existence.

But there were problems too. Hall explained them. 'We're taking about a hundred seals a year, for the dogs. Of course, we fill in the permits as we're required to do under the Treaty. I send these documents back to Cambridge and they're open to anyone to inspect. It's all legal in terms of the Treaty; even so, if I saw that the dogs were really not being used; or if I saw that the amount we were using them for training and for recreation really couldn't be justified in terms of conservation or economics, then I'd be the first to say "no more seals". And that might mean the end of the dog teams because we know already that the people back in Cambridge aren't going to buy "Nutty" or "Lassie" or whatever for the dogs on the base. You just can't justify it in money terms. I'm keeping an open mind at the moment. We'll just have to see which way it goes.'

I saw his point. Killing seals to feed dogs who might in the last resort be no more than glorified pets was probably not the right approach in terms of Antarctic conservation. Hall was big enough to recognize this.

'Of course, recreation is a problem and the dogs help. But the real answer is to get the right people down here in the first place.'

He explained to us how people are recruited to BAS, the informal psychological scrutiny, the interviews back in England. 'One of the first questions we ask is: do you have a serious girl-friend, I mean, a girl-friend you'd miss if you didn't see her. We ask that question', John Hall explains, 'because if they *do* have a serious girl-friend and then they're away for two and a half years, that's a fairly big strain on the relationship. In fact, almost all the people that are down here are unmarried people.'

'Can they communicate with home?' Adrian asks.

'They can send a message of two hundred words a month.'

Two hundred words a month! Barely long enough, I thought, to say what you had for breakfast, let alone try to keep a 'serious' relationship going from a distance of ten thousand miles over a period of two and a half years. What he said made a lot of sense. There were plenty of reasons for coming to Antarctica, but on the whole keeping girl-friends happy wasn't one of them.

It was time for John Hall to go about his business. He seemed genuinely pleased to have met us.

'You're different when you come back from Antarctica after a tour down here,' he said. 'Back home things don't seem to be the same. The crowds, the supermarkets. It takes time to adjust. You're not even sure you *want* to adjust.'

Later that night we came over on the launch for a party at the base. The cook, assisted by numerous amateur enthusiasts, had made a special effort. There were three different main courses: chicken, lamb, and curry, followed by pudding and cakes. The annual visit of the *Biscoe* is worth a celebration.

Like all enclosed communities, these Antarctic bases develop their own highly individual vocabularies. I had already learned about 'mank' and 'dingle'. Now, in the bar after dinner, I discovered 'gash' means rubbish, 'gonking' means sleeping, and 'sploder' means anything you want it to mean, as in, 'Where have I put that f . . . ing sploder.'

The bar at Rothera is not wildly different from what you would find in an English pub or club. Framed photographs on the wall depict ships, like the *Endurance* or the *Biscoe*, pressing on through ice (not so different, if you think about it, from the traditional hunting scenes with horses being set at fences). Other mementoes and trophies – like presentation coats of arms from USARP, the United States Antarctic Research Program, have a similarly local flavour, but the general impression, apart from the fact that it is still broad daylight at 11 p.m. and there are icebergs in the middle distance, is not totally unlike say Surbiton or Ipswich. What is different is the experience of the people who live here.

Dermot Hopkins, to give an example, one of the Rothera Fids who joined me for a pint in the bar after dinner, had spent most of the last three years totally underground. When I expressed some astonishment, he explained why.

'I've been over at Halley,' he said. 'They're on their fifth base now. Halley Four which was only built in 1973 is already sixty feet beneath the snow. Already it's drifted about forty miles out from land; in fact it's only about a mile from the edge of the ice-shelf, so it's going to go in the next two or three years anyway. The new Halley Five is made of wooden tubes. The hut, which is ten metres square, has been erected from panels one metre square which were carried in on board the *Bransfield*. Once the hut has been put inside a wooden tube, you've got an elliptical shape and since there are four pressure points on an ellipse, they hope this will prevent the snow from crushing down on Halley Five as quickly as it has crushed down on the others.

'The tubes are now one hundred metres long. There are no windows there; people tend to go outside every three hours, which means you've got to climb a ladder fifty or sixty feet. It's a major operation to get the vehicles indoors. We have a tunnel going down at a twenty-degree angle.

'When you're all together, there's the strain and stress factor to be taken into consideration. The old base was very cramped. The new one will have much more space. The work on the new base has started. They're putting in the generators now. The *Bransfield* brought them out in December. Generators run on aviation spirit, of course. Almost all the mechanical equipment there runs on aviation spirit. Diesel freezes solid at minus twenty, and you've got temperatures much lower than that at Halley. They've got 4,000 fuel drums there; they get dug out every fortnight. The IH – International Harvester – will haul three sledges, with fourteen drums per sledge and each drum weighing 400 pounds. They recover heat from the generator.'

He himself, he said, had just left Halley to come to Rothera. Unusually, he had gone from one British Antarctic base to another without any stint in England in between.

'We stopped to refuel at the Russian base – Druzhnaya. The Russian advance party had just arrived. The helicopter had flown ahead of the ship. They hadn't unpacked their vodka yet so they gave us de-icing fluid instead!' He laughed – I suspected the joke had been made before.

'Like Halley, the Russian base is buried every year,' Dermot explained, 'but they pull the huts out. It's a smaller operation; there are only twenty people there. The Russians also have a permanent base at the Pole of Relative Inaccessibility, the place in Antarctica that is farthest from everywhere. The air is too cold to breathe there; temperatures can go to $-88°$; your lungs freeze. If you throw a kettle of water in the air, it will quite literally explode. They have a big tractor operation each year to resupply the base. Those tractors go thousands of miles across the Polar Plateau. If a tractor breaks down, they leave it. They have a whole fleet of tractors with very few spares. What they do is take a workshop with them, a caboose, equipped with the proper machine tools, and they actually manufacture the spares they need on the spot.'

He talked with feeling about the way everybody had to 'muck in' at a base like Halley. 'You've all got to get involved. One moment you're out there checking the thermometer, the next you're mending the equipment. Halley is a very good place to listen, there's no disturbance.

'They have an Advanced Ionospheric Sounder, for example. The AIS sends a range of signals up to the ionosphere. Some of them will bounce back; others are absorbed. They pass on through, as it were. You could in fact poke a hole in the ionosphere. It's a bit like poking a hole in a screen with an umbrella.

'It's also a very good place to do other geophysical work, such as measuring changes in the earth's magnetism. The VLF – very low frequency – signals pass along the lines of flux which are concentrated on the poles; the wavelengths are hundreds of kilometres long. If you study them, you can tell a lot about how the upper atmosphere works.'

When I asked him what his own trade was, Dermot replied that he was a diesel mechanic. It was as good an illustration as any I had of what would probably be called in official memoranda the 'spirit of cross-disciplinary collaboration' but which Hopkins himself preferred to think of as good old-fashioned 'mucking in'.

The Falklands War had affected Dermot Hopkins in a directly personal way. He was at Grytviken, in South Georgia, when the Argentines landed on 3 January 1982. He was taken off in an Argentine vessel, the *Bahía Paraíso*, along with twenty-two Royal Marines and thirteen other Fids. They were taken to an Argentine military base at Bahía Blanca, then they were deported to Uruguay. He didn't seem to have been much marked by the experience. The Argentines, he said, treated them very well on board.

I was lucky that evening. Perhaps because it was a party, a special occasion, the Fids seemed ready to open up, to talk freely about their work. When we moved from the bar to the dining-room (dining-room makes it sound grander than it actually is but I can't think of a better term) I found myself sitting between an electrician, Vic Young, and a radio operator, Mark Trotman – both in their twenties, both clearly dedicated to their work.

'What I like', said Vic Young, 'is that there's no difference between living and working. Your job is your life and vice versa. I don't mind what I do as long as I enjoy it.'

Mark Trotman on the other hand had a more specific link with his craft. He had always wanted to go to sea and he had always been fascinated by radios. Working for BAS had enabled him to pursue both interests together. Sitting there that night, I learned from him some of the basic axioms such as: 'The effectiveness of radio is determined as much by its range of frequencies as by its power' or his own more personal motto: 'Operating a radio is just an excuse to break it so you can repair it!'

Across the table from me was Mike Evans, bearded, with a dauntingly intelligent look and a BSc degree in electronics and electrical engineering. He was down at Rothera for the moment but was on his way back to Faraday where he was working on the measurement of the ionosphere.

'Faraday is a good place for ionospheric work,' he told me, 'firstly because of the lack of interference, and secondly because Faraday has a high latitude as far as the geographic pole is concerned, but a low latitude as far as the magnetic pole is concerned. This difference is more important in the southern hemisphere than it is in the northern hemisphere, because in the northern hemisphere your magnetic pole is in the low eighties.'

I didn't understand all this at first so Mike Evans explained it again patiently until I did. It's the kind of thing that needs a diagram before it can be crystal clear. Evans drew one on the table top. The essential point, which I finally grasped, was that the positioning of the true pole and of the magnetic pole in the southern hemisphere made Faraday a very special place. To find a location with similar characteristics in the northern hemisphere you'd have to go to Siberia – which might not be easy. 'How important', I asked, 'are Antarctic stations like Faraday for weather forecasts?'

'It depends what kind of forecasts you're talking about,' Evans replied. 'If you are only interested in a twenty-four hours forecast, you only need to look around 300 miles as far as the UK is concerned. If you want to have a forecast for more than a week, you've got to look much wider than that. You've got to take into account, for example, the effect of the southern hemisphere weather on the north. Much of the mid-latitude area is affected by the mass of Antarctic air. The weather on the equator moves up and down. If you get an air mass in Antarctica, that could generate a depression at fifty degrees, hurricane conditions and so on, and that in turn could affect the weather in the United States and so the United Kingdom. The weather in the northern hemisphere is generally different from that of the south but there are certainly linkages. The further ahead you look, the easier it is to miss something. Generating data is one thing,' Mike Evans concluded, 'making sense of it is another. You need exceptionally powerful computers to crunch the numbers being generated by weather forecasts. Until the Argentines came in, Grytviken used to collect data from all the Antarctic stations and transmit them to Buenos Aires, which in turn used to send them on to Washington where they've got the equipment to handle them. Now we've had to find other routes. That's another casualty of the Falklands War.'

Like so many of his colleagues, Mike Evans was quite ready to say what it was that appealed to him about Antarctica. The aesthetic involvement was there; the moral aspect also but, at least as far as he was concerned, the intellectual fascination seemed to predominate.

'Perhaps it's the only place in the world where a natural resource hasn't been ruined before you even know what it is you're ruining. I used to be at the BAS base on South Georgia. As you know, that's at Grytviken on Cumberland Bay. Now Cumberland Bay was the place where they first came to whale. You walk on the beaches today and you step on or over whale ribs and vertebrae wherever you go. Only seventy years later, seventy years after the whalers came, you're lucky if you see a whale at all. If you had been there at the beginning, you'd have been surrounded by whales. What I'm saying is that, if we had had biologists before the whaling started, we might have avoided the holocaust.

'The disappearance of the whales is a tragedy in itself. But there's more to it than that. On South Georgia today, on Bird Island which is next to it, there are so many fur seals now, the birds can't nest. The seals increased because we zapped the whales. Back in 1979 the seals weren't encroaching on the birds. By 1982 the tussock grass had been flattened and there seemed to be real competition between seals and birds. The seals simply don't want to make space on their beaches for the birds. The truth is, of course, that by destroying the whales we have made a mess of the whole cycle. Other species have filled up the ecological niche created by the disappearance of the whales. Now the question is: is there still a surplus of krill? Even if there is still a surplus today, which no one really knows given the demands of other now abundant species as well as possible human demands, will that surplus remain to be taken up by the whales as and when they recover? And remember, that recovery could take 200 years.'

On the last leg of our journey we would visit South Georgia as well as Bird Island, which is next door to it. I would have a chance to see at first hand the biological explosion of which Mike Evans spoke.

Later that evening I found myself standing by the hut's entrance, looking at the scenery and thinking what a good party it had been. The day was still bright though the sun had lost its heat. The silence was total: a moment for contemplation. The cook came to stand next to me. He had probably worked harder than anyone today. Peter Forman was in a reflective mood.

'We've got the dogs,' he said. 'We've got the planes, we have the scenery.' He lit a cigarette and pulled hard at it. 'I don't like these skuas much, though. Bloody awful birds, they can go for the top of your head. You have to carry a flag with you if you're going up to the point, and wave it. They're nesting there.' Hitchcock in the Antarctic, I thought, with big brown skuas in the lead role.

'Is the weather always as good as this?' I asked. I'm not just making conversation. The bright sunny days have come as a big surprise to me.

'No, it's normally much grimmer at this time of year. This is exceptional. If we'd had the gear, we could have had a barbecue tonight. When there's no wind, the heat from the sun warms you up.'

He himself, he says, likes taking the dogs out; he likes going off on twelve-day dog-trips, nine dogs in his team, one lead bitch called Yvonne, and four on either side. 'You ought to know the key words. *Ouk*, means "go to the right", *rra rra*, "go to the left" and *ach-now* means "stop". Getting the dogs up the ramp is a bore; we generally tow them up with the skidoos so that they don't have time to make a mess on the ski-way and ablate it. Once you've got the dogs on to the traverse, then you're all right.'

That little exchange makes me understand better the psychological role of dogs and the genuine perplexity men like John Hall must feel as they try to decide whether or not to keep the remaining spans. The equation is not a simple one.

John Hall, when at last I went upstairs to say goodbye, wasn't thinking about dogs at all. He was talking about Chilean schoolgirls – as far as the men on the base were concerned this is a different form of diversion but no doubt just as interesting.

'Four of them visited the base the other morning,' he said, 'and had the men drooling. The Chileans are taking the colonization programme very seriously. The first Chilean Antarctic wedding took place at their Rodolfo Marsh base. The Base Commander had prepared for ninety guests, having been told that seventy were coming. Actually 130 turned up, two plane loads. General Pinochet himself is coming to Marsh to inaugurate some new homes.'

Talking about the Chilean Antarctic base at Rodolfo Marsh reminds Munro (he's spending the night on the base and it looks as though he still has a long evening ahead of him, whereas the rest of us have to catch the last Gemini across to the ship) of the time when the *Biscoe* stopped by to say hello to the Chileans.

'Rodolfo Marsh is right next door to the Russian base at Bellingshausen so we reckoned that as a matter of courtesy we should see the Russians as well as the Chileans. So we agreed to have a drink with the Russians at 11.30 in the morning and then go on later to the Chileans. Well, we arrived at the Russian base and were warmly welcomed. We have a great deal to drink, just about everything, in fact, and then around one o'clock we walk the few yards across to the Chilean base. The problem was: we got our timing wrong. The Chileans weren't expecting us for another two hours because there's a difference in the clocks between the two bases although they're at exactly the same location. As a result of this confusion, we ended up with two more solid hours' drinking, with the result that one of our party fell flat on his face.'

'The Russians came to Signy when I was there,' said John Hall. 'You'll be going to Signy later. We asked them if they wanted some charts, but the Russians said, "*Nyet.* Thank you very much but we have very good charts." I took a look at their charts later. They were Admiralty charts with Russian names superimposed!'

The talk about other nations' Antarctic activities became more general. I learned that there was a Polish base at Arktowski and that the Brazilians had a research vessel which paid regular visits to the Antarctic. The Chinese and the Indians were also sending their people down.

'The Chinese visited BAS in Cambridge not long ago,' says Munro. 'They asked our advice about suppliers of equipment, so we recommended a firm. Later we learnt that for some reason they had ordered a whole lot of deck-chairs and marquees!'

Anne Todd knew one about the Australians. 'Down at Mawson base', she says, 'they have a collection of videos – like the *Pride and Prejudice* series. But they know the plots so well they turn the sound off and just watch the pictures. They even talk like the characters.'

Lunch on board ship on our last day at Rothera was a rather sad occasion. We seemed only just to have arrived and already we had to leave. For some of us, and that probably goes for Adrian and me as much as for Colin and Steve, the chances of visiting Rothera again in the near future are fairly slim.

To mark the occasion Adrian and I went quickly below when the luncheon-gong sounded and put on ties before making our way to the wardroom. We arrived to find Gary Studd and John Hall looking spruce as penguins and toasting with raised sherry glasses not this year's departure but next year's return. This is a place where, above all, you have to think ahead. If you want something to be delivered next year, you have to have ordered it last year. That's why the arrival of the *Biscoe* or the *Bransfield* is in its way as predictable as the seasons. It's something that *has* to happen. Otherwise not one but three years' planning goes up the spout.

Though our captain, Chris, vehemently maintains that about thirty feet above sea level – the height of the bridge – is as high as he wants to fly, Gary enthralls us with his descriptions of the deep, deep blue of the skies above Antarctica. 'As deep and dark as you ever see when you're flying in Concorde at 50,000 feet.'

I had heard about the journey out with the Twin Otters. Now I heard about the journey back.

'We normally go to Goose Bay in Newfoundland and then over to Iceland,' says Studd. 'There's an alternative route via Recife in Brazil, Ascension Island and Dakar, but that raises political problems. It's not just the delicacy of our relations with the Latin American countries after the Falklands. Ascension is not really meant for civil flights.'

'Isn't the Recife–Ascension hop at the edge of an Otter's range anyway?' I ask.

'An Otter's range can be 800 to 1,000 miles,' Studd replies, 'but it's also possible to refuel in mid-air as it were, by carrying drums of fuel and piping them into the system.' He laughs. 'I was flying the Director – Dr Laws – back from Halley and the team was piping fuel in from the spare drums carried on board. I made the engines miss on purpose and shouted back to the crew, "Faster, you bastards". They enjoyed that!' He laughed again. As we sit down to the meal, Gary tells another Otter story. Somehow those little red planes with skis on the wheels and the words British Antarctic Survey painted in bold black letters on the fuselage seem to gather stories and anecdotes as the hull of a ship gathers barnacles.

'We were flying into Miami International Airport once,' says Studd, 'when we received a signal on the radio that the airport was closed because of snow. So we signalled back that it was quite all right with us and went ahead and landed on our skis anyway!

'Another time we arrived in Winnipeg in our Twin Otters with the BAS label on the side. We got out of the plane in our shirt-sleeves only to find the temperature was 41° below freezing. Actually', Gary chuckled, 'I misread the chart in Miami. I thought it said −4.1° not −41°. Anyway, people came up to us and said "Gee" and "Wow, I suppose this is nothing to you, you folks who live down in Antarctica." Well, we didn't want to lose face so we had to go on walking around in our shirt-sleeves. −41° was about the coldest I've ever experienced.'

John Hall is not only Base Commander; he is also a sub-postmaster of the Royal Mail. Even though the Antarctic Treaty is in force – with Article IV of that Treaty effectively 'freezing' claims to sovereignty – Britain, like the other Antarctic powers, still issues stamps for its Antarctic territories. Issuing stamps along with conducting weddings or burials or acting as local magistrate (John Hall is that too) is one way of demonstrating effective occupation, and demonstrating effective occupation can in turn be one basis of a territorial claim. Of course, other elements enter into the equation as well – such as first discovery, prior possession, treaties and agreements of one kind or another. Sovereignty is a mysterious affair as the Falklands dispute between Britain and Argentina conclusively showed. Both sides can be passionately convinced of the justice of their cause – in such cases there may be no objective test, though the International Court of Justice in the Hague, if invited to deliver an opinion, will do its best to oblige.

So John collects our postcards and takes them back with him as he and Gary Studd leave the *Biscoe* after lunch. He will unlock his little office, get out the sheets of British Antarctic Territory stamps, stick them on, frank them (17p is what it costs to send a postcard from Antarctica to the United Kingdom and for that you get a picture of a crab-eater seal thrown in), bundle them up again in time for the last shore-to-ship shuttle to bring them back to the *Biscoe*. And the *Biscoe* will in this instance become the conveyor of the Royal Mail, with our Captain holding his noble and special commission under the Crown. If the Antarctic Treaty breaks down and the whole thing is up for grabs, proof of posting may be taken as proof of 'possession'!

In the event, I returned to England well ahead of the postcards. Some weeks later the crab-eater seals began to drop through the letterboxes of London friends. The Rothera postmark, so I was informed, was clearly legible, so was the date and – an imaginative touch – the geographical coordinates 67°34'S, 68°08'W.

5

Faraday

We had our last lunch at Rothera on Friday, 20 January, on board the *Biscoe*. Afterwards they pulled in the stern warps; John Hall and Gary Studd went back in the launch. The weather was much cloudier, much mistier; snow was falling; it was certainly more typical Antarctic weather than the last brilliant few days; the people here call it 'mank'. As we pulled away, Colin looked pensively across the widening gap of water towards the huts of the base. At the age of seventy-five his chances of returning to Antarctica *qua* Colin are fairly slim though he could possibly come back in some future incarnation as an albatross or giant petrel. I think he would enjoy that.

We headed for the south-west to go round the corner of Adelaide Island, before turning north. I was sitting in the wardroom reading when Jerry Burgan, who was on watch, announced over the intercom: 'Two whales on the starboard bow!' So I went up to the bridge and saw them blow. Standing up there and looking around I couldn't help remarking the contrast with the scene just three days ago – though it seemed much longer than that – when we came into Rothera. Today the mist was lying heavy on the mountains; the sea was grey and choppy; there were bergs all around. We passed one a hundred yards away on the port bow. Jerry, cigarette dangling from his lower lip, gauges it with a professional eye. 'If you ran into that at full speed,' he says, 'the ship would come to a very sudden halt indeed. Probably spring a few rivets; maybe cause more severe denting. It's something to be avoided if you possibly can.' Jerry was never one for overstatement.

He scans the horizon for icebergs, a reassuringly competent figure, dark blue jersey hugging the contours of his body (today is a day for warm clothes). 'If you're travelling at night', says Jerry, 'you have to rely on the radar to pick up the bergs except, of course, at this time of year when it's light virtually twenty-four hours a day.'

By early evening it was too cold to sit outside so I found my old haunt in the ship's laboratory and settled down to read a massive volume entitled *Antarctic Research*, edited by Priestley, Adie and Robin. Adie, of course, is R. J. Adie, now deputy director of BAS, whom I met in Cambridge before flying out to

Chile (in the front of the book there is a photograph of him as a younger man standing in the sun outside Stonington base with Sir Vivian Fuchs). Priestley is one of BAS's earliest luminaries, a man honoured in his habitation.

Antarctic research and exploration, I reflect as I sit there in the 'wet' lab surrounded by volumes which I have borrowed from the ship's library, are linked to human personalities just as much as, indeed possibly more than, most other fields of human endeavour. The same names occur again and again. Bertram, Stephenson . . . , Fuchs, Hillary . . . , Priestley, Adie . . . , small wonder that when Fuchs came to write his account of the origins and work of the British Antarctic Survey, he called it *Of Ice and Men*.

After supper, I'm back in the same place. It's fairly rough now and I have tied my chair on to the legs of the work-table in the lab. I'm afraid I've had to put *Antarctic Research* aside, since it's as much as I can do to keep my balance. The last few sunny days were probably an illusion. Now Antarctic reality will be the order of the day.

It was a rough night, but by morning the weather had improved. At half-past three in the afternoon, as we approached Faraday station, the sky had once more cleared and it was a sunny day. Very morale-boosting. We come into Faraday through a corridor of ice. 'Bergibits more than bergs,' the Captain says. 'But still you've got to watch out for them.' I'm not such a connoisseur of ice as is Chris. Even a 'bergibit' looks imposing enough to me.

They lower the launch for some serious reconnaissance. The plan is to bring the *Biscoe* as near to shore as possible, near enough anyway for a pipe to be connected from the ship to the base. At Rothera, drums of fuel had to be manhandled ashore. Here – presumably because we can go in closer – we plan to pump it across.

By mid afternoon we were still edging our way in through this spectacular harbour. We passed a seal on an ice-floe. Colin looked at it and said confidently that it was a crab-eater seal. He should know. Colin's investigation of the life and times of Antarctic seals, including and especially crab-eater seals, was in its day a landmark of Antarctic biology. In fact he has probably looked at the contents of more seal stomachs than most men living or dead. While Steve measured rocks and sized up nunataks, Colin would be out there on the ice looking for seals. This was a time when the requirements of scientific research and the need to keep the British Graham Land Expedition supplied with good fresh meat went hand-in-hand.

Eventually the base came into view – as at Rothera, a group of huts on the shoreline. We tried one path through the ice, thought twice about it and backed off again after having nosed our way in some distance. We took a second run at it and came round in a wide swoop, passing some rocks to the right which were covered with a spectacular patch of red lichens, the first sign of vegetation we'd seen since arriving.

After we had had dinner on board we took one of the rubber boats over to the base. These are amazingly versatile little craft. They can be lowered over the stern of the *Biscoe* in a couple of minutes, with passengers or cargo already in place. Alternatively, they can be lowered empty, to be brought round to the cargo deck in front of the bridge. Passengers, wearing life-vests of course, then climb down the rope ladder over the side, an operation which should be performed with some care, particularly if the ship is rolling.

Once everyone and everything is ready, the 'driver', whoever he is, gives a quick pull on the rope; the 546 cc 40 horse-power outboard roars into life and away you zoom across the briny. Without its array of boats – the scow, the launch, the rubber dinghies – the *Biscoe* would be a helpless giant. These smaller craft, which it carries with it in much the same way as a rhinoceros carries its tick-catchers, provide the necessary interface which makes the whole supply system work.

Like Rothera, Faraday has a bar equipped with most of the normal trappings, including a darts-board which was clearly much in demand. And, as at Rothera, the Fids tended to congregate in the bar at the end of their day. By the time we got there the place was already crowded. The *Biscoe*'s crew had been there some time already and most of them looked as though they were good for a few more hours yet. When it's still bright outside at well past midnight, and a Royal Research Ship (no less) is paying its annual visit, the concept of closing-time loses some of its force.

I found myself talking, beer in hand, to Dave Burke of Fife. He tells me he's been out here two years already. Since he actually left Britain in August 1981 and won't be back there till May 1984, his contract will be thirty-three months altogether. The British, he says, have the longest tours of duty, even longer than the Australians and the New Zealanders.

There are twelve people here on the base and it goes up to thirteen in the summer, so this is really an all-year-round station unlike Rothera where the main work is done in the summer with a caretaking crew taking over in the winter.

The arrival of the *Biscoe* is doubly welcome, says Burke, because it has been a frustrating winter. Normally the sea-ice in winter will stretch for miles, giving base personnel a chance to move about by way of exercise and recreation. In much the same way as parks in or around a city provide the 'lungs' for that city, enabling it to breathe, so sea-ice allows a cramped Antarctic base like Faraday to expand beyond its immediate confines into almost unlimited territory.

But this year conditions have been bad, limiting the recreational possibilities. A recent tragic accident has made people especially cautious. 'Last year', says Burke, 'three guys from the base got lost on the sea-ice. They went out on a trip to Peterman Island, about twenty miles away. While they were out they had a really nasty storm. We discovered later that it blew down two out of the three huts on Peterman Island. Those were the huts the Argentines left behind when they abandoned the base. Back at the base here at Faraday we waited and waited, but the party never did come back. We went out on the ice but we never found them. The Chileans sent a C130 down, which was good of them, but it didn't help.'

He raised his glass and gulped down a deep draught of beer. Then, looking out of the window to the icescape beyond, he said: 'Antarctica is the most beautiful place I've ever seen in my life. But the continent can turn deadly; in seconds it can show its teeth; you have to treat it with respect.'

While we are standing there talking a striking blonde woman with two small children in tow comes into the bar. One of the Fids immediately pours her a drink. She takes it and stands there drinking and talking, evidently quite at home.

'That's Sally,' – Dave Burke sees the direction of my glance – 'and there's Jérôme over there.' He points to a deeply-tanned man in a frayed denim jacket who is engaged in conversation with a group of Fids at the other end of the bar. 'The *Damien* has been here for a couple of days. Sally and Jérôme were here last year too. They usually come for a drink in the evening.' Later on that night I have a chance to talk to Jérôme Poncet, captain of the *Damien* and mariner extraordinary. In spite of the fact that it is years since he last set foot in France, he's unmistakably French, standing out among the Fids like a thistle among docks. It turns out that his wife is Australian – Tasmanian actually – and he is as happy to speak English as French.

'I like it here, that's why I am here,' he says simply. 'I prefer the southern oceans to the Mediterranean any day.'

'How do you live?'

'We have written books about the *Damien*. They bring in a small income. But you don't need much to live on if you live like us. A few thousand dollars, that's all we've spent over the years.'

One year, he says, they actually wintered in the Antarctic. They went on down the Peninsula to Rothera, pulled the *Damien* up on to the ice with a winch and simply hulled down for the winter, living off seal and, as a supplement to that monotonous diet, some tinned supplies of fruit and meat.

Jérôme has sailed to the Falklands recently and is very cross about what he believes is happening there.

'How can you tolerate a situation where 3,000, 4,000 soldiers are simply imposing themselves on the Islands, overwhelming the 1,800 inhabitants there? It's a tragedy. These marvellous islands are now going to be turned into an outpost of NATO.'

I began to explain that the reason the troops were in the Falklands was that President Galtieri had invaded and that the principle of self-determination had to be safeguarded. But these were not arguments to carry weight with Jérôme Poncet. He didn't have much time for the sophistries of civilization. He had left France ten years ago to avoid all the nonsenses of so- called polite society and he didn't expect to encounter them again down here in the Antarctic. He gave vent to a classically Gallic expression. 'Pah!' he said.

After the late night we made a slow start the next morning. While the *Biscoe* discharged oil through the green plastic pipe which now connected her – umbilically – to the shore, Adrian and I boarded the launch to go over to the base. We planned to have serious conversations about ozone and the ionosphere. In the event, most of the base's scientists were lending a hand with the unloading so our discussions had to be postponed. But one kind soul volunteered to take us on a tour of the island.

It takes a while to get used to the cross-country skis (what the Germans would call *Langlauf* and the French *ski de fond*). Instead of being firmly clasped in place by the binding, the heel is left to rise and fall according to the movements of the skier. If you are used to normal skis, turning with these long thin wands can be difficult and braking next to impossible. The only advantage, as far as I could see, was that walking up-hill was easy.

Because it *was* so easy we trudged up-hill – in fact right to the top of the little island (a mile long and three-quarters of a mile wide) on which the base is situated. When we reached the small cairn which had been placed to mark the summit of the island, we could look around us to see a great sweeping arc of mountains and glaciers, icebergs and floes. Half a mile away the buildings of the base showed up grey and green against the backdrop and behind them, her outline contrasting with the dazzling white backdrop, we could see the graceful form of the *Damien*. It was a strange sight – one of the strangest. I never expected to come to Antarctica and see a three-masted yacht riding at anchor among the icebergs. I stood there, on my awkward skis, thinking about the kind of man Jérôme Poncet must be to spend ten years sailing the southern oceans, putting into places like Stanley or Grytviken – hardly the hub of civilization as we know it. And what kind of woman must his wife be? Her children, so I was told, had both been conceived within the Antarctic circle and one, the latest, had actually been born on South Georgia. I couldn't help thinking that if I ever came to know the two of them, I would probably understand and respect their motives. Failing that, the sensible thing was to buy their books.

After our morning on skis Adrian and I decide we have earned our lunch. We sit upstairs among the scientists. Adrian, who is after all the science correspondent of the *Daily Telegraph*, informs the gathering with his customary conviction: 'Nobody knows what the mass of a neutrino is. The Russians think it has a finite mass. They've even put a device at the bottom of Lake Baikal to catch them! Everyone else thinks a neutrino's mass is zero.'

This is the day we meet Tweeky for the first time. Tweeky's real name is Peter Fitzgerald and he is, as we were to discover, a computer genius. An amiable, deeply intelligent man, on more than one occasion during the course of the *Biscoe*'s visit to British Antarctica he would work thirty-six hours or forty-eight hours at a stretch, ironing out the bugs in some computer programme so that lesser mortals would be able to carry on where he had left off knowing that the basic logical structures and operating commands were all lined up correctly.

Tweeky now replied to Adrian, a gloss rather than a contradiction: 'The Americans *used* to think the neutrino had a finite mass.'

After lunch, another scientist – Justin Koprowsky – takes us off to show us some of the instruments. He's a reddish-haired soft-spoken young man. This is his first job. He went to Edinburgh University where he got a First.

He introduces us to the flux-gate logger which monitors the earth's magnetic field continuously, and also to the ionosonde which measures the ionosphere every fifteen minutes. Then we climb up a ladder into the roof to see the Dobson spectrophotometer which measures the variations in the ozone layer.

The loft turns out to be a rather friendly place. Storage space is always at a premium on these Antarctic bases so the scientific equipment is surrounded by piles of cornflake packets, Bovril jars and tins of Horlicks. Adrian gets very excited because he thinks that the fact that no long-term changes in the ozone layer have been detected by this expensive machine aimed at the heavens from an Antarctic attic means that the whole aerosol scare has been disproved. Later that day he rushes off an article for the *Daily Telegraph* to that effect and is delighted to receive a telex almost instantly in return which tells him that London plans to give the story prominent coverage. The same telex indicates that his various reports of icebergs and skidoos have been well received back in England. So Adrian on the whole was in an extremely good mood.

'I always knew the aerosol theory was nonsense. It stands to reason. The ozone layer is much too big to be damaged by a few CFCS (chloro-fluorocarbons). I think the acid rain theory is nonsense too, by the way. They've just got the wrong kind of trees in Scandinavia.'

'Is nothing sacred?' I ask rather plaintively. Over the years I have spent a good deal of time on these fashionable environmental hazards. It's hard to believe that *all* of them are figments of an overheated imagination.

Justin tells us that the Dobson spectrophotometer cost £30,000 when new. 'There are about 120 of them in the world as a whole. The ozone measurements made here in Antarctica are used in the World Meteorological Office's global ozone research project. They are also made available to the United Nations Environment Programme and its group of experts concerned with ozone problems. The Americans use our ozone measurements to calibrate with their own satellite-mounted sensor programme. If all the ozone was brought down to ground level, it would be 0.3 millimetres thick. The volcanic eruption in Mexico changed the pattern of measurements. It's difficult to measure ozone in winter when it's dark down here. You're meant to be able to take measurements off the moon but that's not very satisfactory.'

I've been involved myself, when I worked with the EEC Commission, in the ozone controversy. I remember, back in 1977, going to Washington to what the United Nations billed as 'first high-level meeting on the ozone layer'. (I suggested in a speech on that occasion that you could hardly have a higher-level meeting than that!) After that 1977 meeting there was a follow-up meeting organized by the Germans in Munich at which the main aerosol-producing countries were supposed to announce restrictions on the production of CFCs. The leading light of that conference was the Honourable Barbara Blum, deputy director of the United States' Environmental Protection Agency. Her task – and she discharged it with eloquence and charm – was to try to persuade all of us dull, sluggish, not to say recalcitrant Europeans to bring in restrictive measures at least as severe as those already adopted by the United States. Equality of misery was the essential concept. The British delegation, I recalled, took a typically phlegmatic view, although Barbara succeeded on the whole with most of the other countries.

Later we sat outside in the sun. Munro, who has finished his own tour of inspection, comes to join us. 'In scientific work like meteorology', he tells us, 'you need results from a number of stations over a number of years. The variation in the earth's magnetic field is caused by currents in mid latitudes. There's also a current system near the Pole. We've looked at magnetograms as far back as the ones Scott took when he came south. Continuity of measurement is important. That's why BAS is here – and will remain here.'

I don't think either Adrian or I needed to be persuaded of the importance of the BAS scientific programme but Munro that afternoon summed it up very well: 'Data from the ionosphere and the magnetosphere are both needed by people working in atmospheric physics. People tend to characterize phenomena in terms of the levels of atmospheric disturbance. There are a limited number of stations around the world measuring atmospheric disturbance and Faraday is one of them.'

In the afternoon I went on a short tour of Faraday. Inside, it was not so different from Rothera. There were pictures of the Queen and Prince Philip on the walls and photographs of various ships which had obviously come down here at one time or another – a US coastguard vessel pushing its way through the ice; another French yacht, called *Le Kim*, the picture being inscribed *à nos grands amis*, with the crew standing on skis on the ice in front of their boat. (French sailors, it seems to me, must be a particularly intrepid breed.) Then there were group photographs, showing BAS personnel at Faraday year by year, almost like a school rugby XV. Further on there were presentation shields from the various groups and organizations who have been down here; the Chilean Antarctic expedition, 1978; the United States Antarctic Research Program, 1980; even the medallion of a Soviet ship.

It's clear that there is a camaraderie among those who live and work in Antarctica no matter what nationality they may be. One evening when I was at Faraday at least half a dozen of the Fids were wearing T-shirts given to them by American colleagues from Palmer Station about fifty miles away across the sea as the skua flies – and no doubt there are inscribed photographs of the *Biscoe* at Palmer. (In the event the *Biscoe*, running late, wasn't able to stop at Palmer. I would have welcomed the chance to compare USARP's facilities with those of BAS. According to all reports, the American set-up is considerably more 'up-market', which is not hard to believe since the British Antarctic bases, though comfortable, could hardly be described as luxurious.)

Before going back to the ship I had time to put on my skis again and pad off over the snow towards the distant *Damien*. I saw a Gemini zipping through the ice-floes to approach the French yacht, its passage disturbing a line of blue-eyed shags that took off brusquely across the water. Chris Elliott climbed aboard the *Damien* to pay a courtesy call. There may be a difference in tonnage between the two vessels but as far as sheer endeavour is concerned, the *Damien* probably comes out top and Chris – a sailor to his fingertips – knows when to salute a kindred spirit.

I continued my quiet perambulation of the island. It was slow work since the sun was very warm and the melting surface of the snow made skiing difficult. And anyway I came to a halt every few paces to absorb the scenery: the penguins, skidding and floundering across the ice, occasionally stopping to preen themselves; the skuas, squawking and veering dangerously close; the shags arcing back to their vantage-point.

At last I was on my way back to the base, having made a small circle of part of the island, when, from across the water, I heard Gemini's motor start up again, and saw the Captain scramble back on board in what seemed to be something of a hurry. I concluded, rightly it turned out, that he had for some reason been summoned back to his ship. The explanation, I suspected, might lie in the looming presence of a fair-sized iceberg which had caused the *Biscoe* to pull back from the shore and, therefore, a temporary suspension of unloading operations.

The launch came over in due course and we went back to the *Biscoe* on it, making a detour to see some leopard seals basking in the sun on an isolated bit of ice. As we chugged round and round the floe (the Geminis and Zodiacs zip and skim; the launch is more stately), the seals seemed barely disturbed by our presence. Once or twice they raised their heads and glared balefully at us. But it was not a hostile reaction; nor one of fear. In fact one of the most striking things about visiting this wilderness is that here there is very little evidence that the animals have learned to fear man. Contact between human and animal species has been limited. Apart from the early days of whalers and sealers there has been little large-scale exploitation of wildlife and, on the whole, patterns of behaviour reflect that fact. This is a place where, metaphorically speaking, the lion and the lamb still lie down together – that is an important part of the beauty of Antarctica.

I was sitting on the after-deck, contemplating a good day, when there was a great roar. I looked out and saw a tidal wave sweeping across the bay. An iceberg had just split in half and in doing so had turned turtle. I suppose if you're down here long enough you get used to the sound of the ice breaking up, but for me, an Antarctic novice, it's an extraordinary phenomenon.

At five o'clock I went up to Dallas's radio-shack and rang Jenny in London. Even today, used as one is to the wizardry of telecommunications, it seems absolutely amazing that you can dial directly through from Antarctica to Britain. Here you are, from the geographical point of view about as removed as you could be, and yet within a few seconds you can be talking to nearest and dearest. Pleasant as it is to catch up on the news from home, I can't help wondering whether the concept of wilderness, however that is defined, should not include also some element of total isolation, including telephonic isolation. But perhaps banning telephones in Antarctica would be to introduce an element of artificiality. If the technology is there – and it is – people may say: why shouldn't it be used?

After my telecon with England – timed by Dallas with a stopwatch because after all someone has to pay and there's no reason why it should be the government – I returned to the after-deck to fill in the time before dinner with iceberg-spotting. Charlie Cutsforth, Chief Petty Officer, came on deck. Something seemed to amuse him: 'I saw you skiing over there today. Trying to ski, I should say. I went skiing once in Norway. Couldn't get the hang of it, even though I had a good instructor. He told me to keep my legs together. Imagine you've a hand-grenade between them, he said, with the pin pulled out. Heaven knows how many times I would have blown my balls off!'

'I enjoyed it anyway,' I tell him.

As we stand there by the rail of the after-deck some leopard seals – perhaps the same ones we had seen on the ice-floe – swim by.

'Look at the scars,' Charlie says. 'They get scarred because they fight each other. They fight the crab-eater seals. If you see a crab-eater with scars, it was probably a leopard seal that caused them. Sometimes the leopards eat the crab-eaters.'

The second engineer, an Indian called Sakti Chaudhuri, comes out to join us. Sakti came to the *John Biscoe* two years ago. His family home is in Chittagong in what used to be West Pakistan but is now Bangladesh. In practice he lives in Liverpool.

'I went back to Chittagong with my family on a visit recently. We went to our ancestral home there. Actually, I didn't much like staying there. Too many dacoits around. Finally we moved into town.'

You could hardly have a greater contrast, I reflect, between Bangladesh, one of the most crowded countries on earth, and Antarctica with its all-pervasive solitude.

We stand there together talking about the Indian subcontinent.

'I used to live in Bally Gunge in Calcutta,' says Sakti.

'Oh, did you?' I reply. 'I stayed in the Tolly Gunge Club in 1961 – I was travelling through India on a motorcycle and I had an introduction to the Club's secretary who was the father of a school-friend.'

I don't know what the leopard seals made of this conversation.

At dinner Chris speaks enthusiastically about his visit that afternoon to the *Damien*. He approved totally of the Poncets' way of life, and wasn't the least bit concerned about their children.

'If the parents can hack it, the children certainly can.'

He talked with something like nostalgia of his own boat on the Hamble. 'In summer I tend to move out from the house and live on the boat itself for two months. They've got to know me quite well on the river.' I can well imagine it.

Chris says he'd prefer to go round Graham Land in the *Damien*, a fifty-footer, than in the *Biscoe*. 'You can tuck a boat like that in anywhere.'

I told him that I had seen him zipping back in the Gemini from the *Damien* to the *Biscoe* that afternoon and he explained what had happened.

'There was a berg on the starboard bow nudging us. We pushed that one away, but the anchor chain snagged it. Just then another berg came up to port while we were still snagged and there was a growler behind, plus the wind was getting up to ten knots and the tide was pushing us back. It looked as though we might go on the rocks and damage the propeller or the rudder. That's not a very clever thing to do, so I took her out.'

He made it all sound so easy, but I knew it wasn't.

Next morning I stood on deck waiting for the Gemini to come and take us on a tour of some of the outlying islands. It was a grey day. There had even been some rain. The water was dark and somewhat uninviting. Over on the island, across the water from the *Biscoe*, I could see a young biologist called Paul Copestake padding off on his skis. He had told me earlier he was going to look for the nests of some Wilson's petrels. He was easy to pick out against the snow as he set off from the base, since he was carrying a blue haversack, wore an orange balaclava and had grown an impressive ginger beard.

As I looked around, the little bay on which Faraday was situated seemed to have suffered a positive invasion of rubber dinghies. Geminis and Zodiacs were skimming hither and yon. The reason for all the activity was that the *World Discoverer* (run, as I knew very well, by Society Expeditions, Seattle) had come to call and groups of tourists were being ferried over – a boatload at a time – to visit Faraday station. One boatload, on its way back from the base, had decided to make a quick circle of the *Biscoe*. Well remembering that, had it not been for

Ray Adie's timely intervention, I might have been at the other end of the viewfinder myself, I waved encouragingly at them while doing my best to look intrepid.

As the boats buzzed about the bay, the *Biscoe* and the *World Discoverer* were in radio communication with each other. The *World Discoverer* has a German crew. Mike Jenkins, the ship's Third Officer, comes over with a walkie-talkie in his hand. I hear a voice saying, with heavy Teutonic intonations: 'Ve haf ze Frenchman still on board; but ve vill bring him ofer later.'

Mike explains that we are to have the pleasure of Jérôme's company, as well as that of his wife and their two children, at lunch on the *Biscoe*. 'Captain's invitation,' he says.

In the event our expedition that morning was cancelled. The ice started to crowd us again. Once more Chris had to roar back in his Zodiac – this time he was visiting the *World Discoverer* – to manoeuvre the ship. The pipe to the shore had again been disconnected, which meant that our final departure would probably be delayed. As I stood at the ship's rail, I could see that the ice was pressing right up against the side. A party of gulls and skuas, perched on top of the berg, had a ringside view of the happenings on deck.

These icebergs weigh a huge amount and the ship is not strengthened anyway except in the bow. It would be only too easy for the plating to be dented or even pierced. You don't argue with icebergs.

Jerry, the First Mate, comes by and says that with the wind getting up he is worried about the propeller and the rudder on the beach. He's followed by the Captain himself who comes aft to inform us that the wind is getting hold of the ship and there's not much the anchor can hold on to, since it's a smooth bottom.

The tension, modest but real, is broken by sight of Colin and Steve being winched back on board in a Gemini. They have been visiting the *World Discoverer* and are in a state of stupefied amazement.

'It's like a super de-luxe hotel in the middle of Paris,' says Colin. 'Cinema with plush seats; bars all over the place, entertainment of every sort, souvenirs for sale in the dining-room.' A far cry from the *Penola*.

Steve chips in: 'On the bridge they have special seats for passengers, special charts so they can follow where they're going. The only thing the Captain doesn't let them do is take the wheel. The crew is Filipino.'

'The average age of the passengers', Colin laughs, 'is about the same as ours, up there in the seventies, though some of the younger ones were away looking at the base!'

It appears that this is the last year the *World Discoverer* will be coming to the Antarctic. The German company which has chartered her for the past seven years has decided to refit in Cape Town or Singapore and run cruises in the Far East. My immediate reaction on hearing this is that it is probably a good thing. Tourism can bring in its train a host of problems and even though you may increase the number of people dedicated to the preservation of Antarctica, you will probably increase also the pressures on the environment. And there's the safety factor to be considered as well. How do you deal with the tourist ship which gets into trouble? Any rescue operation is likely to require the cooperation of those who have bases in Antarctica and that means diverting resources from existing scientific programmes. At the worst, rescue may be impossible. It was a tourist plane which crashed on Mount Erebus with the loss of everyone on board. It is not impossible to imagine a ship foundering under equally tragic circumstances.

Jerry Burgan comes back aft shortly afterwards looking much less worried than he had been before. He says he's got the engine going at around 200 horse-power; the bow-thruster is on and, on the whole, the ship is holding its position now with the warps quite tight.

'What happens', I ask, 'when the wind changes?'

'Well, we'll just have to work that out if and when it occurs. This is a seat-of-the-pants operation,' says Jerry. 'You take a look at the situation and you take the appropriate action.'

I spent most of the time at lunch that day talking to Steve about his wartime career in the photo-interpretation part of the RAF. 'The main PI centre was at Marlow,' says Steve, 'a fascinating unit of artists, writers, photographers, eccentrics. Our motto *Nihil lynxi latebit* was vulgarly translated as 'no lunch if you're a bit late'. By the way the author of that witticism was Leslie Durban who was a silversmith. He made the hilt for the Stalingrad Sword which was presented to Stalin after the battle of Stalingrad.

'We used to carry thirty-six-inch cameras, giving pictures six miles to the inch. Over Brest our Mosquitoes could see the clay-pits of St Austell.

'After a bombing raid "Bomber" Harris would call for a "dicing Spit" – a Spitfire that would dice with death – to see the damage. The dicing Spits were white Spitfires and carried arms. Normally the PI Spitfires travelled unarmed. They were blue with black spots. The pilot had the camera switch on his joystick.

'Later in the war, when flares were dropped by the Pathfinders, accuracy improved. A radar station at Cap Gris Nez was spotted by PI. So they landed some commandos. It was a dish-aerial set in a garden in front of a bungalow. We made a model of the installation and then photographed it by moonlight so when the commando team went in they knew what they were looking for.'

After the war, Steve told me, he became an assistant professor and reader in surveying in the Civil Engineering department at Imperial College, London.

Adrian and I finally set off in the Gemini after lunch to go round to the other side of the island to visit Wordie base, built in the 1940s and now abandoned. According to Colin and Steve, who should know, the base was situated on exactly the spot where they were first landed by the *Penola*, the British Graham

Land Expedition's mother ship. While Adrian and I were talking about ozone, Colin and Steve had already been off looking for traces of their earlier presence – some tinned supplies from the *Penola*, for example; a shivered timber or two; a pair of shoes which for some reason they left behind. In the event they returned a little disappointed. Colin said he found no relics of their stay of half a century earlier except a roll of government-issued toilet-paper which he produced with a flourish. Though we knew already, therefore, that we were not going to be seeing any ghosts from the past, we were still keen to visit Wordie. One of the strange things about Antarctica is that the way things are, as the poet put it, so they remain. Put up a hut on a rock somewhere and, apart from the natural effect of the wind and weather, that hut will still be there long after time has moved on. There are no demolition crews in Antarctica; even if you could find a way of using material satisfactorily from hut A in the construction of huts B or C, it will usually be difficult and/or prohibitively expensive to do so. New huts, new homes tend to be brought out pre-packaged from Britain and erected where they are needed (the most recent example being, of course, Halley on the Weddell Sea). As a result Antarctica is a kind of permanent historical museum. Those who have visited the Ross Sea area, for example, report that Scott's old base camp – not far from the current American base at McMurdo – is exactly as he left it, supplies still on the shelves, stove still waiting to be lit and beds to be slept in.

We zipped round the island in a state of some anticipation therefore, overtaking a leopard seal though these, as Mike Jenkins tells us, can be very fast through the water. 'Ugly brutes too', Mike shouts through the spray.

As we rounded the corner of the island, there was a line of blue-eyed shags on the ice-cliff, one of the sights which still sticks in my mind. They were, in their way, majestic sentinels. They didn't move as the Gemini passed at a distance of, I suppose, thirty yards. Just watched us curiously.

The other side of the island the ice had filled the channel. We slowed down to negotiate our way more carefully through the leads, passing – at close range – a couple of Weddell seals and a crab-eater.

Wordie base itself is, as we expected, a gloomy and decrepit place. There is still a sad little pile of coal outside. The base ran out of time before the stove ran out of supplies. The Union Jack still flies on the flag-pole but it is now badly frayed. The door creaks on its hinges.

Inside, the three or four small rooms remain just habitable, though hardly luxurious. Even when newly-minted, Wordie was probably fairly spartan. Those were the days of Operation Tabarin, when Britain was – amongst other things – concerned to forestall any Argentine claim to the Antarctic Peninsula. What mattered was having a team on the spot in a hurry – comfort was a secondary consideration.

Faraday's Base Commander, Martin Lewis, otherwise known as 'Mouse', came over for dinner with David Cotton, one of the Fids. I remember Cotton as one of the four Fids who came down with the *Biscoe* from Faraday to Rothera to help energetically with the unloading there. He had now returned to his permanent station. He is a short, tough-looking, fair-haired young man, whose uncle, so Munro tells me, was at Halley with him in the 1964–65 season. The Antarctic spirit, one sees, not only spreads from one base to another; it also passes from one generation to the next. Sometimes, in the most literal sense, BAS is like a family.

Munro – sitting opposite me at dinner – talks about the problems of having women on the Antarctic bases: 'The US has tried it, so has Australia. Neither has made a great success of it. You can see the difficulty. One year the US had a woman at their Pole station. She was about fifty and she became a kind of mother to the men there, so that wasn't so bad. But normally, if you put a woman in a base, it's a recipe for disaster. If you've struck up a one-to-one relationship, and then for some reason it's over, you can't just drift off down the hut and chat up another bird. One woman applied to BAS for a job and they asked her how she would handle all the men and she replied: 'No problem, I'd have it off with all of them.' She wasn't accepted. It's much more difficult', Munro adds, 'to live in a restricted environment like this. Finn Ronne came down with his wife. So did Harry Darlington. But they were both married. The Sex Discrimination Act doesn't apply to BAS jobs because they're conducted mainly overseas and I don't think it *should* apply either.'

There was no mistaking the note of disapproval in Munro's voice. I couldn't help feeling that his Scottish forebears would have been proud of him. 'I know they've got women in the men's colleges at Oxford now. I'm not sure that's such a good idea as it is, but anyway there's a world of difference between a college staircase and an Antarctic base.'

'What about the lady geologist we met in Punta on the way down?' I ask. 'She had spent the winter here, hadn't she?'

Munro reluctantly admitted that in this case BAS appeared to have broken its own rule. 'But that's not necessarily a precedent.'

The conversation drifts away from the dangerous subject of women to the much safer topic of ice, especially thin ice.

Steve tells the story of how they landed at Terra Firma. 'We were camped on an ice-floe. It was carrying us down the King George VI Sound. We had to work out where it was taking us; we had to decide at what moment, as it were, to bale out. If we stayed on too long, it could have broken up and left us in the water. On the other hand, it was taking us in the right direction. Finally, as the ice was cracking up all round, we decided to go our separate ways. There was a tremendous tide-crack and we had to jump for it, getting very wet in the process. So we called the place Terra Firma. It's still called that today.'

Chris Elliott, hearing us talking about ice, chips in; 'I heard that the *West Wind* ripped itself on the pack-ice as it was pushing up against the ice-shelf.

And the *West Wind* is a fully ice-strengthened vessel. The *Biscoe* has an ice-strengthened bow. There's a one-inch plate but that ends at the bridge. The *Bransfield* has a 1.5 inch plate. Lloyds give the details on all ice-strengthened ships.'

Chris has our full attention. It is one of the Captain's prerogatives. His table; his audience. 'The more power you have,' he comments, 'the more strength you have in dealing with the ice. You can come at it slowly and increase the power as you go in. If you don't have enough power, you may have to ram it and that's the way to damage a ship.'

After dinner we went over for some farewell drinks at the bar at Faraday. With so much to do in so short a time, there is inevitably a hail and farewell atmosphere about the *Biscoe*'s visits.

The bar on the base is called the Green Cow. As we arrive a darts match is in progress, the home team (Faraday) playing the away team (*Biscoe*). Sakti Chaudhuri, the engineer, has come over with us. He says it's the first time he's been to the bar at Faraday. On the whole, he doesn't come to Antarctica for the beer. Today he pulls the ring from the can and says: 'What I like about the Antarctic is that you can just focus your eyes on one thing when you're down here and watch for hours and hours. There's a penguin colony at Palmer station. We went in there once and I spent an afternoon just sitting watching the birds.'

'I'm looking forward to my first penguin colony,' I say. So far the penguins which I have seen have come in dribs and drabs. Single spies, not big battalions.

I look at the scene, finding it hard to believe that I am where I am. If you forget about the icebergs and the midnight sun and concentrate instead on watching the men, quick as a flash (far quicker than you can follow), subtracting double twenty and triple eighteen before throwing for – and getting – that last impossible double, you could believe you were in the Bull and Bush down the road on a Saturday night.

When I returned to the *Biscoe* I joined a party being given by the crew in their own bar on the lower deck. Some of their colleagues from the base have come over and the evening is in full swing.

In the corner of the crowded room I find Dallas Bradshaw, our loyal and long-suffering radio-operator. She tells me that she is the first full-time woman radio-operator to serve on a UK merchant vessel. She first joined in 1970. We talk about dolphins, always a favourite amongst those who go down to the sea in ships. 'The first time I came into Punta,' says Dallas, 'three dolphins led the way.'

Ray Jones, who is our friend from breakfast (without Ray and his two white-coated colleagues there would be no grapefruit for breakfast and probably no breakfast either), explains that dolphins are highly territorial.

'They'll guide a ship through their own area; then when you've reached the limit, they'll turn back and often another set of dolphins will take you on.'

'Did you read about the dolphin-kills in Japan?' Dallas asks. 'Do they really need to do that? Do they need whale oil to light the lamps of China?'

The *Biscoe*'s crew (who do the sailing) like the Fids (who do the scientific work) are employees of British Antarctic Survey. For them, coming down south is more than just another job. They feel themselves to be part of a larger team, and appreciate – or so it seemed to me – the spectacular nature of the environment in which they are called to work.

For example Martin Smith, who is by the bar, comes over to talk to us in the corner of the room. He is a tall young man, still wearing his engineer's boiler-suit. He looks faintly belligerent as he tells us that he joined BAS as a 'greaser' after a period on the dole. 'Greasers are called motor-men now, but I don't suppose you'd know about that.'

I know I look silly standing there like a prune trying to learn too much in too short a time. Instead of boarding the ship as a passenger, I should probably have joined as crew and actually earned my keep – and the acceptance of men like Martin Smith. 'No, actually, I didn't actually know that.' I have found that an extra 'actually' or two, even though technically superfluous, often helps to lubricate sticky dialogue.

Martin relaxes and begins to talk lucidly and poetically about Antarctica.

'As soon as I clapped eyes on this continent, I knew it didn't belong to Britain or Chile or Argentina. It belongs to all the organisms on earth. Even the micro-organisms', he adds for the sake of the record.

And Ray Jones, less poetically, chips in: 'You spend too much money on film, that's the trouble. It's unpolluted bloody everything, ain't it?

There aren't too many places in the world which are so beautiful that you spend too much money on film.

Later that evening Brian Stanswood, a radio operator from the base at Faraday, tells me: 'My view of life has changed. You live in a closed environment back home. Down here your job is your life.'

Stanswood is another of the Fids who got picked up by the Argentines in Grytviken. Contrary to expectation, he says they weren't badly treated. 'We had steak on the ship coming back from Grytviken. We were ten days at sea meandering around aimlessly as far as we could tell. In Argentina we were kept as political detainees for ten days along with the marines before we were sent off to Montevideo.'

Norman, the ship's electrical officer, comes in. He is a Scot, fair-haired and slight of build. During working hours I had got used to seeing him walking around the ship in overalls with a perspex-handled screwdriver stuck in his belt.

'You're a radio operator,' he says to Brian Stanswood, 'but I'm not sure we need all this communication with the outside world. In fact,' he says, 'BAS are worried about increasing means of communication. You can know what's going on back home and yet you're without the capacity to act. For example, your wife can ring up and talk about a money problem, a health problem, or whatever, but what can you actually do about it? If you're limited to letters, everyone is aware of the time-lag. At the very best they take a month, normally they take several months. That's a different perspective altogether and I think it's the right one. One of the marvels of the Antarctic is that you can be so completely out of touch.'

Mike Evans, the man from Faraday who talked to me about the upper atmosphere, laughs. 'We didn't even know there was going to be a general election in England last year until the day before it happened!'

I ended the evening listening to 'Tweeky' talk about his new computer which is going to measure weather automatically. 'It can transmit 600 characters or bytes eight times a day in under a minute. It can tell you temperature, pressure, humidity, wind, wind-direction, rainfall and hours of sunlight. It can't really do cloud cover except by inference from hours of sunlight, but if there's a man in the vicinity my machine asks in plain English about the clouds. The clouds are categorized in eight main types. Have a look', he says, 'at the *Observer Book of Clouds*. The machine codes the information into five-digit groups, sends it on to the satellite which in turn transmits it to NOAA – that's the National Oceanographic and Atmospheric Agency – in Washington which pipes it into the World Meteorological Office (WMO) trunk circuit. The information goes to Bracknell, Tokyo, Moscow, Melbourne, Buenos Aires, Paris and so on – about ten places altogether. We'll be working with a dummy terminal for the next six months; after that, we hope it can become a commercial operation. Normally', he adds, 'we also run upper-air measurements by balloon from Faraday – in fact we've been doing them every day for the last twenty years. But the hydrogen generator caught fire so we've had to stop for the moment. The balloons go from ground level to a height of thirty kilometres in about two or two and a half hours. They measure temperature, pressure, humidity and so on. The ozone balloons often go up to forty kilometres. Until three months ago we were doing that once a week. That was in addition to the work we're doing with the Dobson spectrophotometer. The purer the gas you use, the greater the height you achieve.'

In the most literal sense, Tweeky has his head in the clouds. He obviously thinks and dreams about them. 'Total cloud cover means eight-eighths. But you need to be able to know not only the degree of cover but also what height the cloud is at, what kind of cloud it is. Low would be below 2,000 feet; medium would be between say 3,000 to 8,000 feet; high anything above that. The type of cloud may depend on its height. Antarctica is one of the best places in the world to see nacreous clouds. You find them at around 120,000 feet. They're made up of minute ice particles which refract the sun's rays before dawn and you get a multi-coloured display.

'Stand on the balcony at Faraday station,' Tweeky advises. 'Look up to the north-east in the third week of May. That's the time of the year when the sun rises exactly in the gap in the Le Maire Channel. And just an hour before the sun rises it lights up the nacreous clouds.'

I decide there and then that if I ever come back to the Antarctic it will be to the Le Maire Channel in the third week of May.

6

The Richest Seas in the World

At around 6 a.m. on 24 January we went through the Le Maire Channel which separates the Peninsula from Booth Island. Even outside the third week in May it is one of the classic beauty spots – the Grand Canyon of the Antarctic. On a fine day the mountains rear their sunny crests on either side higher than the channel is wide. The effect of this breathtaking spectacle is doubled and redoubled by the reflections in the water. Even on a grey day, which is what we had, the setting is imposing enough.

I went for'ard into the fo'c'sle of the ship to stare ahead into the wind and spray as we pushed into the channel. I had my camera out with a telephoto lens in place when a humpback whale blew about two hundred yards in front of the *Biscoe* before sinking out of sight. It was a magic moment. My very own whale as it were. Later I had the photograph developed and there it was – smaller than I remembered it, more of a blob than a leviathan but recognizable to an expert as least. I shall not forget it.

By 9 a.m. we are out of the channel and have anchored off an old British base at Port Lockroy. Like Wordie, this is another relic of the time when BAS had a considerable number of smaller bases rather than concentrating its activities, as it does today, in five or six places. It's rumoured that the Brazilians have visited Lockroy, or even moved in, so a shore party from the *Biscoe* is about to go and have a look. We have quite a bumpy run in with the Gemini as the wind is fresh and the water rough. As we land at the base the Antarctic terns blizzard round, hundreds of them, thousands, making a terrific noise. They obviously don't want us to invade their territory. While the others go to look for Brazilians, I climb up the hill behind the base to see on a rocky promontory half a mile away across the water my first full-blown colony of penguins. They occupy every available inch of space and I can hear the noise they're making even from this distance and against the strong competition of wind and snow, not to speak of the high-pitched garble of the crowding terns who are still conspicuously agitated by our visit.

It's hard for me to describe the pleasure I had in the scene. The wind, the driving snow; the birds in the air, the birds on the rocks; the terns' nests on the ground with eggs in them, shortly to hatch; and a mile away, barely visible through the storm, the shape of the *Biscoe*, fount and origin of all good things.

I walk down at last from my vantage point because I can see that the shore party, having inspected the abandoned base and having found no trace of Brazilians, is preparing to climb back over the rocks to board the boat.

We go on across the water, five or six miles this time, perhaps more. Our objective is Damoy, a BAS refuge hut which also serves as an airport. Damoy is where, as I had learned during the course of the visit to Rothera, they fly up to pick up scientists who have come out from Britain, thus saving time – a procedure which becomes vitally important if there's too much ice for the ship to go on down the peninsula.

We walk over to the little hut after tying the dinghies up to the shore. Jerry and Mike, who are with us, each one in charge of a Gemini, are particularly careful in view of the harsh conditions to insist on a proper mooring. As Jerry puts it in his typically understated way: 'It can be a bit embarrassing if you're on shore and you find the dinghy has been swept away. Up the creek without a paddle, if you follow me!' We followed him.

Inside the hut, hardly bigger than a telephone kiosk, we at last found a trace of the Brazilians. There was a note in the visitors' book which I reproduce the way we found it:

TO OUR BRITISH FRIENDS, WE ARE TWO EXPLORERS FROM BRAZIL LOOKING FOR A PLACE TO LIVE OUR ANTARTIC ESTACION. CON-GRATULATIONS TO YOURS REFUGE. WE DON'T USE ANYTHING HERE. BIGS HOLDS (by which I suppose they meant big hugs or something like that). And then the note was signed – OUR NAMES NOGUEIRA AND DANTAS, 22 JAN 1984 – in other words two days before we got there.

It was an intriguing moment. I wondered by what means the Brazilians had arrived at Damoy. Where had they come from? Where were they going? There is no law of trespass in the Antarctic. On the contrary, the tradition is very much that facilities – shelter, food and warmth – are to be shared wherever they are found. If Nogueira and Dantas helped themselves to some chocolate from the hut here at Damoy, a party of Fids might well do the same in some unoccupied Brazilian base if they happened to find themselves in the vicinity. More seriously, even though national 'sectors' are depicted on the maps, at least while the Antarctic Treaty is in force any country may establish a presence anywhere. If they wanted to, the Russians could build a base right next to a BAS base – and the British would have no cause for complaint. Perhaps the Brazilians had their eyes on the area around Damoy and were 'casing the joint'.

On the way back to the *Biscoe* we stopped to say hello to some Frenchmen on board a yacht, smaller than the *Damien*, which had sailed down from South Georgia. They had obviously been sleeping late. The sound of the Geminis' engines roused them and they came up on deck, somewhat bleary-eyed, as we approached. I suppose when you have taken the trouble to sail all the way to the Antarctic, you don't expect people to drop in unannounced.

Jerry invited them to come over to the *Biscoe* later in the morning. But it was a rough day and the Frenchmen's dinghy didn't seem particularly robust so they declined. 'Have you seen any Brazilians lately?' Jerry asked in his best French.

It turned out that the previous day the Frenchmen had seen a large Brazilian ship (bigger than the *Biscoe*) with a helicopter which had been flying around the area. The ship had now departed but they had no idea where. They also said they had encountered two Chileans who were staying on Deception Island in an old base there.

'What about your own plans?' Jerry asked. Inevitably, down here the big ships look after the little ships, however informally. It's good to know where people are going.

The Frenchmen, standing up on the bobbing deck of their small craft and looking down at us in the dinghies, answered that they would probably go on down to Faraday or else put in at the US station at Palmer. I could see Jerry mentally filing the information. It would be logged later.

'Where are you going after the Antarctic?' I asked.

'South Africa,' came the reply. 'We expect to find work there.'

We returned to the *Biscoe* after our morning's excursion. Weighing anchor around mid morning, we steam up the Neumayer Channel which runs to the east of Anvers Island and to the west of Winky Island. Just the other side of Winky lies the southern end of the Gerlache Straight, named after the famous Belgian explorer who was the first to winter in the Antarctic, albeit involuntarily.

At lunch we talk about noises in the Antarctic. I decide to play a recording I have made of the noise of the Antarctic terns at Port Lockroy. I prop the tape-recorder on the table in the wardroom and for a moment we are all transported to the scene of a few hours earlier.

'Wait till you hear fur seals on a beach,' Colin says. 'It sounds like a crowd at a football match. Two million fur seals in the Pribilovs, they make a noise I can tell you. That's about the largest gathering of large mammals you'll ever see anywhere on earth. It probably even beats the migration of wildebeest and hartebeest in the Serengeti. The pup of the fur seal, or at least of the Pribilov fur seal, carries the placenta around for a few days after birth. It's like a little anchor. It stops the pup wandering off.'

The following day we headed straight up from Smith Island to the Falklands. We left Deception Island far over to starboard (it would have been interesting to have put in to the spectacular natural harbour there – the result of the island's volcanic origin – and to have visited the abandoned whaling bases, but the *Biscoe*'s timing was too tight to permit unscheduled detours).

There was no land at all in sight. The most striking thing I could see from the back of this tossing deck (it was really quite rough) was a profusion of seabirds. I was beginning to be better at identifying them. A scud of Wilson's petrels went past and a Cape pigeon. Then there were the gulls – I was not sure what kind – and various sorts of albatross, which I had not yet learned to distinguish correctly.

The albatross as usual seemed to take up a position further astern than the other birds. You could see them wheeling and beating in a kind of virtuoso display a hundred yards or so away from the ship. Since the rubbish or 'gash' – the slops and leavings – from our time at Faraday was still lined up in barrels on the afterdeck waiting to be tipped into the sea, this was going to be a red-letter day for the birds.

For the rest of us, the non-bird population, it was a grey murky (or 'manky', as the Fids would say) day. That didn't really matter. We had had our share of fine weather. I wondered as I stood there how many whales had passed silently in the night.

After breakfast Paul Copestake – my biologist friend – came on to the bridge to do a preliminary bird count. He starts by noting three black-browed albatross and some dove-prions.

'Those are the little grey ones with M patterns on the wing,' he explains. Paul isn't counting the birds astern of us, just those which are flying past us or else are out in front. An albatross about 150 yards away is a grey-head, he says. And then he points out a raft of feeding albatross. There must be about twenty of them over there, I reckon, but Paul actually counts sixteen. They're just sitting on the water ahead of the ship now.

'They would have been feeding at night,' he tells me. Two fur seals leap through the water as we watch. 'Fur seals are totally pelagic,' Paul says. He also notes a mass of Cape pigeons. 'Very rich pickings this morning. We're bang in the middle of one of the main feeding areas. This is one of the places where the krill swarm.'

He points out a black-bellied storm petrel, white underneath with a dark stripe down the middle. 'On the whole the black-bellied storm petrel is less common than the Wilson's petrel. The petrels seem to line up astern more than in the front.'

Just before noon we come up again to continue the bird count. This time we stand on the afterdeck and add a southern fulmar, darker than the albatross, to our list. The ship is rolling fairly severely now, though the sun has come out and the day looks brighter than it did. After one forty-degree roll I thank Paul for his company and retire to my position in the wet lab.

Tweeky comes by and talks to me about the ship and the weather. He looks out of the window and says scathingly: 'The waves could be five times higher than that. You can have eighty-foot waves from trough to top. Now we've only got about fifteen feet.'

I ask what happens when the boat hits an eighty-foot wave and he says: 'That doesn't happen because before that you heave to and are lined up head into the wind. It's up to the people on the bridge to interpret the state of the sea. Mind you,' he says, 'this ship has taken a sixty-foot roll. There have been times when the lifeboats have been touching the water and still the ship has come back. If it *did* turn over, it would probably float for a while because the hull would form a giant air bubble.' Even Tweeky with his optimistic view of things doesn't find the thought very comforting because, he says, it would be difficult to get out.

'But you have tremendously experienced captains on these BAS ships,' he reassures me. 'The four captains of the two vessels – there are two captains per vessel – have been on this Antarctic run for twelve years. They know the waters. Know them probably much better than the captain of the *Endurance*, for example. He's a naval man and likely to be down here only for two seasons.'

The bell rings for lunch, but I think that today I'll give lunch a miss.

I spent much of the afternoon sitting in my customary place in the wet lab, mainly reading. I looked again at the book on Antarctic Research edited by Adie, Priestley and Robin. However dated it may be, it seems to be the only book where the whole range of Antarctic sciences is brought between the covers of a single volume, though more comprehensive treatments of single branches of science, e.g. geology or biology, either have been or are about to be published.

I also read Nigel Bonner's book on whales. (Bonner heads BAS's biology department; knows about seals as well as whales – I recall that we had lunch together once in London when I was involved with the EEC campaign to prevent the import of Canadian seal products.) Later we would see the tiny wooden hut, still known as Bonner's bothy, where as a young man Nigel Bonner spent his – and anyone's – first winter on Bird Island. Another book which I have been reading is Apsley Cherry-Garrard's *The Worst Journey in the World*. He tells the story of how he led the search for Scott and his companions after they had failed to return to their base. I couldn't help feeling that if Cherry-Garrard had not respected Scott's own instructions as scrupulously ('don't hazard the dogs'); if only the rescue party had pressed on that little bit further, the tragedy might have been averted. And it was clear to me as I sat amidst the towering waves digesting his account that Cherry-Garrard himself must have entertained similar thoughts. There is more than a note of self-justification about the book.

On a more practical plane a book to have close at hand wherever possible is Watson's *Birds of the Antarctic and Sub-Antarctic*, published by American Geophysical Union in Washington DC. Watson is a great help if you're trying to sort out one albatross from another. He is, as it were, the literary complement to Paul Copestake.

Towards the end of the afternoon Paul himself came through the wet lab and saw me determinedly learning, from Watson's book, how to tell one albatross from another. He perched himself – rather like a bird – on the metal top of one of the sinks to give me a gentle lecture on the subject. 'Their dynamic soaring makes use of currents of air created by the wave patterns. The albatross works with a long flight-range. Like prions and petrels it uses the full extent of food resources. It feeds mainly on fish or krill and some amphipods but the different species have different feeding patterns. The grey-headed albatross on the whole takes squid and some krill. It has a long breeding cycle because squid has poor nutritional value. The grey-headed albatross can't get back into condition quickly so it breeds every other year. The black-browed albatross on the other hand breeds annually and is a krill-feeder. But then sometimes – as may indeed by the case this year – the krill can crash. Normally the grey-heads have the more reliable breeding record. Sixty per cent of their chicks survive. Of course we're talking about one chick every two years. The life-span of an albatross is thirty to forty years.

'In fact,' Paul continues, 'the key biology is known for all breeding species at Bird Island. We know diet, incubation, growth, the energetics of chick rearing. Theoretically you can work out how much food is required from the ocean to meet those requirements. You're talking about a pretty substantial biomass. For example we have a group estimating penguin numbers. Jérôme and Sally on the *Damien* did some work for us – in fact I came down with them on their boat once, doing the penguin count. There are 2 to 5 million penguins just on Willis Island, which is more or less next door to Bird Island.

'You *do* find diversity in the sea-birds here. What you miss out on are the shelf-feeders, the gannets, the gull groups. All of the birds here are truly pelagic. They don't need land apart from nesting which is why you have such enormous concentrations on the sub-Antarctic islands. With penguins you've got to be within three hundred or four hundred kilometres of good feeding grounds, the good areas for swarming krill, for the mega-swarms if you like. One of those areas is off South Georgia. There is another one in Scotia Bay, and another in the Weddell Sea. The albatross on the other hand can forage about one thousand kilometres. There's a chap at Bird Island called Peter Prince – we'll probably meet him – who's invented a device which measures the total time flown by an albatross and the time spent sitting on the water. It shows when an albatross is feeding at night, when the krill come up to the surface and the squid come up to feed on the krill. From this machine – from the daylight hours registered – you can work out the range of a bird and the average latitude and longitude where the albatross has been. There's one albatross breeding-group at South Georgia. Another at Tierra del Fuego. They're both grey-head groups. If you work it out from the information given by the machine it turns out they seem to spend quite a lot of their time feeding exactly where you'd expect, in a krill-swarming area half-way between the breeding grounds of the two populations. The US research vessel *Hero* actually found one of our birds exactly where we'd expected it to be. We put the ring on the leg and then when the bird comes back after about ten days' foraging for its chick, we get a read-out from the device.'

Like that of the albatross itself, Paul's range as well as his stamina was considerable. It was clear that he enjoyed talking about birds. I enjoyed listening.

'There are two kinds of skua: the brown skua and the south polar skua. The south polar skua actually looks brown but it's possible to tell the difference between them. Prions are burrowing petrels. Diving petrels also burrow. The point is they also require a slightly warmer climate than you get on the Peninsula. You've got to be able to dig down to make the nest and of course you can't do that when the land is frozen or ice-covered. Mollymawks are what we call the small albatross: the grey-headed, the black-browed and the yellow-nosed albatross. Mollymawk is a term the whalers used to use.

'But the birds that don't rely on actually burrowing, the Cape pigeons, the snow petrels, the Antarctic petrels, are all down here. Having nested, they become pelagic. They are wanderers in their non-breeding year. The wandering albatross, for example, can circumnavigate the globe. Birds breeding here one year have been recovered in their non-breeding year in Australia. They're caught when they moult. Or sometimes they're washed up on beaches. You need the ring numbers of course. An organization called Euring covers Europe and North Africa. Then there's the British Trust for Ornithology (BTO). The US operates through the Fish and Wildlife Service.

'Virtually all the sub-Antarctic islands are packed with birds. They were also the centres for sealing and whaling operations. That's how the rats and the cats were introduced. These seriously affected bird populations. Rats, for example, will eat the eggs of the smaller species or disturb them.

'There has been an expansion of the chin-strap penguin population. Jérôme and Sally made their own penguin count. This was extremely useful because their information could be fitted in to the information we have gathered. The biomass programme has shown a great increase of penguins on the South Orkneys and South Georgia. This increase is probably related directly or indirectly to the availability of krill. The chief threat to bird-life down here now is over-fishing of krill.'

Colin happened to be passing through the lab at this point in our conversation. Hearing Paul's last remark, he expressed his view on the survival of the penguin and indeed most other species clearly and succinctly: 'The chief requirement is for populations to exist in viable numbers and to be well distributed.'

Paul agrees: 'The great thing about wide distribution is that it leaves the possibility for the natural forces of speciation to operate.' He says to Colin: 'In your day the giant petrel was just one giant petrel. Now we see the northern and the southern giant petrel. In biological terms you get the lumpers and the splitters. Of course there is an overlap and there's also hybridization. The northern petrel tends to feed off carrion and penguin; the southern on krill and prions. The whales became too specialized, too highly adapted. It took such a long time for their reproductive cycle to work. If you accept the idea of evolution and speciation, it's not really surprising if we find some species in the process of splitting. Under some biological definitions, man himself could be referred to as several species although we can still interbreed, which is a rough test.'

Colin nods his agreement. He says there used to be – probably still is – an antelope in the museum at Khartoum with ancestors of three different antelope species.

The conversation circumnavigates the globe and comes back to albatross. Possibly it was the Ancient Mariner syndrome; more probably the sheer magnificence of the birds themselves which drew us back to them. For me, unquestionably, the albatross in their variety and abundance, in their size and strength and power, were king of the Antarctic air and it was a treat to hear men who knew about them talk about them.

'The grey-headed and black-browed albatross look virtually the same,' says Paul, 'and yet they have very different strategies. The genetic imprint is different. The black-browed reaches maturity in 100 days from hatching to fledging; the grey-headed in 125. Peter Prince in South Georgia swapped the black-browed chicks with the grey-headed chicks. He fed squid instead of krill to the black-browed chicks and krill instead of squid to the grey-headed chicks. Both chicks followed the inherited growth curves but the black-browed chick fed on squid did very poorly and the grey-headed fed on krill did very well. Became super grey-headed if you like. Prince has a system for weighing birds:' – he turns to Colin – 'I believe it was your son who first invented the machine . . .'

It is clear that biology runs in the Bertram family because Colin acknowledges the truth of Paul's last remark and says he hopes to see the device in action when we reach Bird Island.

For the time being Paul has to content himself with merely describing its operation: 'It weighs the chicks every four minutes or every ten minutes. You have to allow for the distortion when the parent-bird lands. You put a radio-transmitter on the parents and you can tell which parent is feeding which chick.

'Last year', says Paul, 'we were looking at the domestic budgeting; at the sharing out of duties. We'd see the male come in first. He'll spend anywhere between two and three weeks building up a nest. Then the female comes in and recognizes the male. She makes two or three short trips during which time copulation occurs. The female goes off to produce the egg. She lays it and almost immediately returns to sea. She'll only spend ten to fifteen per cent of the time on the egg at the beginning. Over the incubation period as a whole the male does sixty per cent of the work. It's the male that puts in the first ten to twenty days' incubation. You see his weight drop from five kilos to four. The female goes off to feed; then she does a shift. The shifts gradually equalize over the ninety-day incubation period until they're both doing about two days at a time. So there's a very good chance that when the chick hatches there is still food in the gullet of the parent. Then you have the brood/guard period and that lasts two, three weeks. The birds are dependent in this initial period on their parents for thermal regulation.

'Wanderer chicks get to a peak weight of sixteen to seventeen kilos and then drop off as they are feathering. Some chicks think they're on to a pretty good number and just wait to be fed. Others are really working at it. You can see them flapping their wings. There was a helicopter came in to Bird Island and rotors created a marvellous down-draught. I could see all the chicks really working trying to take off in the slipstream of the helicopter. When the helicopter left, of course, they just fell back bewildered. In the end the parents will desert lazy chicks so they either die or they have to get on with it. They spend about ten months as chicks. You have egg-laying at Christmas, hatching in March, fledging in November.

'It seems odd for the birds to feed during the winter, but the food comes up at night. Possibly the clue is the phospholuminescence. The concentration of krill goes up at night. The marine ecosystem of the Antarctic hinges on krill. This in turn depends on phytoplankton and zooplankton. The Antarctic convergence produces nutrients. In the tropics you don't have much mixing of surface water. Here you've got a lot of mixing. All the sub-Antarctic islands fall within the convergence at some time of year. And the Antarctic can be defined as everything within the convergence.'

It was a long lecture but I think I absorbed most of it. Talking to Paul and Colin that day on board the *Biscoe* made me realize how much I missed by *not* studying biology – or indeed science of any kind except for a brief spell of agricultural economics which, I suppose, has something to do with physical reality. There was so much to learn and no chance at all of learning it. In the end I could only envy men like them who can point a pair of binoculars at some wheeling mollymawk and announce with certainty that what they're looking at is a young grey-headed albatross which has not yet entered on its breeding cycle. And of course that conversation – with its references to places like Bird Island and the South Orkneys which still lay ahead of us – served only to increase the sense of anticipation.

I asked Paul, banally, what the great moments of his life as a biologist so far had been. He thought about the question and then said: 'There have been many. One of them certainly was when I was on Laurie Island in the South Orkneys and I found penguin colonies which had never been seen before.'

At dinner that evening Chris told us he sailed single-handed in the *Observer* transatlantic race. He was seventeen days late starting because he had to go to hospital at the last minute but even so he came thirty-fourth out of fifty-three.

'At night', he says, 'you could hear the sound of whales and dolphins through the hull of the boat. At Southampton boat show Greenpeace bring in the *Rainbow Warrior*. They have a stand there and they play the records of those sounds.'

That same day we saw six whales on the port bow. They were probably hump-backs. We were having dinner and the Officer of the Watch called down through the intercom: 'Whales on the port bow!' We rushed up and were in time to see them. Up there on the bridge the general scene was one of grey seas and rain. The windscreen wipers were working at full speed and the little fan was whirring in the clear-view window. A pair of wandering albatross were sweeping low across the foredeck. Our position, as recorded by the satellite navigator, was 63.4°S, 61.28°W.

The next day, 26 January, was finer. I went up on deck early to talk to Paul, who said that the birds seemed to have disappeared. He was delighted with their performance yesterday morning. If they weren't around today, it was probably because we had moved out of the feeding area.

Things weren't much better in the afternoon. He had seen a fairy prion but not much else. It was a sunny day; not much wind, not much swirl. We were at the end of one leg of the journey, before starting the next. Paul had been talking on the radio with 'the lads at Bird Island'. Since we were going to be visiting the Falklands before going on down to the South Orkneys, South Georgia and Bird Island, he had asked them if they wanted the *Biscoe* to bring anything from Stanley.

Inevitably, as we approached the Falklands, conversation in the wardroom tended to focus on 'the campaign'. I found myself sitting at dinner that night with the Second Mate, Peter Kerry, and the electrician, Norman. Peter was obviously something of an *aficionado* of naval strategy. He explained to me how the Sea Dart system mounted on our two frigates *Sheffield* and *Antelope* actually worked extremely well until the *Sheffield* was blown up by an Exocet. 'It forced the Argies to come in low and it meant that their bombs didn't have time to arm. So even though many of our ships were hit, often the weapons didn't explode. The system worked.' Meanwhile, back in the east, the frigates *Brilliant* and *Broad Sword* were guarding the aircraft carriers. For his money it was on the whole a most successful operation. 'After all,' Peter claimed, 'our systems were geared for the North Atlantic to bring down the Russian bombers. We transposed the whole operation to the South Atlantic and won.'

To what extent Antarctica was behind the Falklands campaign is an open question. Explicitly, probably not at all. But, implicitly at least, Antarctica was one of the issues over which the Falklands war was fought. One of the first things we did, for example, was to remove the Argentines from South Thule in the South Sandwich Islands – British territory falling outside the Antarctic Treaty area but which had in fact for the last several years been the site of an Argentine base. South Georgia itself, the scene of the first actual hostilities between the two countries, is regarded by many as a 'gateway' to Antarctica. Certainly Grytviken is a good deal closer than Grimsby to the White Continent. As for the Falklands, though these islands (biologically at least) are rich in their own right, they could be of interest too as a staging-post for Antarctic operations. A government wishing to undertake major exploitation, say of minerals or oil, might find it exceptionally handy to have the title-deeds to the Falklands in fee simple.

We also talked at dinner that night about our route home. Why weren't we stopping in Montevideo, I ask. (I know that BAS ships used to stop there.) Jerry Burgan tells me that that particular port of call is another casualty of the Falklands War. Since the Argentines are enforcing a two-hundred-mile zone for British ships, the *Biscoe* would have to do a long sweep to the north before coming in to the mouth of the River Plate. Peter, the Second Mate, tells me that the name of our equivalent area around the Falklands has been changed from an 'exclusion' zone to a 'protection' zone. *Plus ça change* . . .: I bet the Argies aren't fooled.

The temperature of the sea today is 8°C. It's getting warmer. After the Falklands, we shall go south again to the icy cold of South Georgia. But it's good to have this interlude.

At two o'clock the next day I'm up on the monkey-deck. We're six miles away from the Falklands. We can't actually see the islands yet, because there's a light mist over the sea but they're somewhere to the north of us. Over to port I notice a flock of albatross sitting on the water. There must be another forty or fifty birds whirling around in the air. The Falklands are one of the great breeding-areas for the albatross. Calm day, calm sea. The sun is beginning to peek through the mist; it's difficult to imagine that two years ago a nasty little war took place here and about five hundred people were killed and several ships sunk.

Looking out over the rail of the monkey-deck, I've just seen the wonderful sight of half a dozen albatross paddling themselves through the water so as to get up enough speed for take-off. I think this is the largest quantity of albatross we've so far seen. The ship is really surrounded by them. As far as I can make out they are mainly the black-browed variety. Paul agrees. He makes a quick ornithological inventory.

'See that small bird skimming over the surface with light patches under its wings? That's a sooty shearwater. Over there you can see immature black-browed albatross in the water. The black or dark-brown birds are giant petrels, although they fly in a manner rather similar to the albatross. Giant petrels get lighter as they get older.'

Paul tells me he saw some rock-hopper penguins this morning and points out some Magellanic penguins in the water some distance away, also some white-chinned petrels known as 'chinnies'. 'You'll be confused at Signy because there they call the chin-strapped penguins "chinnies".'

An hour later land was clearly visible. I can understand exactly what people mean when they say the Falklands look like Scotland. They do. The hills, like Scotland's, are brown-green with heather-covered stone outcrops. As we turn into the harbour, we have the first sight of Stanley itself. A tiny little town running up the hill away from the water and the harbour front. I couldn't have imagined that the place would be as beautiful as it is. It's the Western Highlands; it's the Shetlands; it's the Western Isles. It's what we fought a war for.

On the way in we passed the *Uganda*, which saw service as a troopship during the Falklands War and is still being used for that purpose. Further in, the *Andalucia Star* and the *Tor Caledonia* ride at anchor. There are a couple of container ships waiting to discharge their cargo. Coming closer to the town one can see how neat it looks. Rows of little box-type houses with coloured roofs, not much bigger really than the containers themselves which are stacked up on the quay-side.

I can see the cemetery up on the hill. That must be one of the old cemeteries. I expect there are new ones now. In fact I know there are. The church, over there to the right – more properly called the Cathedral of Port Stanley – looks very English, its red-tiled roof contrasting with the green of the hills in the background.

At this distance – we're still half a mile out – it's difficult to see any signs of war damage. Apparently, they filled many of the shell-holes, though we'll probably see some burnt-out helicopters. On the quay there I see a building which bears a sign along the whole length of its façade: Falkland Islands Company. A helicopter flies overhead and I can see another parked opposite the town the other side of the water.

I can understand why they built the town here. It's obviously a perfectly sheltered inlet. The harbour itself I'd say is about five miles along by one mile wide. Looking to the right-hand side of the town I can see Sapper Hill, the top of a Rapier missile poking out from behind the crest. The hill behind that is Tumbledown which is where one of the main battles took place. In the water ahead of us are the floating fuel flubbers. These are great balloon-shaped tubes which get towed out to the tankers to be loaded with fuel and are then towed back again so that they can be discharged into the oil tank. And crossing now from one side of the harbour to the other is a maxi-float, a flat transporter which can carry men and material including vehicles.

Another helicopter sweeps overhead. An albatross follows it, heading for the skyline across the water where cows and radio-masts commingle. Not far from the cows, or so it seems, I hear an explosion and see a cloud of smoke.

Somebody or something, I presume (possibly a cow), is blowing up a mine. From the other end of the inlet where the great floating 'coastels' for the troops are to be found, comes yet another helicopter. It is flying low and fast and slings a heavy object from a cradle beneath its belly. Adrian, looking through his binoculars, says it's a gun and he's probably right. This is a gun-toting place at the present time. Everywhere you look there's military activity of one kind or another. Helicopters, boats, troops, guns, planes – I can't believe Britain is planning to hand this one back on a plate to the Argentines.

Looking once more towards the shore I can see, now that we're close in, that even there the traffic seems mainly to consist of lorries or jeeps or Land Rovers. Down towards the end of town, in the direction of Mount Tumbledown, the new radio-dish stands out as a sign of the times. They didn't have it when they needed it, but at least they've got it now. The dishes point day and night at INMASAT – the International Maritime Satellite – which orbits 22,300 miles above the equator.

The black ball at our mast indicates that the *Biscoe* has anchored. (Two black balls would mean that we're out of command or have no engines.) We are waiting our turn to go in. As the helicopter comes back again, this time gunless, the gong goes for dinner.

We were still waiting to berth after the plates had been cleared away. The delay was due to the fact that the *AES*, a Danish charter vessel from Svendborg, which usually makes the run from England to the Falklands, was still taking up our position at the jetty. Paul was up on deck with me spotting different species of helicopter. He wasn't sure what the big civilian model was – he thought it was a Sikorski of some kind. But anyway he had positively identified a Sea King, a Sea Lynx and a Gazelle. As we stood there a small cargo boat registered in Stanley called the *Monsunen*, which had been drawn up next to the *AES*, pulled across to the other side of the harbour. The *AES* winched herself round by hauling on the anchor which had been dropped out from shore. As she eased away from the jetty we made ready to go in.

7

Falklands Interlude

After we had docked I decided to go for a walk along the front. The road runs between the water and the town. The main landmarks of Stanley are all there by the water's edge. I passed West Store, Stanley's main shop, which is owned and managed by the Falkland Islands Company – probably one of the neatest monopolies or near-monopolies that still exist in these last few years of the twentieth century. I surveyed the cathedral from close range, noting the massive arch of whalebones – each one of them fifteen or twenty feet long – that had been erected in front of the door. (There was whaling from the Falklands as well as from South Georgia and throughout the Antarctic, until they ran out of whales. Putting whalebones up outside the church was, I suppose, all part of the Judaeo-Christian tradition of 'subduing the beasts of the field' – or, as in this case, water – and 'having dominion over them'. Judaeo-Christians, it seems to me, have a lot to answer for.) Then I walked on all the way down until I came to a large and graceful white house with a red roof and trim green lawn. The Union Jack was flying briskly in the breeze above the gables so I reckoned, correctly, that I was looking at the seat of power. The Governor – since the Falklands War – is called the Civil Commissioner, but the change of name has not really produced a change of role. There was a distinctly colonial air about Government House. When, later, I met Sir Rex Hunt, the present incumbent, I could understand why. Whatever his title, Hunt is a man who knows how to wear a cocked hat and ostrich plumes.

Standing outside the house, on the gravel forecourt, was a London taxi. For a second or two I'm surprised to see it. Then I understand the explanation. The taxi – maroon-coloured like the Royal cars in London and with the Royal coat of arms emblazoned on the passenger doors on both sides – is the official vehicle of the Queen's representative. That the total mileage of metalled road in the Falklands scarcely runs into double figures (as I was to discover to my cost) is neither here nor there. Whether you are a Governor or a Civil Commissioner, you need an official vehicle even if it spends most of its life on its pad looking at the upland geese on the water across the way. In terms of capital investment, a London taxi makes more sense than a Rolls. Altogether an imaginative touch, I thought.

The Marconi Communication Centre, newly installed, with its satellite dish and ancillary equipment, is right next door to Government House. I examined the huge saucer pointing at the sky. Whereas before the war the islanders had to rely on whatever ramshackle means of contact with the outside world were at hand, now they have the finest, most up-to-date system in the world. Seven pounds sterling buys you about six minutes of prime-time clear-as-a-bell conversation with London or other European centres (it's a bit more expensive if you want to call the States). You buy a card and you shove it in the slot, dial the number and three seconds later you're talking to Peter and Joyce, Cyril and Edna, and all the other loving folks back home. There was a time in British politics when, as far as the Falklands were concerned, out of sight meant out of mind. Galtieri and Marconi (why is it always the Italians who are responsible for the big changes?) have altered all that. Some of the really canny islanders even know the direct-dial numbers of a few key London journalists. The Falklands 'lobby' no longer depends on the good-will and sympathy of occasional visiting firemen who can carry their message back to London (as certain Conservative backbenchers did most effectively during the 1970s). Now they call Britain direct to make their views – and news – known. Any idea that the British Foreign Office, or anyone else for that matter, can 'cook up a deal to get shot of the Falklands' without there being the mother and father of a row is totally naïve – there are enough people here to see to that and now, with that surrealist white saucer tilted up to the sky like a young girl waiting to receive her first kiss, they have the necessary means at their disposal.

I walked on past the Marconi office – a temporary structure like contractors' offices on a building site – in the direction of Mount Tumbledown. My objective was a house on Racecourse Road where, so Colin Bertram had told me, I might find a gentleman called Tom Davies who was Chairman of the Falkland Islands' Trust and as such deeply involved with the preservation and protection of the historical and natural beauty of the Falklands. I found Racecourse Road easily enough. As its name suggested, it ran alongside the Port Stanley racecourse, a location which itself was distinguishable by its white railings and a rather homely grandstand. A flock of sheep grazed on the turf in the middle and I couldn't help wondering whether on race-meeting days, whenever these were, one set of four-legged animals remained *en poste* to encourage and exhort a different brand of quadrupeds about its business. No point, surely, in wasting grass.

Tom Davies's house was to be found half-way down Racecourse Road. It was a newly-built affair, rather Scandinavian in appearance, standing with a group of houses of similar design, some half a dozen altogether which had clearly been constructed by the same firm at the same time. I subsequently discovered that I was looking at a development known as the Brewster houses to which considerable notoriety attached. It turned out that they had been contracted for by Britain's Overseas Development Administration to make up for accommodation lost in Stanley during the recent hostilities and to provide shelter for 'experts' of various kinds who might be coming to the Falklands to help with the development programme which had recently been approved for the Islands. By the time the Brewster houses actually became habitable, it was estimated that the cost per unit exceeded several times over the cost of constructing similar houses in Britain. Even allowing for the relative inaccessibility of the Falklands and the high cost of transporting men and material, it seemed as though somewhere someone had made a killing and it probably wasn't the long-suffering inhabitants of Stanley.

I didn't, of course, know any of this at the time as I stood on the doorstep ringing Mr Davies's bell. I registered only the somewhat incongruous nature of the development. The Brewster houses on Racecourse Road were, to say the least, an architectural innovation, contrasting rather oddly with the usual Port Stanley style of simple box-type houses, most of them painted white, with coloured roofs of corrugated iron.

When it became clear that no one was home, I left a note on the mat saying that I would call again and walked back the way I had come. It was a grey, windy evening but after several days on the *Biscoe*, where exercise was hard to come by, I was glad of the excuse to stretch my legs.

A quarter of a mile or so from the jetty lying – as do most of Stanley's landmarks – along the waterfront is the Upland Goose. It is, I believe, the one and only hotel in the Falklands, though there are certainly other establishments in town where it is possible to rent rooms. There was no one, as far as I could see, in the dining-room; there was no one in the lounge. There were, however, several old copies of *The Times* and *Telegraph* which must have been flown in on the air-bridge. I sat down and caught up with the news for half an hour. Two of the *Telegraph*s, by coincidence, contained stories which Adrian had telexed during the first leg of our voyage. Rather imaginatively someone had included a little map with each story to help readers unfamiliar with Antarctic geography to locate Faraday and Rothera and the Drake Passage, places which to us were now as familiar as Nottingham and Newcastle.

A few yards from the Upland Goose is the Globe Hotel, now no longer a hotel but a very thriving bar. Still holding the two copies of the *Telegraph*, I was drawn by the commotion coming from within, and opened the door, to find half the British Army there. The place was completely jammed with people wearing camouflage jackets.

'Hello,' says a voice belonging to a man with a beret and no hair on the back of his head. 'Have a Penguin.'

I'm a bit slow off the mark, so the voice explains: 'Penguin is the local brew. They import the malt but otherwise it's made on the island. It's all right for starters.'

It began with starters that evening, but didn't end there. The owner of the first voice had a friend with an equally abbreviated coiffure. They introduced themselves as Ian and Dave. They said they were with the army ('you can tell by the hair cut') out at Mount Pleasant, half-way to Darwin, building the airfield.

'First they called it the "Strategic Airfield",' says Ian. 'Then they changed its name to RAF Mount Pleasant. Now it's just called Mount Pleasant airfield. The object is to reduce the requirement for permanent troops out here in the Falklands by having a place you can fly them into in a hurry – in about eighteen hours actually. The length of the main runway will be 8,500 feet and there'll be a secondary runway as well. Mount Pleasant will be defensible in its own right. It will have Rapier systems of ground-to-air missiles as well as its own permanent garrison – much smaller than the present level of troops on the island.'

I suppose it's all right for me to know all this – the Argentines certainly know it all already. But it shows what a pint of beer can do on a blustery evening. Looking around the crowded bar of the Globe, I have the sense that Stanley is like a sleepy frontier town which has suddenly been invaded by a Klondike-type goldrush. In this case the invasion has been created not by prospectors but by the army. The town itself, like the bar of the Globe, is full of soldiers. There are helicopters in the air; Land Rovers, jeeps and armoured cars on the streets; houses taken over to billet one regiment or another. Even though a serious attempt has been made to get troops out of town, I can well understand the point which Jérôme Poncet made, back in Faraday on the Antarctic Peninsula. In the long run, and probably that is not so very long, the Falkland Islands cannot absorb a military presence of this sort while retaining their own distinctive character. It is not clear, of course, that an Argentine presence on the Islands would be any less disruptive. Certainly all the islanders I talked to were vehement in their wish to have nothing further to do with the Argentines. The tragedy is that this remarkable outpost of the Antarctic wilderness should have been caught up in the games of national – and nationalistic – politics.

Later David and Ian come back with me to the wardroom of the *Biscoe* and we continue the discussion with Peter, the Second Mate, who signs in the bar-book for a round of beers, the first of several.

'You may say, leave the Falklands the way they were,' says Peter, 'but I think you're wrong. Before the war, the place was still bloody feudal. The Falkland Islands Company owned most of the land; most of the people were FIC tenants, the FIC was taking more and more out of the island and putting back less and less. It was dying on its feet. Officers joining the Royal Naval Reserve used to be asked the standard question: in which ocean are the Falkland Islands. Atlantic? Pacific? The Indian Ocean? And so on. You had to ring the answer. Not many of them got it right.

'Before the war mail only used to come once a month and then it was getting to be once every two months. The *John Biscoe* served as the mail-ship once.'

'Heseltine was here last week,' says Ian. 'He flew into Stanley and went over to the new airfield. It was a beautiful sunny day – a politician's day. He shook hands with the people working here, made a little speech and flew back on a non-stop flight in a Nimrod. Eighteen hours in the air. It had to take off with a very light load. In fact with hardly any fuel on board. Then it gets refuelled over the islands by a Hercules tanker. Janet Young from the Foreign Office was here the other day too. She made a speech in the Town Hall, then answered questions. It was broadcast on the local radio.'

'Where do you live out at Mount Pleasant?' I asked. 'Do you camp?'

'They brought up a ship called the *Merchant Providence* and moored her to the shore with a Bailey bridge. That's our base.'

David has the more poetic soul. 'The wildlife is incredible. The penguins, the geese, the albatross. The scenery is magic. It has all the beauty of Scotland without the roads to mar the landscape.' I was to discover in the next two days what he meant by the absence of roads.

Later still I asked about Antarctica. Was the British presence in the Falklands linked to the defence of British interests in Antarctica? Had the Falklands War itself been fought over Antarctica? My military friends were fairly sceptical. 'That's a four-pints-on-a-Friday-night theory,' said Ian.

The following morning I was up early. My Antarctic clothing had to double up as motorcycle gear. Apart from a crash helmet I had everything I needed – boots, waterproof trousers, bright orange jacket and a long woollen scarf to get caught up in the wheel, like Isadora Duncan's. My plan was to explore as much of the Falklands as I could during the next two days while the *Biscoe* was tied up at the jetty.

Land Rovers are hard to come by; other forms of four-wheeled vehicles are even more difficult to find and in any case anything less than a Land Rover or a jeep would, I knew, be useless since the roads don't exist outside Stanley except for one nine-mile stretch which sets off hopefully across the island towards Darwin before petering out into the usual boggy track. Happily, Ian had in the course of our previous evening's conversation (begun in the Globe and continued till after midnight on board the *Biscoe*) told me about Kelvin's.

'There's a chap come out from England,' Ian had said. 'Simon Powell is his name and he started up a business selling muttonburgers and renting out scrambler motorcycles. He's made quite a go of it. The troops haven't got much else to do on their free afternoons so they quite enjoy hiring a bike for a few hours. You've got to watch out for the mines, though.'

Having discovered where to find Kelvin's Bike 'n' Burger shop, I left Adrian asleep in his bunk, clomped down the gang-plank in the early-morning mist and up the hill. Half an hour later, having dutifully shown a UK driving licence, paid a deposit and acquired a crash helmet, I mounted a 200cc Suzuki with scrambler wheels and an extra can of fuel strapped to the pillion, and headed off into the unknown.

Simon Powell, a soft-spoken young man who had been some eighteen months in the islands already, was sceptical about my plan to get to Goose Green and back in a day. 'The average speed you make on the tracks in the 'camp' – 'camp' is what we call the country outside Stanley – is less than ten miles an hour. Have you ridden a motorcycle before?'

I wanted to tell him that once, a good many moons ago now, I had ridden a 500cc BSA Shooting Star most of the way to China in the steps of Marco Polo, so reckoned I could handle some puny little Suzuki. But I restrained myself. There was a look in the man's eyes which seemed to indicate that he knew what he was talking about.

'Thank's for the advice,' I said. 'Perhaps I'll just head off and see how far I get.'

In the event there was never any question of my getting to Goose Green and back within the day. Though there was only one stretch of gravel road out of Stanley – and that was indeed the road to take if you were heading for Darwin and Goose Green – somehow I failed to find it. Instead I shot off with the little Japanese motorcycle bucking and rearing like a rodeo steer (you *can* forget a thing or two about motorcycle riding if it's twenty-three years since you've last done it) in the direction of Government House. Somewhere behind that seat of power I found a track which seemed to head off into the mountains. At the time I imagined that this could conceivably be the way to Goose Green so I ploughed on, slicing and slewing through the mud and the peat. Quite soon it began to rain heavily and I, in turn, began to get seriously wet. The Antarctic anorak was great for Antarctica, but a Falklands rainstorm was a different thing altogether. Life was full of trickling sensations.

On occasion both I and the motorcycle disappeared altogether into bogs or other sorts of holes in the ground. It was hard to see them coming since my snow goggles were steamed up on the inside and so covered with rain on the outside that to clear them would have required some of those high-speed windscreen wipers such as are found on the *Biscoe*'s bridge. Even if I had seen the holes coming, I could not always have avoided them. A lightweight motorcycle becomes a heavyweight motorcycle once I am on board. In partnership as it were we acquire a certain momentum, particularly downhill, and though the track for the most part led uphill, there were plenty of downhill stretches too with bogs neatly sited to catch the unwary.

Once or twice the motorcycle disappeared almost totally. It was a question then of finding a piece of *terra firma* somewhere and heaving and tugging until first a wheel, then the frame, then the thing itself, as Duns Scotus might have said, emerged.

After an hour or so of this (during which time I calculated I must have covered all of six or seven miles while climbing a few hundred feet in altitude) I decided that I would check the map. If this was actually the main route from

Stanley across the island to Goose Green then, or so it seemed to me, the network of internal communications on the Falklands was even worse than I had been led to expect. So I sat there astride my motorcycle peering at the sodden map for five minutes before concluding that I'd goofed. I wasn't on the 'road' to Goose Green, that was obvious. If I was anywhere, I was approaching a place – a settlement of some kind, I imagined – called Estancia. In so far as I was still on a track at all (and recent experience had given me reason for doubt) I concluded I must be on the 'Estancia Road'.

This was both good and bad news. The bad news was that in view of the weather, the distances and difficulties involved, and the fact that I was very wet and also quite tired from yanking the motorcycle out of bogs, it was clear that I wasn't going to make it to Goose Green and back in the day and therefore wasn't going to have the pleasure of turning the machine back in at Kelvin's and telling the proprietor that it had been a piece of cake after all. The good news was that I knew more or less where I was and had worked out that if I plunged onwards and upwards through the rain and peat for another few miles I would reach the Estancia settlement itself where, no doubt, I would be able to raise a cup of coffee and perhaps even a bit of mutton. My view was that though I had not personally fought in the Falklands campaign, I belonged to the class of people, as my old logics tutor used to put it (he probably cribbed the expression from Russell and Strawson), who *had* fought in the Falklands, namely the Brits, and *qua* Brit if for no other reason – like being hungry or tired – I deserved a spot of sustenance and drying out if and when I made it up the road to the homestead and to the homesteaders whose way of life and irredeemable Britishness had been safeguarded by the expending of so much blood and treasure.

This carefully laid scheme unfortunately came to nought because, soon after establishing my whereabouts, I found myself confronting a large sign. The legend on the sign was written in bold red letters. It said: MINEFIELD RED AREA. Then underneath, just because the world is full of idiots on hired motorcycles who think they are cleverer than they really are, the message was spelled out in detail: 'This is a Minefield Area Situation Map as at 20th December 1983. It supersedes the previously produced Minefield Area Situation Map dated 12th November 1983.'

I digested this information somewhat uncomfortably. The fact that Minefield Area Situation Maps seemed to be following on each other's heels thick and fast indicated to me that the said Situation was clearly fluid. Was the Situation, as perceived by the mappers, better or worse? Were they blowing the mines up? Or were the mines blowing themselves up? Were sheep and cows and motorcyclists being blown up too?

I read on. The notice said: 'The map below shows three categories – (i) *Green*. These areas have been exhaustively checked by the Royal Engineers and are believed to be safe; (ii) *Blue*. There is no evidence at all that these areas contain minefields or boobytraps. However they may contain unexploded bombs, ammunition, missiles etc.; (iii) *Red*. These areas are known to contain mines or boobytraps. Do not enter.'

Stuck on to the map, in the middle of the Red Area, was a playing-card depicting the Ace of Spades. Under the card, someone had written the message: 'You have been zapped by the Black Aces, the Royal Engineers' Bomb Disposal Unit.'

I sat there on the motorcycle contemplating this turn of events. It was clear to me that if I wished to proceed towards the Estancia settlement and the several attractions it offered, I should have to pass through the Minefield Red Area, a course of action which the Black Aces amongst others would obviously strenuously oppose were they around to be consulted. On the other hand, I reasoned, the people who lived up at Estancia must come down to Stanley from time to time. Surely if one actually kept scrupulously to the track, veering neither to the right nor to the left but following in the path of the latest Land Rover there was every chance that unexploded mines would stay that way, and the booby-traps fail of their targets.

So in the end I unhooked the gate in the fence around the minefield and rode gingerly over the next mile of peat and bog. At one moment a helicopter came up from behind the hills and flew low overhead. I thought I was going to be hailed by a megaphone and told to clear out of the Minefield Red Area before I was blown out of it. But instead it took a long close look at me in the still driving rain before clattering on in the direction of Stanley.

I cleared the minefield successfully though there were some nasty moments when the track itself became too boggy and rutted for me to proceed and I had to strike out across fresh ground (I held my breath waiting for the bang and hoping somehow that the motorcycle would take the force of any explosion). But in the event I gave up on my plan to reach the homestead at the end of the track. A ridge too far, I said to myself, as I finally turned back to Stanley.

Yet I was glad I'd gone out that morning. Apart from the helicopter and some sheep I had seen nothing for several hours. Even with the hassle of manoeuvring the machine across country, the beauty of the scenery, the pervasive solitude, left their mark. Once I paused with the engine switched off on a small stone bridge crossing a clear burn where the water gurgled deep amid the peat and heather and then curled away between grey rocks till it was lost in the mist. Moments like that made the effort worth while.

I came back down in the end by the same route I had gone up – including having to pass a second time through the Minefield Red Area. The going was every bit as rough and as slippery but I was beginning to get used to it. By the end of the long morning I found I could manage quite a turn of speed. On the final stretch into Stanley where the track across the peat turned into a stony pathway, I noted with some satisfaction that the needle on the speedometer was reaching double figures more and more frequently.

Tom Davies, wisely, suggested I should leave my boots outside since he could see at once that they were full of mud and muck. I have a feeling that he might have wanted to suggest that I should leave myself outside as well but he was too polite to say so. I was certainly too cold and wet to refuse his hospitality.

'I got your note,' he said, in his cheerful, welcoming Welsh voice. 'I wasn't sure when to expect you. Come on in anyway and have some lunch.'

Over lunch, while I dried out and generally recovered from the morning's exertions, Tom – and his wife Gwen – spoke about their life in the Falklands. Tom had the ruddy complexion of a man who has spent much of his life out of doors. He had come out to the Falklands a few years back on a contract with Britain's Overseas Aid Administration. They had moved into one of the Brewster houses because their own had been destroyed in the fighting in Port Stanley. Tom knew about the 'scandal' – by coincidence there had been a front-page story in the *Observer* a week or two earlier and copies had reached the Falklands – and he thought there was probably something in it. 'They do seem a bit pricey,' he said.

Tom Davies's job was to run the Falklands Islands Agricultural Research and Development Centre.

'It was previously known as the Grasslands Trial Unit. The new title is meant to indicate that we're concerned not just with improving pasture in the Falklands but with agricultural developments on a broader scale. In essence, though, sheep are still pretty damn important,' Tom explained. He gave me a quick thumb-nail sketch of the sheep economy of the Falklands.

'You've got 640,000 sheep on 2.8 million acres, that's three-fifths the size of Wales. That means the stocking ratio is one sheep to four acres. The Corriedale is the main breed. They've tried Cheviot and similar breeds but the quality of the wool isn't good enough. And remember out here wool is the crucial thing. The basic problem is gross nutritional deficiency. In schools out here, the teachers ask what colour the sky is – and the answer's "blue". They ask what colour blood is and the answer's "red". Then they ask, what colour grass is and the answer's "white". The Falklands is covered with white grass, *Cortaderia pilosa*, which is very poor quality herbage and for four months of the year there's damn all to eat. Even if we could get fat lamb here, the prospects of exporting mutton are poor because the slaughtering facilities are not up to EEC standards and it probably wouldn't pay to bring them up to those standards. So you're left with wool which is in fact a super product for an isolated community. Falklands wool is very high-quality knitting-wool. It has "loft" and by that I mean a light texture. The problem is: Corriedale sheep have low fecundity; the lamb ratios are around 65% at marking times; the cost of fertilizer is high and you've got a structure of ownership whereby the FIC holds 43% of the land, and even the other farms – or many of them – are owned by absentee landlords.

'Patagonia', continued Tom, passing his plate up for a second helping and making sure that I had some too, 'has exactly the same system as the Falklands, except that there you have one sheep in twenty acres. As a matter of fact, the Argentine part of Patagonia is pretty arid. It's desert scrub around Comodoro Rivadavia. Stanley has the highest rainfall in the Falklands – about twenty-six inches. Normally we have a water deficit for eight months a year. Today was very untypical. Usually it's windy, but with clear bright sunny weather. If it wasn't for the peat's moisture-conservation, it could be as arid as Argentina.'

The conversation turned to the environment. Tom and Gwen Davies explained that the Falklands Islands Trust was a small group of people interested in the conservation of both fauna and flora as well as sites of historic interest such as the original British settlement at Port Egmont or the remains of the early French colony at Port Louis. The wrecks which were scattered around the islands were also of considerable importance.

'Our chief task, mind you, since the invasion,' says Tom, 'has been educating the military. They were landing by helicopter in the penguin colonies, lighting fires in the peat. There's been a sudden doubling of the population in the Falklands and that's bound to have an impact. And the population has become more mobile too. With their helicopters they can get to the most isolated islands and cause a lot of damage. I'm glad to say they've appointed a Military Conservation Officer now and things are improving.'

Before I left the Falklands I would have a chance to talk both to the Military Conservation Officer and also to the Senior Naval Officer. I formed the impression that, whatever the initial shortcomings may have been, the military was now trying to take more seriously its responsibility for conserving the environment. The essential problem seemed to be one of attitude. Whereas I might look at a sweep of hills, bare and bleak and empty of human life, and think of it in terms of its landscape and ecological interest, your average military man tends to view the same prospect as a marvellous place to practise with his artillery, a 'magnificent natural firing range' in a world where, from his point of view, such facilities are sadly becoming increasingly scarce.

I realized the size of the problem – and just how much was at stake – when Tom produced for me a verbal synopsis of the wildlife of the Falklands.

'There are 5,000,000 penguins on the Falklands give or take a couple of million. There are five kinds of penguins here, in fact – the Magellan, gentoo, rock-hopper, king and Macaroni. They don't have the emperor or the Adélie. This is also one of the great reserves for the black-browed albatross, particularly on Beauchene and Jason Islands. The tussock grass provides a marvellous habitat. Fifty per cent of the world reservoir of albatross is here in the Falklands. You've got a whole range of burrowing birds – petrels, prions, shearwaters; there are kelp geese and flightless steamer ducks, a wide variety of waders, two sorts of oyster-catcher, teal, black-necked swans – there's an enormous heritage of bird life. As far as marine mammals are concerned you've got elephant seals, sea lions, fur seals in profusion.'

It sounded like – as indeed it was – a veritable cornucopia. 'Aside from the military landing their helicopters in the wrong place, what's the chief threat to the wildlife?' I asked.

'Over-fishing,' Tom replied promptly. 'The waters around the Falklands have become a free-for-all. The Poles are here; the Japanese are here; the Spaniards are here; the Russians are here. The Russian mother ship comes right into Berkeley Sound. Quantities of fish and krill are being taken around the islands – I've heard estimates that put it as high as 400,000 tonnes a year. You can't keep up that kind of fishing for long without damaging the base on which the whole marine ecosystem depends in these parts. The islanders have been pushing for a 200-mile fishing zone to be declared. Lord Shackleton recommended it in both his reports to the Government. That 200-mile fishing zone would make economic sense – we would get some revenues from the fish caught in our waters by those foreign fleets even if we weren't doing the catching ourselves, although', Tom added, 'there are plans to develop the fishing industry in the Falklands. And ecologically speaking, some form of control over the fishing is indispensable. Janet Young – Lady Young – from the Foreign Office was down here a few days ago as you may know. She held a public meeting with the islanders in the Town Hall. They pressed her on the fishing question, but she wouldn't give any assurances. She kept using phrases like "Be assured the Government is considering the matter". That didn't go down very well.'

'Surely the Government has to think about what the Argentine reaction might be if we unilaterally declared a 200-mile zone around the Falklands?'

Tom Davies had the answer to that one too. 'Better controls are in the Argentine interest as well as ours. Biologically speaking, the resources of the Patagonian shelf – that's the area between the Falklands and the South American mainland – are shared. Fishes swim. The Argentines must suffer if uncontrolled exploitation takes place on our side. And vice versa.'

This was a theme which I was to hear more of in the course of the next couple of days. Later, as the *Biscoe* steamed up on the last leg of its journey from the South Orkneys to South Georgia, I was able to appreciate at first hand the extent of the foreign, especially Soviet, invasion that is taking place in these southern waters. Even then, during that lunch on Racecourse Road, it seemed to me to be ironic that Britain was making so much effort over the Falklands only to throw away what was possibly its richest asset, namely the resources of the surrounding seas.

'With all its wildlife, with its marvellous scenery' – and in spite of the rain I had, after all, seen a good deal of scenery that morning – 'the Falklands could attract more tourists than they do, couldn't they?' I asked. Tom wasn't sure about that.

'Even if tourists can be flown into the new airport,' he said, 'and it's not yet absolutely certain what its status is to be, it's incredibly difficult to move people around as you have probably already discovered.' I nodded feelingly.

'Simon Lyster is here at the moment for the Falklands Islands Foundation,' Tom continued. 'He wanted to go out to New Island over on the West Falklands and of course we did our best to help him. But it still meant that a chap had to give up three days of shearing to take him round in a boat. With the best will in the world, coping with tourists can be very difficult.'

I took his point. The Falklands is the kind of place that can absorb people, whether soldiers or tourists, only in small doses. Overload the environment, drive too many roads across the 'camp', too many heliports and hotels and you can find, suddenly, that the place isn't what it used to be, that, in the most literal sense, the birds have flown.

'I'm glad you were able to help Simon Lyster anyway,' I said. 'He's a good friend of mine. Give him my regards when you see him.'

Tom and Gwen Davies had another guest that day at lunch, a young man called Steve Whitley who was also working on the agricultural side. He left before I did, having remained rather silent throughout the meal. When he had gone Gwen Davies explained that Whitley's wife had been one of the three civilian casualties, all women, killed in error by British troops as we recaptured Stanley. While I was in Stanley I bought the *Sunday Times* book on the Falklands campaign which was being sold in the NAAFI. According to the book, the house in which the three women died had been shelled because Jeremy Moore, the officer in command, had been led to believe that all the houses lying to the west of the War Memorial had been abandoned.

'With Steve here today, we didn't want to make too much of the Falklands conflict,' Gwen explained. 'I'm sure you understand.' I did. Meeting a man whose wife was one of the three Falklanders killed brought the Falklands conflict into a different kind of focus. It may have been a relatively small war as wars go but for one man at least its effect was cataclysmic.

It was still raining after lunch, but I had hired the motorcycle for the whole day and decided to have my money's worth. Tom Davies explained how to find the gravel road which runs for those nine enticing miles in the direction of Darwin. 'Turn right up the hill after the hospital,' he says. 'You can't miss the hospital, it's got a red cross on the roof.'

Soon after I returned to England the hospital in Stanley burned down in a fire with tragic loss of life. But it was still in one piece that afternoon, the huge Red Cross on its sloping roof having successfully protected it against the effects of the battles which raged round. So I found my road across the island, tried out the motorcycle's paces over the measured distance and finally returned to the *Biscoe* in time to get ready to go off to drinks with the Governor along with the captain, officers and assorted members of the crew.

Stanley is the port where the *Biscoe* is actually registered. For Chris Elliott and his men this is very much home ground. They – and the British Antarctic Survey – may have their differences with the Governor of the Falklands (one of those differences concerns revenues which the Governor collects from ships which put in at South Georgia and which BAS argue should properly be spent in and on South Georgia where they have – or had – a base, rather than being diverted into Falkland Islands coffers), but on the whole the relationship between BAS and the island authorities is a long and close one. For years now the distinctive red hulls of the *Biscoe* and the *Bransfield* have been a familiar sight in Stanley harbour.

Walking along the front to Government House, I came across a load of wooden crates piled by the roadside. Some of the packing had come open. Peering inside, I could see grey marble slabs with gold lettering: IN MEMORY OF THOSE WHO LIBERATED US. There followed a list of regiments and a rollcall of the ships involved in the recent Falklands campaign. The names seemed to go on for ever.

Since I had some minutes to spare I walked on up past Government House, past the Marconi hut and the satellite dish pointed towards London to that now much-weathered memorial commemorating the earlier but no less crucial engagement of the Falklands. The granite pillar set above the water, where the road bends and curls upwards, is surmounted by the bronze model of a warship, while to one side stands a statue of Victory. Beneath the statue I could read the words: 'In commemoration of the Battle of the Falkland Islands, Fought on the 8th Day of December 1914, in which the British Squadron Invincible, Inflexible, Caernarvon, Kent, Cornwall, Glasgow, Cannabis and Macedonian, under the command of Vice-Admiral Sir F. C. Doveton Sturdee, KCB, CO, CME, destroyed the German Squadron under the Vice-Admiral Graf von Spee, thereby saving this colony from capture by the enemy.'

Government House is a large, rather pretty, white building. Wide French windows look on to the lawn which in turn sweeps down towards the road to the harbour. When the weather is fine the Governor – one imagines – must enjoy holding his official celebrations outside within sight of the upland geese winging their way across the Sound. It is not hard to imagine him moving decorously among his guests as they cluster on the grass toasting the Queen's birthday, or the Recapture of Stanley, or Empire Day, or some other similar event of enduring significance in the Falkland Islands calendar. Of course the Governor is no longer called by that title. Some wimp in Whitehall, believing that there will be less fuss about the islands' colonial status if an alternative designation is used, has thought up the phrase 'Civil Commissioner'. But no one is deceived. Everyone knows Rex Hunt – Sir Rex Hunt as he now is after the war – was the Governor, is the Governor and, at least as far as the islanders are concerned, ought to remain the Governor, until death or disability removes him from office.*

Today the French windows are closed. Though the morning's rain-clouds have moved on towards the West Falklands and Patagonia, the wind is still gusting fiercely. The party takes place indoors. I arrived to find the Governor, a genial quick-witted man with a lifetime in the colonial service behind him, talking about the events of the Falklands War and their impact on the daily routine of Government House.

He points to the life-size portraits of the Queen and Prince Philip which hang at one end of the reception room. 'Menéndez took them down when he occupied the house. He propped them up against the wall there. He put up a picture of Galtieri and San Martín. When Jeremy Moore took over he said to me: "It's your house; you put them back up."'

Glass in hand, he takes me by the arm and steers me across the room. 'Look at the carpet,' he said. 'It's amazing it's in such good shape. The Argies had piled sandbags outside the house all along the window.' Lady Hunt – Mavis to her friends and intimates – is with us. She too, she tells me, was agreeably surprised to find the house in such good condition when the Argentines left.

I'm lucky that day. Sir Rex takes time off from entertaining his other guests to give Adrian and me a private tour of the main landmarks. (Adrian, I'm glad to say, is still with us, though he'll be leaving the *Biscoe* and the Falklands to fly back to England on the air-bridge. Happily, I will be able to continue with the *Biscoe* until the end of its Antarctic voyage.)

We move from the main reception to the little office which is in the back of the house. 'The Argies', explains Hunt, 'came down over the hill and fired from outside, about fifteen yards away.' He shows us the bullet-holes in the walls of the room. 'I was lying on the floor behind the desk here with a 9mm pistol the marines gave me. Mike Norman, the Marine Major, was in here too.'

We stand there for a while in the office. It seems to me to be a tiny, flimsy room. I decide that Sir Rex Hunt is probably lucky still to be alive.

'You're lucky still to be alive,' I say.

'I think so too.'

Outside the house Hunt shows us the spot where the marines shot an Argentine captain. He speaks without relish, in a matter-of-fact tone of voice, yet I could sense the faintest hint of satisfaction. At least the fight hadn't been totally one-sided.

'His guts were hanging out, he was dying. We could hear him groaning all night. But instead of surrendering when one of us went out to him, he put a grenade to his mouth, pulled the pin out with his teeth, so that we had to go back. He died during the night. Later on, when García took over, he told me:

*His retirement is now imminent, but the title of Governor is to be reinstated.

"You killed my best Captain." So I told him: "I never asked him to come here."'

While we are outside we see the maids' quarters at the back. At some point during the battle of Government House, three Argentine soldiers found themselves trapped here. 'They surrendered to us when it was morning,' said Hunt. 'But we didn't really know what to do with them as we were about to chuck it in ourselves.'

We go back inside, past the kitchen, to the dining-room, another splendid room whose windows give out on to the lawn at the side of the house where the Union Jack flies proudly on its flagpole. There is a glass-fronted mahogany sideboard in which place-mats and other table furnishings are stored. Some of the place-mats have been damaged by rifle or machine-gun fire.

'They fired from outside into the room. You can see the holes in the walls too. When Menéndez occupied the house, they had dinner parties in here.' He points to a splendid life-size portrait of the Queen above the sideboard. 'They kept that portrait in place all the time they were here – illuminated, too, when they dined.'

As I stood there beside the Governor looking at the Queen in all her Majesty, then at the long polished table, the well-kept lawns beyond the window and the flag flying stiffly in the wind, I couldn't help imagining Menéndez sitting in this very room during his brief moment of glory and wondering how he must have felt when, between the dessert and the cheese, some aide-de-camp came in with the message that a British task force had sailed for the South Atlantic.

Nor could I avoid the thought, as Rex Hunt threw in that little touch about keeping the Queen's portrait lit for dinner, that if the Falklands War had not been tragic it would have been comic, even absurd. Here were two great nations, Britain and Argentina, quarrelling over a straw, as Hamlet put it. We were not historic enemies. Far from it. We were historic friends. The Queen presided willy-nilly over Menéndez's dinner-parties. A couple of months after I returned from Antarctica and the Falklands, I had a chance to visit Argentina in person. Ten days in Buenos Aires convinced me that there was a reservoir of goodwill towards Britain just waiting to be tapped. 50,000 Argentines are of British descent; 20,000 actually hold British passports. A British Foreign Secretary, George Canning, in Verona in 1822 refused to lend the British fleet to the Spaniards to enable them to reconquer their River Plate colonies. British money helped build the railroads, the public utilities, expand the cattle industry. Yet all these links were being jeopardized – at incalculable cost both in economic terms and in terms of our general strategic interests – because we could not come to an agreement over the Falklands.

Across the way from the dining-room is a pantry of sorts. This too looks out on to the lawn with the flag-pole. Hunt describes how Don Bonner, his major-domo, who today is helping to serve drinks at the party and who throughout the Argentine occupation came in each day to check up, took a gun and stood by the window all night. 'Bonner said: "If any Argie tries to take the flag down, I'll bloody shoot him."'

We go upstairs to the bedrooms. Hunt shows us the room where the British Prime Minister and Denis Thatcher slept when Mrs Thatcher visited the Falklands. This room too still has bullet-holes in the ceiling. I have a feeling that they will probably stay there for ever now, as part of the furniture of the room. 'Maggie wanted to sleep under the Argie bullet-holes,' says Sir Rex. 'So she slept over here in one bed near the door and Denis slept near the window.'

Next to the main guest bedroom is a room in which the Hunts' daughter used to sleep. 'There used to be a Picasso painting in here. My son-in-law gave it to my daughter before they got married. It was a nude from what I believe they call Picasso's Blue Period.' He smiled. 'That blue nude had a bullet-hole drilled in it bang in the right place. My daughter's got the painting in her new home now. Pride of place. The bullet-hole is still there too.'

Once more we go downstairs – this time into the Governor's study. 'Menéndez took this room over during his time,' says Hunt. 'This was where he worked. See the picture of Shackleton behind the desk. Menéndez didn't take it down, but he put another picture above it.'

On the table is a large leather-bound volume containing copies of *Illustrated London News* of 1919. 'Menéndez obviously liked to look at the book because he had taken it out of the shelves.'

He shows us other relics of the Argentine occupation: an illustrated book about the exploits of San Martín, the Argentine national hero; some pills which Menéndez had left behind in the drawer of the desk; some rose-coloured lip salve. It is a bizarre moment. Though Menéndez had been unceremoniously kicked off the island, his presence – through these relics and mementoes – could still be felt. We were probably witnessing folklore in the making.

I considered myself to be especially privileged that day. Not only did I have this personalized Cook's tour by one of the principal actors – if not *the* principal actor – in the battle for Government House; I was also lucky because Sir Rex – in a genial and forthcoming mood – took the time as we stood there in the study to give his own account of how it had all ended. He had certainly told the story before and no doubt he would tell it again many times (after all he became a national figure as a result of the Falklands and there are many besides me who will be curious). But he recounted his tale that evening with gusto, with imagination and with a sharp eye for detail, as though the events he described had happened only the day before yesterday.

'When I finally decided to pack it in – there was no point in everyone getting killed – I had to deal with an Irish Argentine intelligence officer, a chap called Major Dowling. We didn't really see eye to eye. Dowling wanted me to hand over the keys to the safe, but I said "Blow it in yourselves. The keys have already been taken and thrown in the harbour."

'Then I got word that I had to meet General García. I said: "Let him come here." "No," replies García, "come to the Town Hall." The stand-off continues for a time, then I hear that García is losing patience so I decide I'd better go along. Dowling says, "No uniform", but I put on my uniform and when Dowling wasn't looking I had the car brought round – you've seen it, haven't you?. The taxi with the Royal coat of arms on each door – and I went on down to the Town Hall. García was waiting. He wanted to shake hands. But I wouldn't shake hands with him. García said: "It's not gentlemanly of you to refuse to shake hands with me." I replied: "It's not very civilized of you to invade my country."

'After that I was whisked off the island. When I got back to Britain I met Healey, Foot and Silkin. Healey said in his usual blustering way: "Why didn't you sustain any casualties?" So I said to him: "Why do you want my marines to have been killed?" and Healey replied: "It would have looked better." I think Healey was looking for ammunition to beat the Tories in the debate the next day.'

As we walked back to the reception, Hunt talked about the problems they had had in communicating with Britain at the time of the Falklands War. There was a disturbance in the ionosphere at the crucial moment. 'The last signal I got from the Foreign Office said: "An Argentine fleet will be gathering at dawn off Cape Pembroke. Make your dispositions accordingly."' He laughed, somewhat mirthlessly I thought, and then he added: 'Now, of course, we have the dish.'

Before we left, Hunt took us to sign the visitors' book. He showed us the entries on the previous few pages. The Thatchers had signed; so had Jeremy Moore and other British officers. 'The Argentines all signed too,' said Hunt, pointing out the signatures. 'All, except for García. He never signed.'

David Taylor, Chief Executive of the Falklands, whom I visited the next day, lives in a white clapboard house, set back from the water just opposite the wreck of the *Jhelum*, a guano ship which – Taylor explains as he greets me at the garden gate – put in here around 1870 and never left. 'It was probably badly damaged after passing Cape Horn.'

We go inside. Taylor is around fifty years old, slim, with short hair and an alert, interested face. We start off by looking at a map, fifty or sixty years old, which has been framed and hung up in the passage outside the kitchen. It shows how the Falkland Islands have been split up into various holdings. A different colour is used for different owners and I can see immediately that the Falkland Islands Company – FIC – has well over 40% of the land.

Over lunch our talk, inevitably, focuses on the role of the FIC. 'The FIC is in a very strong position not just in terms of the land it owns, but also because of its other enterprises. It owns West Store – that's the supermarket which you will have seen – which is virtually a monopoly. It has all the faults of a monopoly.

Look at the Food Hall and you'll see what I mean. You can buy food there stamped with a date which is two years old. And the non-food section is a bit like an Oxfam shop. The trouble is the Falkland Islanders are very passive. Mutton is very cheap, and they grow their own vegetables so they don't really care if there aren't any vegetables in West Store. Many of them, if they need clothes, will shop by mail order. You don't have here the pressure from the consumer, the customer, that leads to improvements in the quality of goods and service. The managing director of the FIC is based in London; he comes out here from time to time, and the local manager here is a chap called Terry Spruce. He's been here for twenty years and is married to a Falkland Islander. Of course there are real problems getting goods out here. The *AES* comes out four times a year and that's about it.'

The FIC had been taken over by Coalite, a company which had its headquarters in Bolsover. Taylor tells me that he went to see Coalite's chairman, Ted Needham, a blunt north-countryman who had come up the hard way, before taking up his appointment in the Falklands.

'I was working with Booker McConnell before I was trawled by the Overseas Development Administration [ODA] for the job. Needham professed not to know what Booker McConnell was, so I asked him whether he had heard of the Booker Prize. Needham said to me, "You'll be running for that, lad, after two years in the Falklands." Now that Coalite has bought FIC, Needham has a larger stage to posture on. He tends to say things like: "I only talk to Maggie."'

The rumour in the Falklands is that FIC exacted a very high price for the land it sold the British Government for the airfield at Mount Pleasant. It is a notion which has gained currency in Britain too and the FIC has not been able to refute it.

'Selling the land at Mount Pleasant for a high price', Taylor speculated, 'could set the pattern for FIC holdings in other parts of the island. Remember the farmers here for the most part aren't even tenants of the Company; they're employees.

'I have a feeling', Taylor continues, 'that when the Government first sent Lord Shackleton out here – the first Shackleton report was in 1976 – they secretly hoped that he would say it was all hopeless so then they, the Government, could get shot of the problem. But actually Shackleton came up with a very positive report in 1976 and developed his ideas still further in the report which he made in 1982 immediately after the Falklands conflict.

'Shackleton recommended that there should be a Chief Executive who would take over the role of the old Chief Secretary reporting to the Civil Commissioner. He proposed the creation of a Falkland Islands Development Corporation and recommended that the chief executive should be executive vice-chairman of FIDC, the chairman being Sir Rex Hunt who would therefore head FIDC as he heads the Government.

'Parliament approved a £31 million programme of development aid to the Falklands to be spread over six years. We've had one year already, so we've got five to go, drawing down from ODA. Quite a lot of these funds are to be spent on infrastructure projects: electricity, roads, water-supply and so on. FIDC's task will be in areas which are commercial or semi-commercial: inshore fisheries, for example, small businesses of various kinds. I'll give you an example. I was at a New Year's Eve party given by the *Lindblad Explorer* which had put into Stanley. After the party I went back to my Land Rover – by the way this place has the highest ratio of Land Rovers to population of anywhere in the world – and found out that someone had been sick in the front seat. Actually, I sat in it! I then discovered that there was no dry-cleaning facility at all in the Falklands. That's the kind of venture that is needed.

'Another venture which is under way at the moment is the woollen mill at Fox Bay East where FIDC is putting in £160,000 which will improve the island's ability to process its own wool.'

'What about the land tenure system itself?' I asked. 'Surely that's one of the key questions, the pattern of ownership, the semi-feudal structure. How are you going to tackle that?'

We were sitting in David Taylor's dining-room looking out at the wreck of the *Jhelum* a couple of hundred yards away and pushing pâté and biscuits back and forth across the table. I didn't expect a snap answer and I didn't get one.

'The logic of the Falkland Islands', said Taylor, choosing his words carefully, 'is that you have large estates. On each estate there's a settlement and all of those settlements, if you come to look at it, are on the coast. Each settlement has its wool-shed, its shearing-shed and its jetty. That's because you get the wool out by water. You've probably seen the *Monsunen* in the harbour, haven't you?'

When I nodded, Taylor continued: 'Well, the *Monsunen* goes chugging off round the islands on its wool-round. It brings the wool back to Stanley and loads it on to the *AES*, which is a Danish-registered vessel chartered by the FIC. The *AES* takes the wool off to London. Some of it is sold by J. G. Field on a commission basis; some the FIC buys speculatively.

'This is the structure and it's not easy to change. The FIDC has plans to divide some of the large estates. We'd like to see land sold first to Falkland Islanders. Then to immigrants. We'd finance 90% of the costs at a fixed interest rate – at the moment it's 11% – over twenty-five years. The subdivisions themselves of course have to be approved by a subdivision committee. It's a long job. Greenpatch is one farm which is being subdivided and it's taken from 1977 till now to do it. That was 100,000 acres split into ten lots of 10,000 acres each. The difficulty isn't so much dividing the flocks or the land; it's getting the legal aspects right. And then you have to consider: do these new units have the facilities – the wool-shed, the shearing-shed? Do they have the jetty to get the wool out by water or are we going to have to build roads all over the place?

of course, roads could make a difference. It will be easier to organize education; the isolation out there in the "camp" wouldn't be so great. But we're dealing with limited resources and we have to consider what's the right investment.'

As he spoke I was, naïvely perhaps, struck by the images he had conjured up. He ran through the names of the settlements, names of course familiar to me and to many from the context of the Falklands War: Darwin, Goose Green, San Carlos, Fitzroy. I could imagine the *Monsunen* making its rounds, its decks piled high with wool. I could understand that this was a system which worked. However daunting it was to cross those peat-tracks, was it really sensible to replace them with a network of tarmac roads even if we could afford it? Was this what the islanders themselves wanted? There were after all other forms of communication. There was an air-taxi service, known as Figas, which could ferry people about from one part of the island to another. There was the radio, including a radio doctor and schools programmes for those children who had stayed on in the 'camp' instead of coming – as many did – to boarding-school in Stanley during the term. (There are also itinerant teachers who go from settlement to settlement.)

It was easy to talk, in sweeping terms, of programmes of 'land reform' as though one were dealing with some Central American dictatorship. But was it right, I wondered, for the people or the environment? On balance, I think I supported David Taylor in his gradualist approach. The Falklands is not the kind of place which can absorb too much change too fast.

Looking back at those few weeks in the southern hemisphere, I find that the afternoon which sticks in my mind as vividly as any other is the one I spent after that friendly lunch with David Taylor, going out to Fitzroy. Taylor told me that Fitzroy was certainly worth a visit – a settlement in the traditional Falklands pattern – and one which I should be able to reach (and return from) in the course of an afternoon's hard riding.

By now I was much more familiar with the terrain and with the quirks of riding a motorcycle across wet and slithery ground and unlike that first day, the weather was fine, half cloud, half sun. I headed off down the first good stretch of road towards Bluff Cove, then began on the cross-country stretch towards Fitzroy. It was, as always, hard work but it was also immensely rewarding. No one else passed me on the way, going in either direction. The heather-covered hills rose to my right. To the left, the land stretched to the sea.

I gave Bluff Cove itself a wide berth. Simon Powell, the Bike 'n' Burger magnate, had warned me that the farmer there had taken a strong dislike to Suzuki motorcycles and their riders (I could see his point). Leaving half a mile between myself and that particular settlement (the scene of considerable action during the campaign), I swung right-handed over the moor and up the hill beyond.

I had been going for about two hours in a broadly westerly direction, had just climbed up along a rough peat track full of rocks and boulders, come to the summit of a hill, switched the motorcycle's engine off and paused to look around, and then saw – and can still see it now as I write – one of the most magical sights I can recall.

Down below me, about two miles away, was a cove where the sea pushed inland between the coast and some outlying islands. At the edge of the water, grouped rather casually together, were a dozen houses or buildings. From where I was they had a pretty matchbox quality, dolls' houses from another world. It was hard to imagine that in the sound beyond the settlement, within sight and hearing of those gentle homesteads, one of the sharpest, and in terms of life most costly, engagements of the Falklands campaign had taken place. Why the *Tristram* and *Sir Galahad* waited so long in the sound – in full view of Argentine spotters on the top of Tumbledown Hill – before putting their troops ashore remains something of a mystery to me. I can understand the preference the commanding officers may have had for a Bluff Cove, rather than a Fitzroy, landing. Having covered the terrain myself between Bluff Cove and Fitzroy, I can see it would have been hard slogging or hard yomping – and the creaky wooden bridge which you have to cross on the way (some 200 yards in length) could easily have been mined or destroyed, another incentive to try a landing farther to the east. But there was no doubt about it that the *Tristram* and *Sir Galahad* were sitting like ducks in the water when the Argentines hit them out of a clear sky, and that by any reckoning had to be an error of judgement on somebody's part.

I let in the clutch once more and bumped down the hill. Two white blobs leave the settlement below and come towards me up the hill. The first blob is a hundred yards in front of the second blob. As they get nearer I hear the sound of powerful engines and realize that these are Land Rovers approaching, bound, I imagine, for Stanley. In fact I'm tempted to say to the drivers as they pass: 'Stanley, I presume?' But the vehicles veer away from me and find their own track up the hill just as I am finding my own way down. Like policemen on the beat, Land Rovers often travel in twos in the Falklands. If one gets bogged down, the other is there to pull it out.

It took me twenty minutes to come down the hill into Fitzroy. There is a young lad standing by the gate at the entrance to the settlement.

'Do you mind if I look around? How many people work here?'

'About thirty altogether. I've just started work on the farm myself.'

'How many sheep?'

'About 25,000. That's on 100,000 acres.' Better than Patagonia anyway, I reflect. Tom Davies was right.

I parked the motorcycle and walked on down to the water. Access to the sea – that was the crucial element in the sheep economy of the Falklands. If you didn't get the wool out by water, you didn't get it out at all. Tom Davies had told me that. David Taylor had repeated it, but it was only as I slogged across the island that afternoon that the reality of the message sank in. Shearing-shed, wool-shed, jetty – those were the three vital components of any settlement.

The sun was setting over the sound as I walked out along the jetty, keeping between the iron tracks – rather like railway lines – on which the men of Fitzroy would push out the wool trolleys when they saw the *Monsunen* chugging round the point towards the settlement. At the end of the wooden pier two young boys were fishing.

'What are you after?' I ask.

'Mullet,' the boys answer together. As I watch, they haul in first one and then another silver wriggling fish. Rich pickings here, it seems, for inshore fishermen. No wonder the Russians are interested.

The water beneath the pier is clear and cold. Sniffing the air, I think I detect the smell of mutton. Sheep's bones are very much in evidence, both in the water itself and on the bank. Fitzroy, like the other Falkland Islands settlements, is a place where the sheep in all its forms, dead or alive, shorn or shaggy, tends to dominate.

This perception is reinforced when I visit the wool-shed. Fleeces were piled to the rafters, reminding me of my childhood on Exmoor when we used to pile the wool on the billiard-table in the landing waiting for our own *Monsunen* – in this case the Wool Marketing Board's lorry – to call round to collect it. The smell, rich and pungent, is just as I remember it. And in the shearing-shed next door the equipment hanging from the beam (I counted fifteen posts in all) doesn't seem to have changed over the years. How many ways, after all, are there of shearing a sheep? Or perhaps Exmoor by some geographical kink or warp belongs to the same time-zone as the Falklands and has the same rustic habits.

Apart from the young man I met on first entering Fitzroy, the two boys fishing and a horse and rider who trotted across the skyline against the background of the setting sun while I was leaning on the side of the pier looking at the sheeps' skulls and jawbones in the water below, nobody else seemed to be around. I moved on from the shearing-shed back up the track towards the centre of the settlement. An antique telephone kiosk, painted the regulation red, takes pride of place. The letters EiiR are painted on the side to remind passers-by that this is a land in which the Queen's writ runs. (There is a story, perhaps apocryphal, that some alert British officer telephoned through to Fitzroy from a call-box such as this at the time when British troops were advancing from Goose Green towards Stanley. He was thereby able to discover that the place was empty of Argentines – which piece of information enabled a rapid leap-frog to take place as the paras were choppered in ahead of the rest.)

The journey back was uneventful. I scrambled back up the hill, slipping the clutch and revving the engine mercilessly to thrust up and over the last fifty almost vertical yards of track. I stopped on the brow of the hill and switched off the motorcycle's engine for one last look back at that distant little group of houses so far below. In the immense silence, with the shadows lengthening and the wind freshening as the evening approached it was hard to imagine the howl of jet engines, the crash of bombs and the shrieks of pain from the men on the ships in the sound and on the shore. Yet the attack on Fitzroy happened; the Falklands War happened and down here life will never be the same again.

While I was visiting Fitzroy, Adrian had gone off in a Land Rover to see Mount Tumbledown and the two hills behind it known as the Twin Sisters. When I returned to the *Biscoe*, after surrendering my mud-spattered Suzuki to Kelvin's Bike 'n' Burger shop, he was striding around the deck brandishing a large piece of shrapnel which he had picked up on the field of battle. It looked like a meteorite and if it had hit you in a soft and vital place it would probably have been just as lethal.

'Did you have a good afternoon?' I asked.

'Splendid.' Adrian was clearly in a very good humour. Technology of every kind, even the technology of war, interests him intensely.

That evening we walked up the hill behind the ship to Miriam Booth's house. Miriam was – and is – the BAS agent in Stanley. Both her parents originally came from Chile – and it was in Chile, in Punta Arenas, that I first met her. She had come with the *Biscoe* from Stanley and was to return to Stanley by way of Antarctica, a long way round but in the circumstances the only feasible route.

Throughout the voyage no one had seen much of Miriam because she had been prostrated with sea-sickness. Safely back in Stanley she regained her sparkle and threw a party for the officers, crew and guests of the *Biscoe*.

She had also invited some of the locals (including of course her parents who after years in the islands were totally Falklandized). I spent much of the time talking to George Betts, the captain of the *Monsunen*, the Falklands Island Company vessel which we had seen in the harbour at Stanley on that first day and whose dominant role in the island's affairs I had come increasingly to appreciate in the course of our short visit.

Betts was a rugged-looking individual who seemed quite at home with a glass of beer in his hand (this wasn't his first party of the day since he himself had invited Chris Elliott and some of the other officers for a barbecue lunch where, so I learnt, there had been copious liquid refreshments). With him was his wife, Lucía – another Chilean who had made the trip across the Patagonian Sea to a world where the pubs still shut at 10 p.m. and where the main news was that conveyed by the BBC World Service in those well-modulated accents of Oxbridge broadcasters.

'Forty-seven pick-ups we do altogether,' he said. 'Cargo in; wool out. Each bale weighs forty pounds, eighty fleeces to the bale; four bales to the tonne; 400 bales each load. I was born and brought up at Goose Green, lived there for seventeen years. My father was assistant manager; they had 108,000 sheep. But there's no money in the sheep industry. That's why I got out.'

He saw me with my notebook and pencil poised. 'Don't knock the FIC. They've been good to me. When I told my father I was going to leave Goose Green, FIC helped me to become an apprentice engineer. They paid my voyage to London when I went to take my Mate's Certificate. I failed it once, but I took it again and passed it. FIC backed me. People attack the company, but what about the other companies with land out here? Their record is probably a great deal worse than FIC's.'

It was a salutary experience to hear him talk. There is always the temptation when you are only a few days in a place to form snap judgements. The FIC is an easy target. Here was one man at least who had something good to say for them.

Chris Elliott comes over and joins in the conversation. He recalls how the *Biscoe* did the 'wool run' five years earlier when the *Monsunen* was laid up for repairs. 'The FIC paid the costs,' says Elliott. 'And we were happy anyway because it was good for relations between BAS and the islanders. Those were the days when we still had the after-hold, before we put in the scientific equipment. We also packed the aftertween-deck. We came back in with 250 tonnes of wool. We used to work around the clock. Sometimes we'd arrive early in the morning at a settlement and be invited up for breakfast with freshly-baked rolls.

'The draught of the *Biscoe* is greater than that of the *Monsunen* – eighteen feet as opposed to eight – so we couldn't get into all the jetties. Sometimes the locals complained at the amount of trans-shipping, but there was no alternative. We got stuck in the mud once at San Carlos. Another time I watched them load the scow until it virtually toppled over – and there was probably £30,000 worth of wool on board. Yes,' Chris Elliott muses, 'one of the best trips we had was when we collected the wool.'

On our last day in the Falklands I spent the morning writing letters and postcards, then walked along the front to the post office to send them off. Philatelic sales, as Lord Shackleton recognized in his two reports on the economy of the islands, are an important business, bringing in a considerable revenue. In the post office there were two counters: one for those who wanted to buy plain ordinary stamps and another for those who were looking for the various special issues of the Falklands.

At the end of the morning a staff car drove up to the *Biscoe*'s gang-plank and I was whisked off to have lunch with Captain Peter Erskine, otherwise known as SNOFI – an acronym which stands for Senior Naval Officer Falklands Islands.

Naval headquarters were in a former school up the hill behind the hospital. SNOFI's office was a modest enough room – probably the headmaster's study – in which a table for three had been set.

Captain Erskine, a tall, civilized man, who was half-way through his tour, introduced me to my fellow guest, Ian Strange.

'Ian owns half of New Island, that's out to the West of the West Falklands.'
Ian deprecated the image of large-scale landowner.

'It's only about eight miles long,' he said. 'And it's not very wide. I've got about four thousand acres.'

We spent most of the lunch talking about the wildlife of the Falklands. Ian Strange not only part-owned an island noted for its ecological interest (I envied Simon Lyster his good fortune in being able to get out there); he was also the author of a book about the islands published by David and Charles and newly reprinted which concentrates on the Falklands' historical and biological aspects. And Peter Erskine revealed his own private enthusiasm as a keen amateur botanist when he spoke with sorrow about the damage being done to the wild flowers of Cape Pembroke.

'When you arrive at the airfield, it's a terrible mess. Now the troops are being taught to appreciate wildlife, if they don't already. Most of them are thrilled to bits when they see a penguin.

'There are nineteen endemic flowers in the Falklands: by that I mean flowers which don't occur anywhere else. Otherwise the floral properties of the islands are similar to the mainland. You've got a dusty miller, and a spring-flowering primula – that's a long-stemmed white flower. There's a site right next to the airfield. There are flowers growing in the minefields. I was out at the Mount Pleasant airfield the other day and spent a couple of hours looking at flowers around the site. I found seven things which weren't on the list.'

'The problem is sheep,' Ian Strange interrupted. 'You find the wild flowers in the cliffy bits or the places where the sheep haven't been. Sheep are great consumers of wilderness.'

He was bothered too by the idea of subdividing the large estates, if ever that policy was made to work.

'Many of the large estates own small islands. Some of these islands are very rich in wildlife, including birdlife. If you subdivide, the pressure to intensify is going to be there. I took sheep off my half of New Island and there was a marvellous result.

'Both Darwin and Hooker – I mean Sir William Hooker – came here. Some of Hooker's collections of pressed flowers from the Falklands are in the British Museum. Darwin didn't like the place so much. He probably hit it on one of our nasty wet days. In my view this place is a southern Galápagos.'

A southern Galápagos! The phrase stuck in my mind long after that lunch ended. Men like Ian Strange would not use such terms lightly.

'The biological richness is unbelievable,' he said. 'Look at the birdlife on Beauchene Island. There has to be an enormous concentration of fish and squid in the area for the birds to survive in those numbers. Yet all this is now in jeopardy because of the overfishing. Read a book called *Only on Sunday*. The seabirds off Peru used to eat the anchovies and then the people took the guano for fertilizer. Some bright sparks – greedy men – thought they could take a short cut and convert the anchovies directly into fishmeal fertilizer instead of taking out the guano from the islands. As a result they damn nearly killed off the *anchoveta* industry as well as the guano industry.'

I harp back to what seems to me the straightforward answer. 'Can't we impose a 200-mile limit around the Falklands, regulate the fishing, and derive some benefit from it?'

Peter Erskine gives a studied response, professional caution seeming to win out over his otherwise very evident ecological enthusiasms. 'On conservation grounds I'm sure it's necessary,' he said. 'But as you can imagine there are political ramifications with the Argentines to be considered. And policing a 200-mile zone could be a complicated and expensive operation. I'm not sure that the Navy would want to take it on.'

'Couldn't an Anglo-Argentine fisheries agreement be part of the wider negotiations? Couldn't there be a Joint Scientific Commission and mutually agreed zones of administration?'

But for both Peter Erskine and Ian Strange this was going too far too fast. They both thought that time had to go by, wounds had to be healed. Alfonsín was in power at this moment and things over there looked a little better. But how long would he stay in control? And, if he departed, what policies would his successor pursue?

When, three months later, I had a chance to visit Buenos Aires, I understood better the force of their remarks. Alfonsín's tenure of office was precarious to say the least and the pressures confronting him, both political and economic, tremendous. Any agreement between Britain and Argentina resulting, amongst other things, in a joint conservation policy for the biological resources of the Patagonian shelf would have to have some pretty effective guarantees if it was to be worth the paper it was written on. The sad reality is that seabirds and seals, penguins and squid – and that whole biological nexus which makes the Falkland Islands the wonder they are, do not rate high among the political priorities of either side.

From the window of Captain Erskine's office we could look out at the water of the harbour and at the various wrecks which, at different stages of decrepitude, bulked large. As a naval man, he had a special interest in them.

'Bear in mind', he admonished, 'that these are the Roaring Forties and that the prevailing winds are westerly. Ships coming round Cape Horn through Drake's Passage tended to end up in a bad state off the Falklands. That's why so many of the wrecks are there.'

He looked out to the east to where in the distance the troop 'coastels' floated at anchor. 'About the only wreck which is in fairly good shape is the *Lady Elizabeth*. She was a clipper and you can see her down there at the end of the harbour. And then over at Grytviken on South Georgia there's a Norwegian whaler, the *Petrel*. They're trying to raise money to get that one home. I'm not sure it's worth it. There are other things to spend £500,000 on out here.'

I walked back to the *Biscoe* after my lunch with SNOFI. Our conversation about wrecks was fresh in my mind, so I surveyed the waterfront with interest. One large hull lying a hundred yards offshore but connected to the land by a pontoon bridge had a large door cut into its side and was clearly still in use as a storage vessel of some kind. And not far from the post office a metal plaque had been erected beside the mizzen-mast of the ss *Great Britain*. The plaque noted that 'the great ship was recovered from these waters and returned to Bristol for restoration in July 1970'.

In August 1984, as I was writing this book, I ran into a friend of mine, James Chewton, who – it turned out – had been closely involved in the business of bringing the ss *Great Britain* back to Bristol.

'I went out to the Falklands to cover the story for *The Times*,' Lord Chewton told me at dinner one night. 'Rees-Mogg rang me up and said did I want a job, so I said yes, and he said well off you go to Stanley. So I went. The *Great Britain* was one of Brunel's triumphs. The first iron ship. Brunel saw it as an extension of the Great Western Railway. Paddington to Bristol and on to New York! There were six masts, Monday to Saturday; her best feature was her light steering because she brought a bit of rudder forward. During her lifetime the *Great Britain* actually went backwards in design. She was used to carry wool from Australia to London and the Australians said iron doesn't float so she wasclad in elm. When we went down to the Falklands to bring her back, you could punch your fist through the iron but the elm was still there. The Falkland Islands Company had cut a hole through the main spar so the structure was fantastically weakened, but eighty years later she was still partially floating. We filled the holes with concrete and pumped the water out. Wonderful scene when she lifted off the bottom. Awful night. Terrible weather. Storm coming up. We had the best team of salvage operators from Hamburg. Euan Strathcona rebuilt the mast-house – it took him six weeks – but the Germans cut down the last mast with a buzz-saw and Strathcona's mast-house was smashed in the process!'

As far as James Chewton was concerned, the reason for the large number of wrecks around the Falklands wasn't just the weather and the Roaring Forties.

'Many of those ships were "lost" going east to west,' he told me. 'The Falkland Islands Company in those days were also Lloyds agents. A vessel insured at Lloyds could be written off when it reached the Falklands and still have a useful life ahead of it, pottering around the islands or further afield.'

The whole ss *Great Britain* story had clearly fired his imagination at the time and continued to do so. 'She's restored in Bristol now. We brought her back to the dry dock where Brunel originally built her. He was a real technological risk-taker, was Brunel. He knew the *Great Britain* was too big for the dock when they built her, but there was one high tide they might be able to get her out by. She got stuck half-way out. It looked like curtains, finish. So Brunel dashed around the pubs of Bristol offering the bog Irish five pints an hour to dig her out. It worked. The ss *Great Britain* floated clear at the next tide.'

One of the sad things about saying goodbye to the Falklands was that it meant saying goodbye also to Adrian Berry. He would have two more days in the Falklands before flying out on the air-bridge via Ascension. He appeared to relish the prospect. I had brought the two *Telegraph*s which I had found in the Globe Hotel back to the ship. Other clippings of the stories he had filed had been mailed to Stanley and were now pinned up on the *Biscoe*'s notice-board so that officers, crew and guests of the British Antarctic Survey all had a chance to see how life on board a Royal Research Vessel appeared to one distinguished science correspondent. Now Adrian was planning a last 'exclusive'. He had learnt that the Navy had developed a 'flexiport' – a dock which, like the famous wartime Mulberry Harbours, rode up and down with the tide. This would feature in his last dispatch. As far as the rest of the *Biscoe's* voyage was concerned, he instructed me to cable any news instantly.

'By now you must know the kind of thing our readers like,' he said. 'Keep it lively.'

I took him at his word and sent off over the next two weeks through the good offices of Dallas Bradshaw, our inestimable radio-operator, a fair number of pieces, some of which the *Telegraph* used.

8

South Orkneys

With the *Biscoe* re-supplied and raring to go, we sailed at five o'clock on 31 January. Adrian Berry stood by the side of the dock in his peaked yachtsman's cap – the relic of some distant Cowes Week – waving at us as we pulled away. When we were well clear, the Captain gave a long blast with the hooter, followed by two shorter blasts. Stanley receded into the distance, its red- and green-roofed houses becoming smaller all the time. It was like running a movie backwards. We were on our way south once again.

There was a full turn-out that night for dinner in the wardroom. As we sat with our drinks waiting for the gong, newspapers which had come on board at Stanley were passed from hand to hand. By coincidence, the latest *Daily Telegraph* featured a piece by Sir John Colville, once Sir Winston Churchill's private secretary, which called for the 'internationalization of the Falklands', as one way of solving the Falklands problem. Colville's idea was to turn it into a base for Antarctic exploration (and exploitation) for any and every country that wanted to use it for this purpose. Of course, fees would be payable – to the UN and or some other appropriate trustees – and suitable forms of government devised.

We mulled over Sir John's ideas. On the face of it, it seemed a pretty far-flung notion. Who, after all (apart from Britain) was going to use the Falklands as a stepping-stone to Antarctica? Not Chile and Argentina, each of whom already had a slice of Tierra del Fuego, which was just as near to Antarctica as the Falklands were. Australia and New Zealand were the other side of the globe and it would make no sense for them to use the Falklands. The United States had its own supply routes already worked out and seemed able to manage quite adequately. France had Kerguelen, an island which, like South Georgia, lay within the Antarctic convergence. Perhaps some of the newer Treaty powers might find a Falklands base useful, but on the whole, the internationalization of the Falklands as a means of advancing the development of Antarctica seemed a speculative scheme and one in any case not likely to resolve the immediate problems.

'Anyway,' I said to Martin White, the BAS biologist whose capsule guide to the marine ecosystem of Antarctica I was to find invaluable over the next few days, 'I'm against solutions, of whatever kind, which hasten the exploitation of Antarctica. We shouldn't ruin Antarctica in order to solve the Falklands question. There has to be a better way.'

'Such as?'

'Sheep,' I replied firmly. 'Better breeds, but in the right place. Not everywhere. Conservation and tourism. Talks with the Argentines about fisheries and other shared resources.'

Martin on the whole seemed to agree. When you are a biologist, you tend to look for benign solutions.

We put out to sea the way we had come in. We were seated at dinner – out of sight of land – when someone tuned the wardroom radio in to the local Falklands broadcasting station. They were playing a prerecorded interview with Anne Todd and Carys Williams. (Both ladies blushed to hear their voices across the ether.)

'Why is this the first time women have been down here with the British Antarctic Survey?' the interviewer asked.

'Normally the scientists would be on board,' Anne chose her words carefully – she is a careful, precise kind of person who abhors inaccuracy of any kind, 'but this year they had a winter programme which left space for us. Actually, we're not the first women to come down with BAS to Antarctica. Tom Woodsfield, the master of the *Bransfield*, came down with his wife in 1953. And this year a female geologist – we met her in Punta Arenas at the beginning of our trip – participated in geological landings on the Biscoe Islands.

'Of course, there is no question of scientists taking their wives or families, unless their wives are qualified. It's a tough life. Women have to be extremely good and competent and versatile if they are to contribute.'

And Carys (on the air) chipped in. 'It's an incredible morale booster for us. I think it's a morale booster for those on the bases as well.'

I – and all of us – can vouch for the truth of that last remark. Carys Williams in particular had a cheerful, jaunty personality that seemed to make her a special favourite among the Fids. Many of the BAS people down south would of course have done a stint in Cambridge and got to know the 'girls' there. But even those who were meeting them for the first time seemed delighted.

Two days later at about the same time in the day, I noted the *Biscoe*'s position: 59.31 S, 47.50 W. We were just about to drop down once more below the Antarctic Circle. I was up on the bridge peering out through the mist and spray. Jerry was bending over the radar looking for icebergs ahead of us. He picked up two or three on the starboard bow, and another about eight miles in front of us.

'If you're out there in a sailing boat, you can sense the icebergs. You can listen and hear the waves crashing against the ice or else you can feel the change of wind as you're blocked by the berg. On this kind of ship, there's too much noise for that.' He moved away from the radar to squint through the window at the grey seas ahead.

'You can pick up the bigger bits of ice on the radar – five or eight or ten miles away – but the smaller bits are quite big enough to do considerable damage. So we have a permanent look-out up here.'

At dinner that night Norman, the electrician, tells me that he would prefer to be on the *John Biscoe* than on some cargo vessel. 'The *Biscoe* is registered 100A1 ice-strengthened at Lloyds.'

3 February 1984 was, I noted, another grey, manky day. Ice had formed on the upper deck. We were about five miles away from Signy but it was too misty to see anything. As I stood on the port wing of the bridge an iceberg – deep blue in colour – slid past. It was only a small one but, as Jerry had pointed out the previous day, even the small ones could do a lot of damage. In front of the ship, and at either side, shoals of penguins were popping in and out of the water, 'porpoising' is the word they use. From where I was they did indeed look like porpoises.

Four hours later we finally arrived at Signy. I went up to the monkey-deck above the bridge to look at a rocky island about a mile away. Some Cape pigeons were feasting on garbage which had just been thrown overboard. A Wilson's storm petrel was skimming across the surface of the waves below us, followed by a snow petrel. We were back in Antarctica with a vengeance. It was snowing as we came in; ahead of us, the rocks and mountains were entirely snow-covered. In the distance I could see the great glacier of Coronation Island.

The wireless mast at Signy is up the hill to the left of the base. The whole of the BAS team there seemed to have climbed up to watch the *Biscoe* come in – I counted at least a dozen figures in orange anoraks. I guess when you only see five or six ships a year, you're quite happy to turn out to welcome a ship in. Down on the rocks below I could see other figures moving around – it was another kind of welcoming party: a group of fur seals who, even from this distance, could be heard barking and scuffling.

Later that morning I met Humphrey Smith, a dark-haired man with a beard and glasses, medium-to-heavy build, who is a terrestrial ecologist. We talked in his office at the base.

'The fur seals are more numerous now. There's no doubt about it. They're breeding on the eastern part of the South Orkneys. Fifteen years ago you wouldn't see more than a dozen fur seals here; now there could be two hundred at Gourlay Point. They come in to moult.'

'Gourlay Point?'

'A mile or two away across the island. You should go there if you can.'

I decided then and there that I would visit Gourlay Point, even if I did nothing else during my time at Signy.

Humphrey Smith expounds further on the subject of the 'fur seal explosion' at Signy. 'There might be 150 million tonnes of krill in these seas, but that isn't evenly distributed. One of the areas where you find the greatest concentration of krill is here in the Scotia arc.'

'Is this still the Antarctic?'

'It's the Maritime Antarctic. The pack-ice comes off Antarctica. It dampens the sea down, then the sea freezes which is when you get sea-ice. The sea-ice can go 200 miles north of Coronation Island. To get good sea-ice you need a temperature of minus ten degrees and calm weather. Our technique of testing whether the ice is strong enough to walk on is to thump it three times with a bog chisel. If it doesn't go through, it's safe.'

Next door in the microbiology lab Roger Worland explained that he was studying the mechanisms that enable mites to endure the cold. 'How cold can they get before they die? What are the mechanisms that enable them to survive at very low temperatures? That's one of the things we are trying to find out.'

'How do you find the mites?'

'Scrape them off the rocks with a paintbrush. We're also studying wingless insects – springtails. Mites and springtails are the dominant terrestrial arthropods. There's a very small number of species here. Very low diversity. One two in fact. In the UK, you'd have fifty species. The number of organisms in the soil, on the other hand, is quite high. You've got bacteria, nematodes and so on. One of the main projects here at Signy is the fellfield ecological project. You'll see that while you're here. Fellfield is a term for the terrain which is left behind once the glacier has gone.'

It was inevitably something of a Cook's tour. As a layman, I tried to focus on the practical utility of the studies.

'The work on cold resistance,' Roger tells me, 'has to be taken hand in hand with other work on cold. It might be useful for example in biochemical studies of the freezing of sperm.'

Ray Cannon, another scientist, says: 'We're also looking at nitrogen fixation in algae. We're trying to link together light and temperature. Does the rate at which the blue-green algae fix nitrogen vary according to how bright it is or how warm it is? Blue-green algae', he adds for the benefit of people like me who wouldn't know one if they saw one, 'are now classified as bacteria because they have no internal cellular membrane.'

Cynan Ellis-Evans, head of the biology work at Signy, looks round the door and joins in the conversation. 'Biology here covers the freshwater work and the limnology. Our definition of a freshwater lake is one that doesn't freeze to the bottom. The highest form of life in the freshwater lake is the fairy shrimp. Some of the lakes near the beaches have elephant seals and fur seals who obviously like them because they're warmer. The fur seals get everywhere. They're wrecking the moss banks.'

Colin Bertram arrives in the middle of this explanation. '"Modifying" would be a better word, surely?'

Dr Ellis-Evans stands corrected. 'Modifying the moss banks,' he agrees. 'They are certainly having an impact. The fur seals first came to Signy in 1975–76. There were a couple of hundred of them then. Now there are maybe twelve hundred. We count them each year on 22 February. The Weddell seals breed here in winter too.'

We continued our tour with a visit to the marine wet lab. On a bench is a penguin with its head cut off. Somebody back in Cambridge, I learn, collects penguin skulls so when they find a carcass on the beach they send the head back to England.

In a bucket beneath the bench is a selection of fish. We talk about the British housewife's reluctance to buy new sorts of fish. Paul Harris, who looks after the wet lab, tells us: 'Ice-fish, for example, are perfectly good eating but they don't look nice. We send the fish back to Sainsbury's and so on and they try them out but there's a lot of consumer resistance. One day Antarctic species will be made into fish fingers.' He peers down into the bucket. 'There are quite a few species here, but they are all so closely related that you'd find it hard to tell the difference.'

Our last stop that morning was with Dr David Walton who is studying the micro-climate. He has a collection of rocks in his office. He picks one out of a case to show us. 'You can see the marble here is cracked and that algae are actually living in the cracks. There are also endolithic algae who live inside the rocks themselves. We're studying the weathering of the rocks here to see to what extent it is related to the creation or weathering of soil.'

He takes another rock from the case. 'I'm looking at the effects of lichens, algae, mosses and so on. Lichens on the surface actually peel bits off the rock and loosen them to the soil below. The soil here is a broken-down rock matrix but you've got bacteria, algae, protozoa. This is the first attempt to look at the early stages of soil formation in a cold climate. Very little is known about this. The questions we are examining here are of significance for any understanding of soil development anywhere in the world.'

One of the glass-fronted cases was heated. Inside were rocks which had been taken up from the bottom of the lake. 'They had probably been there for 2,000 years,' said Walton. 'What was interesting was that water had never penetrated into the interior of these rocks. This sort of information is useful if you're looking at the freeze-and-thaw theory of soil formation, by which I mean the notion that soil is formed when rocks explode as the water inside them first freezes and then thaws.'

We had lunch on the base. Cynan Ellis-Evans, who comes up from his lab to join us, says: 'On a hot day the elephant seals really smell. They can lie in a hole for a month or two at a time. It's not too bad today but sometimes it can be overpowering.'

The radio is on in the canteen as we eat, picking up short-wave transmissions in the surrounding area. Russian seems to be the dominant language of these overheard exchanges and when I ask why, Cynan says: 'They're out there somewhere; we're not exactly sure where. The Russians used to come in here quite a lot but frankly we don't encourage it now. Too much socializing distracts from the work of the base. We don't allow the cruise ships in here either now. *World Discoverer* has been here twice this year, *Lindblad Explorer* three times. Nowadays we go out and meet them and go over in the boats to Coronation Island.

Cynan picks out, from the shelf in the canteen, an illustrated book about the Soviet Merchant Marine fleet. He shows me a photograph of a ship called *Sovietskaya Rossiya*, 25,720 tons. 'That one was here last year,' Cynan says. 'It anchored about five miles off Signy. When the Russians come down here, the mother ship just sits tight the whole time and you see a line of trawlers coming up to her.'

Martin White, who probably knows about as much about Soviet fishing in the Antarctic as anyone, intervenes: 'The Russians have probably fished out South Georgia; that's maybe why they're here in force. There's certainly talk about this being a bad season in South Georgia. The first time we saw a big fleet down here was in 1978–79 and those were Russian or Sovbloc ships. The Soviets are not sending their junk down. They're sending their best. They leave the fleet down here including the mother ship. From time to time other ships come down to take off personnel who need a change, to refuel the mother ship, and transport the processed catch back to Russia. We're seeing an extended effort by the Eastern European fleet since the late 1960s. There are the FAO statistics as well as West German, Russian and Polish statistics. All these show a change in the composition of the catch, as well as a change in actual totals caught. When one type of fish is fished out you go on to the next. That's what they did with whales.

'There is a 200-mile limit around the French island of Kerguelen,' Martin continues, 'and the French enforce it. They just put their two little trawlers from St Malo in among the fleet. Britain could do the same for South Georgia. Thirty or forty trawlers were seen there this year – the *Bransfield* spotted them at the north end of Bird Island, Polish or Russian ships, but the Japanese are down here too.'

I realized as we sat there having lunch that this question of fishing in the Antarctic is clearly of overwhelming importance. I had already been made aware of the issue during our time in the Falklands. Later on, as we steamed from the South Orkneys to South Georgia, there would be more first-hand evidence of a massive Soviet presence in southern waters while at South Georgia itself the military have no hesitation in confirming the position.

Talk about fisheries leads to talk about oil. Munro joins in. He sounds a note of caution. It is far too early to talk about an Antarctic oil-boom.

'Even the *Glomar Challenger* was doing basic work,' he said, 'and the *Glomar Challenger* operation was never repeated. As far as BAS is concerned our oil-related work is mainly confined to onshore studies of structures. Of course onshore structures can relate to offshore structures too. I mean you can deduce that something might lie offshore by your studies of the onshore geology. An area which is thought to be promising is the area east of the Peninsula, the Ross Sea in particular and the ice-shelf. In the future, we're going to use more marine seismic techniques.'

He said they were going to buy a forty-eight-channel seismic recorder which might be expanded to ninety-six channels. This was going to be part of the NERC – National Environment Research Council – equipment pool. BAS was going to use it 25% of the time although they would probably pay for all of it.

Next year they were going to use the *Discovery* off the ice-free parts of the Peninsula and also in the Weddell Sea area. 'In addition to the seismic recorder there is another instrument called "Gloria" which is a side-scan sonar developed by the Institute of Oceanographic Studies. The main object of all these studies is not exploring for oil as such, but to elucidate the basic structures. There may be some core-drilling involved. But they won't be going very deep.'

I asked whether the results would be published under the terms of the Antarctic Treaty and Munro said, yes, of course they would.

I cannot pretend that during my tour of Antarctica I was left with the overwhelming impression that major discoveries of oil or minerals were just round the corner. But I only saw a part of the continent. There may be other areas where the prospect of exploitation of oil and mineral resources is a great deal nearer. If that is so, the need for agreed regimes – whether to control or deter such exploitation – is altogether more evident.

Our conversation drifted around like the Weddell Sea gyre. At the end of lunch I found myself talking to Kenny Cameron, one of the divers on the base. He told me how one day he put on his wet–suit and, instead of scraping up the blue-green algae from the bottom of Signy's semi-frozen inland lakes, spent the afternoon diving alongside the southern right whale.

'The whales were spotted first of all by the tourist ship, *World Discoverer*, which was over at Coronation Island. Some of our lads were with them. When the whales were seen our lads radioed back to the base and three of us got kitted out in diving suits and went over in a rubber boat. We zipped along in our Zodiac keeping a parallel course with the whales and when we got close everyone jumped over the side. The whales were covered in callouses like warts, five foot wide warts. We swam in the water with the whales.'

Kenny Cameron is another bearded man. There are a lot of beards in Antarctica. Quite apart from the problem of shaving, beards tend to insulate the face against the cold.

'I spent fifteen minutes down there taking photographs,' says Cameron. 'The side of the animal was like a massive wall. It was a light-brown colour. Then I came up and the whale came up at the same time. It sat there blowing fifteen feet in the air at least. Its back was about fifty foot long and it stuck out about three foot above the water. The third time I dived, I was just on top of its head. You could see the rakers, the baleen plates, in its mouth. When it had its mouth open it was like a black hole. I looked at it and thought, "It's not interested in me, I'm too small. That whale is just interested in cruising along and getting where it wants to go."

'Before I went over the side, I thought to myself, "How do you dive?" Well, the way you dive is to jump into the water as soon as you can. Whales have a wide variety of sounds and frequencies. I could hear the noises it was making. There are only two thousand southern right whales left. You see them at the Valdes Peninsula, Argentina; also off Southern California. The irony is that now that whaling is finished the data we have on whales is more and more incomplete. We don't know much about the southern right whale or the blue whale. It's difficult to do whale counts. If you're going to try and use remote control methods, you've got to find some way of attaching the equipment to the beast. It's got to be able to be picked up by the satellite. It's easier to use remote control systems on birds, but even then you've got a problem of weight. Your transmitting device mustn't interfere with the bird's ability to fly or with its normal flight pattern. There's a chap called John French in England. He's a one-man commercial concern, he's interested in developing a system for tracking polar bears. In fact he did develop a pretty substantial system based on a device that had to be put on the back of the polar bears. It had to be made waterproof because the bears kept on jumping in the water. It was an expensive system but in the case of the polar bears both the Russians and the Americans were interested in paying. The Sea Mammal Research Unit in Cambridge is trying to develop a package which can be put on a seal.'

We talk about killer whales. Cameron says: 'Look at the accounts given in Shackleton's book *South*. Shackleton says he found holes up to three or four foot thick in the ice. That was where the killer whales drilled through in order to find the seals lying on the ice. Shackleton recounts how he'd see the whales take a look over the edge of the ice-floe and then come in underneath.'

'Lyall Watson tells the same kind of story,' I say (I have just been reading Watson's book on whales). 'He saw two killer whales tilt up an ice-floe so that the seal on the top of the floe the other side slithered off into the waiting mouth of a third killer whale.'

Soon after lunch I set off with two BAS scientists – Roger Worland and Paul Tarle – to walk to Gourlay Point at the south end of Signy Island. To get to the plateau you have to climb up a steep rock face, known as the Stone Chute. The view from on top is spectacular. Coronation Island lies across the water, two or three miles away, its immense glaciers glinting in the afternoon sun. The rock cliffs which surround the base seem to be covered patchily in snow.

'Those are the Cape pigeons nesting,' Roger tells me. 'We've been ringing them for about twenty years so we know more or less what's going on. Some of the birds have been here as long as we have been studying them.'

We walk up the valley which lies between the mountains to our left and the ice-cap which covers most of the interior of Signy Island. It is known as Moraine Valley because of the line of stones which have been pushed out by the glacier.

'This is the fellfield,' Paul Tarle says. 'See how the weathering has given rise to some sort of crude soil formation.'

I can see what he means. There is a thin covering of soil, a flaky crust which is the first step in the transformation of rock into earth.

'Could you plant anything there?' I ask.

'Conceivably,' Paul replies. 'But you wouldn't be allowed to under the rules of the Antarctic Treaty. No exotic importations are allowed. You can't even grow tomatoes. In South Georgia you have a number of exotics like rats and, in particular, the reindeer which the Norwegians brought down for skins and meat in the whaling days. But down here we're trying to do things right.'

After an hour's walk, first up the valley, then across the corner of the ice-cap, we begin to descend once more towards the shore.

When we are still half a mile from the coastline, Roger says: 'Look out for fur seals now. They're very agile; they can go a long way inland. They look just like rocks and suddenly they are there at your feet, growling. You can get nipped quite badly and if you do you must have a course of antibiotics. A chap on Bird Island got bitten on the back of a leg when he was bending over. They can run faster than you can. There's a theory that if you fall over and lie still, they won't bite because they think you are another seal. The ones that come down here are the non-breeding males, probably because it's so overcrowded in South Georgia. Ten years ago you would have hardly dreamed of seeing a fur seal here and now there are more and more.'

For me, those few minutes as we approached the shore were another of the high points of my Antarctic trip. We threaded our way through a mass of seals, holding out sticks we had brought with us to fend off any that seemed aggressive. They growled and barked, feinted towards us, then at the last moment backed and slithered away. And all the time, as we pressed on towards the sea, the sound of the penguin rookeries on the rocks and cliffs behind the seals grew louder and louder until finally even the noise of the seals was drowned by the clatter and bustle of the birds.

It's hard to describe the sight as we arrived at Gourlay Point. The penguin rookeries stretched out to the right and left, thousands upon thousands of birds. The snow had a pinkish tinge from their droppings and was crisscrossed by footprints and skid-marks. There was moss between the rocks and this, too, was marked by the passage of thousands, of hundreds of thousands, of webbed feet.

By some faculty of social organization, the penguins have managed to create roads and avenues and streets dividing off one part of the rookery from another. It's like some vast housing estate seen from the air. Birds are walking busily up and down and back and forth, using the tracks and the pathways wherever they can so as to avoid – I imagine – stepping on or over another bird's territory.

I took one of these tracks myself, climbing up after a friendly pair of chinstraps whose habitual perch seemed to be high up in the upper circle of this dramatic natural theatre. In fact this particular colony consisted entirely of chinstrap penguins; some of them – many of them – have chicks with them, grey and furry little animals that quite soon will become as sleek and active as their parents.

There is another cove or bay the other side of the promontory. Here again, unbelievably, there is a vast acreage of penguins – Adélies this time, rather than chinstraps – which extends down to the water, around the bay the other side and over the rocks as far as the eye can see. There is a bare strip of earth, hardly more than ten yards wide, which runs along the top of the territory and separates the chinstraps from the Adélies. This is a kind of no-man's-land and I suppose that all hell would break loose if one or other side tried to colonize it.

Roger and Paul had gone off in another direction. I stood there alone, feeling like Cortez on his peak in Darien, surrounded by this multitude of birds. When you consider how few breeding sites there are in the Antarctic – places where the rock is free of ice – then it is not surprising that there should be these vast congregations of animals. But that is an intellectual appreciation; from the visual and emotional point of view nothing had prepared me for the sheer biological abundance that confronted me at that moment. Wherever I looked there were penguins – plunging and strutting up their walkways, tobogganing down the slopes and splashing into the water, porpoising in the bay while the waves crashed on the rocks. And some of the rocks, when I looked closer, weren't rocks at all but huge elephant seals lying close to each other in great mounds of blubber, not bothering to lift their heads as the birds bounced past.

I spent a long time that afternoon just standing and watching, absorbing the sight and the sounds of this Antarctic miracle. It could well be that I shall never again visit a penguin colony like this, never experience nature in this superabundant mood where penguins and seals and skuas and petrels have free run of sea and earth and sky, and man, if he is there at all (and most often he is not) is a tiny and insignificant spectator. None of these animals showed any fear of man; none of the birds stepped aside to let me pass. On the contrary, as far as they were concerned, I was just another penguin, expected to respect the rules of the rookery like anyone else. Even the elephant seals, naturally more belligerent, showed no sign of being disturbed by human presence. If you walked very close to them, they might roll their thick necks around, stare at you with brown-red eyes, open the gullet wide and bare their teeth. But because the threat was not serious the response was not serious either. Only the fur seals were to be guarded against and in their case, as far as I could tell, the motive was not fear but a healthy aggression directed not against man *per se*, but against any and all intruders into their particular domain.

I am not a biologist and it is too late to become one now. Men like Konrad Lorenz and Gerald Durrell, women like Jane Goodall, understand and write about 'territory' better than I ever will. But I had glimmerings that afternoon of what it all means and could begin to grasp how it is that some men and women can spend a lifetime watching animals in the wild.

There was a tiny hut set back on the hill above the bay and the penguin rookeries called, by some quirky humour peculiar to Fids, the Hunting Lodge. The place is hardly larger than a potting shed, but there's a primus there and paraffin and powdered coffee on the shelf.

Roger took a saucepan, went outside and filled it with snow which he melted and heated over the primus. He found some chocolate in a tin and handed it round.

'We play poker for chocolate on Friday nights at the base. The winner generally brings the chocolate over here.' He loaded some more snow into the pan.

'Monday evenings we have slide-shows. People develop their own photographs on the base. Things can get quite raucous at times. No one has much hesitation about criticizing someone else's pictures, but it's all pretty good-natured.'

'Do you all get on with each other?' I asked.

'Pretty much. Some people, like the Americans, go in for psychological screening before they send someone down here. On the whole, the BAS approach is that if someone wants to go back, then they go back on the next boat.'

'One of the people who works hardest on these bases', Paul adds, 'is the cook. He might have a couple of people to help him, but it's still his responsibility six days out of seven to do his best with limited material. Ironically, one of the limitations is shortage of freezer space. So he has to use a lot of dried products. Batchelors, for example, make a dehydrated mince, and whenever it appears people will say "Oh, not Batchelors again!" The cook has to learn to live with that.'

I realized that food on the ship is obviously a good deal better than food on the base. There's more storage space on the ship and we can stop at ports to pick up fresh meat and fruit.

After an hour or two at Gourlay Point, it was time to go. We trudged back up the slope towards the plateau.

'We call this the Khyber Pass,' says Roger. 'You have to watch out for crevasses. Sometimes you can see the slight indentations; otherwise you've just got to probe. Dogs have an uncanny sense of when they're coming to a crevasse, which is one of the arguments – though not necessarily decisive – in favour of dogs versus skidoos. Sometimes you can see the snow's a different colour which can indicate that a crevasse is there.'

As we reached the ice-cap we turned round and looked back towards the point. The roar of the elephant seals came to us on the wind. It is amazing how far the sound carries. We must have been over a mile away from the shoreline and could still hear them.

Nearer at hand the wind on the plateau had wrought strange patterns in the ice. 'We call it *Sastrugi* – snow-sculptures,' says Paul. I can see what he means.

As we walked on the weather closed in; visibility dropped; I stared at the knapsack on the back of the man in front of me and was grateful to be escorted. It had all looked so balmy and simple when we set off, but if you don't know what you are doing or where you are going a gentle afternoon's hike in the Antarctic can quickly end in disaster.

I caught up with Roger and we walked together, with Paul leading the way.

'Signy is probably one of the most isolated of BAS bases,' Roger tells me. 'We sometimes only get a couple of mail-drops a year. This year one of the tourist ships actually brought the mail on from Stanley. Getting the mail is quite an emotional occasion for the people on the base. Once the German vessel – the *Polarstern* which supplies the German Antarctic base – helicoptered our mail in. Helicopter operations are something which BAS can't afford. To run a Sea King for a year would cost us £12 million, allowing for amortizing the capital as well. Running an Otter costs £1 million a year. They're relatively economical. One of our people was flying over Rio in a DC10 which had to jettison fuel and he commented that the amount of fuel being jettisoned could keep the Otters flying for a year.

'Mind you,' Roger continued, 'we didn't complain when the German helicopter brought the mail in. Communication of any kind is precious down here. As you may know, we're allowed to transmit two hundred words a month to our families. You can break that down into two lots of one hundred if you want to.'

We passed a ski-stick stuck in the snow. 'That marks the place where a skidoo broke down last season,' Paul explained. 'It hasn't as yet emerged from the snow.'

We came up to a small, yellow hut about five feet high and three feet wide. There's a solar cell on top of the hut, whose purpose is to collect power for the batteries inside.

'This is the Moraine Valley fellfield site,' says Roger. It is not his particular responsibility, but one of the features of operations at a base like Signy is that everyone knows, at least in broad outline, what everyone else is doing. Certainly Roger knows enough to convince me he is an expert.

'Here we have automatic recording of ground temperature at various depths. We're also measuring humidity, wind-velocity and direction, as well as light. All that gets put on a reel or disc which can be picked up from time to time and taken back to the computer. The machine is called a data logger. It could tell you the number of freeze/thaw cycles, for example, over a period of time and that might be an indication of nutrient release which in turn might give you a sudden growth of bacteria. You might then be able to relate that to a change in one of the other variables which you are measuring.'

We trudged up the last hill before reaching the steep pathway which takes us back down to the base, and passed, to our right, five plain white crosses. Four have Norwegian names inscribed; the last is blank.

'Five whalers are buried on Signy,' Paul says. 'One of them doesn't seem to have a name.'

We came to the brow of the hill and looked down into the bay where the base is situated.

'That cove is called Factory Cove. They used to bring the whaling ships in there and then process the whales on the ship. That was in the days of pelagic whaling.'

The tide has come in since we left. We have to scramble over the rocks as we make our way round the cove to the base. We said we would be back by 6 p.m. and we have ten minutes to spare. (Had we not returned on time, a search party would have been sent out to look for us in accordance with established procedures.) The only noise we can hear now, as we approach, is from the new generator.

'We used to have some old Rolls-Royce generators,' Roger tells us, 'and the mountains used to shake.'

In the background, the *Biscoe* is pumping oil across to a storage tank on shore.

Later on that day I walked round to the end of one of the huts on the base. It is called Tonsberg House and was built in 1955 on the site of the Norwegian whaling station at Signy. A piece of whalebone has been fastened to the wood with the following inscription: 'Antarctic whale catches South Orkneys and South Shetland 1911–1930. Right 78; Blue 61,336; Fin 48,023; Sei 1,796; Humpback 6,742; Sperm 184.'

That brief record, as cold and factual as a tombstone, brought home to me as nothing else could the sheer scale of these Antarctic whaling operations in their heyday. I was reminded as I stood there at the end of the wooden hut looking at that sad message (was that dead whale itself included in the statistics?) of the time when the Japanese Ambassador to the EEC told a meeting of Euro-MPs in Brussels: 'We shall continue to hunt whales as long as there are whales left to hunt.'

Sometimes I wonder how any whales at all have managed to survive.

I stayed on the base for dinner that night. It is someone's birthday and bottles of champagne are being passed around. Those who aren't drinking champagne are drinking gin and tonic with slices of lemon. Birthdays are important down here. They are landmarks in an otherwise monotonous landscape.

I had a long talk with David Walton, who is mainly responsible for the fellfield project, about the future of Antarctica.

'It's very easy to say "Let's make it an exclusive club",' Walton comments. 'That's not necessarily the wrong thing; but it's not necessarily the right thing either. How can people share in this beauty? I think that the *World Discoverer* and the *Lindblad Explorer* are on the whole a good influence. They take great care to discipline the tourist parties. They don't interfere with the rookeries. On this island we don't allow any parties from tourist ships but we give them our cooperation. We go over with them to Shingle Cove on Coronation Island. There may be six visits altogether by tourists ships between the beginning of the season and May. But with the Argentinian and Chilean vessels it's a different story. The Argentine ships have been known to land 1,000 people at a time. There you *are* beginning to make an impact on the environment.'

We moved on from tourism to talk about the wider exploitation of Antarctica.

'In Alaska, when development took place, you had massive disruption. In spite of the re-seeding, you see enormous scars about the place, for example on the mountains where they took the stones for the road. In the Arctic you're working on consolidated tundra; here you're working on snow. There'll be dust and dirt, a change in the albedo. And it's not just the impact on wildlife or climate. You've got to take into account the effect on landscape as well. The US base at McMurdo is the slum of the Antarctic. It's the biggest garbage dump. The New Zealanders have their own base near by – I've heard of them going over to the American dead vehicle park and finding that some car has been junked merely because the battery is missing. They've also got a garbage dump at Palmer Station. One of the visitors who came in on a tourist ship was so appalled by the state of the place that she wrote to her Congressman. Since then some cleaning up has gone on. It's a matter of balance. How can you show people penguins when you've got an ore-extraction plant next door? That's not the Antarctic.'

We went on to talk about the 'krill surplus' theory and the expansion of the seal population. The idea is that since we have eliminated the whales (more or less) the krill which the whales would have eaten is available for other species, particularly seals and penguins. But those species are now expanding in such a way that they may threaten other species; may even jeopardize the recovery of the whales themselves because the whales may find there just isn't enough krill around for them to climb back up to their former levels or anything like it, even if whaling does stop completely. So shouldn't we, therefore (so the argument runs), intervene and 'take out' some of the seals and penguins – just as they used to 'take out' villages in Vietnam? Wouldn't that give the whales a better chance?

Round the table that night at the BAS base in Signy there were proponents of intervention (or 'rational management' as they preferred to call it) and proponents of non-intervention. Scientists often have a self-confidence that borders on arrogance. Even though the examples where intervention or 'rational management' has had disastrous results are legion, many scientists (including some BAS scientists) seem to have a powerful belief in their ability to understand, and therefore control or manipulate, more or less complex ecosystems. The notion is that somehow one disequilibrium (in this case the disequilibrium created by massive whaling over a forty- to fifty-year time-span) can be put right by intervening somewhere else in the system.

Munro Sievewright asks: 'How do you preserve the South Georgia pippit?' And he answers himself by suggesting that since the expansion of the fur seal population on South Georgia is threatening the habitat of the South Georgia pippit, the solution may be to reduce the number of fur seals.

David Walton has his own example of the effects of disequilibrium. 'How long are we going to let the fur seals wreck the moss at Gourlay? Why should fur seals be preferred to a 4,000-year-old moss bank?'

My own point of view – and it is one which I expressed that evening with all due deference – is that it is better to leave ill alone. Let nature restore her own balances without man's helping hand. We should not add insult to injury. And in any case from a political standpoint the notion of taxpayer-funded 'culling' of seal and penguin populations in Antarctica (unless conducted under a cloak of secrecy which is hardly good science) boggles the imagination. Even if the scientific calculations were unassailable, the moral and aesthetic price to be paid (all the blood on the ice) would be altogether too high. 'I'm sorry about the moss banks, though,' I said.

Inevitably the conversation comes back to whales. David Rootes, the Base Commander, has been down at Signy for seven years. When they saw the whale the other day, head and flukes right out of the water, it was a rare occurrence indeed.

'First time I've seen one like that,' Rootes says. 'We could see the barnacles. There are people working in the Pacific now who are beginning to be able to identify individual whales by the barnacles, building up a picture of barnacle growth for each individual, in much the same way as you can identify elephants by the tears and holes in the flaps of their ears.'

The closing down of the BAS base in South Georgia has put pressure on Signy. Munro says: 'It's never been like this. Normally there are only twelve scientists here. You ask anyone who has wintered here which they think is best, summer or winter? They'll all say: winter. You've got good sea-ice, you've got water clear for diving; things are more settled down. You've got a small community here then. Over at Halley, you only get one ship a year. The ship comes in for a week and after a few days people are looking forward to seeing the ship go. At the end of two years people at Halley have horribly mixed emotions about going home.'

The launch came over at 10 p.m. and we returned to the ship. One moment of drama occurred when Dave, a diesel mechanic, who had obviously dined well if not wisely, tried three times to climb up the ship's ladder. Each time he failed. Finally he lost his footing and fell between the *Biscoe* and the launch into the icy water and had to be fished out. In the end, they sat him firmly on the engine hatch and winched the whole launch on board. Anne Todd, whose memory for incident and anecdote is as inexhaustible as her knowledge of Antarctic geography and history, tells me: 'We lost a chap like that two or three years ago. If there's a current running, you can fall in and get swept away. Or else you can get crushed between the launch and the ship.'

Back in the wardroom, the Captain offers us all a round of drinks. At this time of night liqueurs of various kinds tend to flow freely. Chris Elliott has been coming down to the Antarctic for a long time. Though his job is sailing a ship, inevitably he knows a great deal about BAS and its work.

'BAS took a new direction under Laws,' he says. 'Right up to 1969–70 we were still sending sledging parties out from Stonington to do original survey work. Laws moved BAS from exploration to science.'

Anne, who spent years working for Vivian Fuchs, intervenes in defence of her former boss. 'Dr Fuchs had a real interest in science.' But she agrees that it was probably when Sir Raymond Priestley took over for the 1955–58 period (when Fuchs was away on his Trans-Antarctica expedition with Sir Edmund Hillary – the first overland trip to the Pole since Scott) that the transition took place and BAS was put on a properly scientific basis.

The next day dawned fine and clear. We finished pumping the oil, but Tweeky was still on shore making adjustments to his computer program, so it was not absolutely clear that we would leave at ten o'clock next morning as we planned. I put in an appearance at breakfast which was a departure from my recent practice. One of the drawbacks of shipboard life is that you eat too much so I had been tending to skip meals. However, after the previous day's walk across the island, I felt I could do with a fried egg and bacon.

An hour or two later we were setting off in the base's launch down the coast towing our rubber Zodiac. The plan was to visit a fresh-water lake where diving was in progress. (The Zodiac would take us ashore from the launch; after that we would walk inland to the lake.)

As we chugged round the island, I found it hard to get over how beautiful this coastal scenery is. These hills have much more colour than those of the Peninsula. The great cliffs which rise sheer from the sea are covered with moss and multicoloured lichens. The yellows and greens, reds and rust colours contrast with the white of the snow on the face of the rocks. The snow petrels and the Cape pigeons are wheeling and whirling in front of us as we come up to a little rocky beach to anchor a few hundred yards from shore.

We made a quick run across in the Zodiac, then walked up off the beach through the massed ranks of elephant and fur seals. Colin, always a reliable guide and mentor, explains: 'The elephant seal is polygamous. It's the only true seal which actually has a harem except for the grey seal in Scotland which is also polygamous to some extent. The fur seals here are mainly immature. The elephant seals actually breed here though.'

Colin points to a massive patch of blubber where a dozen huge elephant seals are lying close to each other. 'The big elephant bulls are here at the moment. They come ashore in October and then disappear again as soon as they have mated.'

The smell of the seals is strong. These are powerful animals in every sense.

Half a mile from the beach is the fresh-water lake where they are diving. It is not a huge lake – not much more than three hundred yards long and about three hundred yards wide. Two men in wet suits are swimming around, bobbing up and down and occasionally disappearing from view entirely. It is a weird scene. One of the Fids who has come with us from the base gives a running commentary: 'He's trying to fix a light-meter at the bottom of the lake so we can discover how much light penetrates to the bottom.'

'Who is diving?' I asked him.

'Kenny and Allan.'

I remember Kenny Cameron. He is the one who talked with such enthusiasm about his experience diving with the whale.

There is a control box where we are standing with the wires leading from it into the water. 'A log is taken every thirty minutes of water temperature and the light-value.'

Kenny surfaces in front of us, black and sinister, canisters of air strapped to his back and flippers flapping as he walks up out of the lake. 'Look!' He removes his mask and holds out one rubber-clad hand. 'A fairy shrimp. The highest form of life in the inland lakes of Signy.'

I look at a tiny shrimplet, only a few millimetres long. It's hard to believe I'm observing the highest form of life.

'We're also trying to determine what the take-up of nitrogen is by the algae,' explains Kenny. 'I've put a canister at the bottom and we'll look at it from time to time.'

We walked over to a second lake, Kenny coming with us.

'This lake is eutrophic. There have been so many elephant seals in the vicinity that the nutrients in the lake have increased considerably. This has led to a growth in the phytoplankton. There's been an increase in sediment at the bottom because the light has been screened out.'

I see what he means. There are seals everywhere, some of them stretched out by the edge of the lake, some of them wallowing in the water. Many of them are moulting; most are scarred or chipped; all of them snort or rumble or bellow, depending on mood and moment. Not the prettiest sight – certainly not furry and cuddly like the young harp seals so often pictured in the anti-cruelty advertisements. Nevertheless it was good to know that down here in the South Orkneys the elephant seals are flourishing – even if they do spoil the pristine purity of the occasional inland lake.

We walked back along the beach, littered with whalebone, including some gigantic pieces of bleached porcelain which I take to be the skull of some monster of the deep which must have met its end in Factory Cove. The elephant seals are stacked up against these relics of yet larger mammals, though I doubt whether they appreciate the poignancy of it.

After lunch at the base I joined Carys Williams and Dave, one of the Fids from the base, on a small chick-ringing expedition. We climbed up into the rocks behind the huts where the Cape pigeons are nesting. The adult birds fly off when we approach, leaving their chicks, grey fluffy balls, behind.

'One of the habits of these animals,' David warns us, 'is that they spew up at you as you come near them.'

The first chick we approached vomits a massive gobbet of orange-coloured half-digested krill as Dave picks it up. He avoids this offering and holds the bird firmly while Carys rings it.

'Don't leave a gap,' Dave instructs. 'If you leave a gap, the ring could get caught in something.' He examines the chick. 'This one is already getting its flying feathers. It will fly in another two weeks. Once you ring the chicks, you have to be careful to put them back on the right nest because the parents don't necessarily recognize them.'

They have been marking birds at Signy for twenty years. The numbers are issued by the British Trust for Ornithology.

On our last afternoon at Signy we went out to have another look at the penguin colony at Gourlay Point, this time by launch rather than on foot. Coming in by sea you can see the penguins standing up on the skyline like sentinels. And you can see them on the lower ledges of the cliff as well, some of them well within reach of the sea-spray as it crashes up on the rocks. There was a leopard seal dead ahead as we came into the cove. It was probably waiting to get a bite at a penguin.

We transferred from launch to Zodiac and climbed out of the water like penguins returning from the sea. While the others in the party explored – as I did myself yesterday – I perched on a rock, listening and looking.

Someone has left a knapsack on the beach which causes a momentary ripple of interest. One or two birds poke at it. Apart from that, armies of penguins are going about their business as they did yesterday and will, I hope, continue to do for the foreseeable future. As I sit there an elephant seal surfaces just in front of me and sinks out of sight again and a fur seal pulls itself up on to the rocks.

There are large numbers of chicks at every level of the cliff. The chinstrap chicks don't seem to have the actual chinstrap marking itself. They're grey-black in colour with down on their wings and a brownish tuft on the top of their heads. One chick, about three-quarter size, has parked itself at my feet and is squawking as though it has lost its way. I'm sorry I can't help it.

The launch is bobbing away on the waves fifty yards from me. The radio on board has been left switched on and I can clearly hear – over and above the background din of the rookery with all its squawking and screeching, cheeping and squeaking – the voices of the Russian trawler captains. It is an odd juxtaposition. How evil it would be, I reflect, if the Soviet fishing fleet and its East European counterparts were even now hoovering up the marine resources which these animals need if they are to survive.

A few yards from me a South American sheathbill is pecking away at a dead penguin chick. Next to the chick are the carcasses of two adult penguins. Richard Price, a scientist from the base who has come out with us for the afternoon, walks over and comments: 'They've probably been wounded at sea. Maybe they tangled with a leopard seal and dragged themselves ashore to die.' He looks around with a practised eye. He is used to estimating numbers.

'There are probably 50,000 or 60,000 birds just in this one colony. And there are seventeen colonies on the island. We've noticed a big increase in the number of chinstrap penguins here. That's probably due to the increased availability of krill. The penguins have been able to take advantage of the decline of the whales.'

Eventually we left Gourlay Point to run back round the island to the base. From a distance the sight of the penguins standing stiff and upright on the rocks above the water reminded me of the cemetery at the top of the Golden Horn in Istanbul. The launch disturbed a giant petrel scavenging in the water ahead of us on the floating carcass of a penguin. It propelled itself into the air, paddling energetically through the water over a long runway before lifting off above the waves. A school of penguins porpoise alongside keeping pace with the boat.

'They breathe as they leap,' Richard explains. 'Also, if they're being chased by a leopard seal, the seal can't really see them when they're out of the water.' He points to the horizon. 'You know, I found it very hard to imagine, when I first came down here, how this sea on which we're travelling can transform itself into ice sixty feet thick in the winter. If there's good sea-ice, parties will go over to Coronation Island and stay there from two to ten days. The pack-ice from here down to the Antarctic Continent is solid all the way. And it can freeze two hundred miles north of the South Orkneys. The seals will haul out and breathe when they see a tide-crack between the sea-ice and the islands.'

We turn in towards the base. This time Richard Price points not at the sea but at the cliffs. 'Look at the lichens. The colour is most vivid at the end of winter when the snows are melting. That clears the muck off them and you get wonderful yellows and oranges.'

We passed a small island called Outer Island. Five years ago there were no penguins here. Richard says he counted fifty-seven chicks last week. Coming into the base we pass a gulley on the cliff.

'We call it Capey Gulley,' says Richard, 'because there are so many Cape pigeons there. We've marked about 500 nests. There are also fifty or sixty snow petrels.'

At dinner on board the *Biscoe* that night was Mark Sanders. He is Australian in origin but lived in England for twelve years before coming down to work with BAS at Signy.

'The main reason', he tells us, 'that the lakes are studied here at Signy is because they are untouched. You have a wide variety of lakes: mesotrophic, eutrophic or oligotrophic. The second lake you saw this morning was eutrophic. It had a high level of nutrients mainly because of the elephant seals all around it. The first lake was oligotrophic but that could change as the seals are beginning to invade that lake as well. Where else', asks Sanders, 'can you study every type of lake? The highest lake in Signy is ice-covered, but you still get an input of nutrients through the ice and snow. We've given all the lakes numbers. There have been reports of fish in lakes 2, 5 and 6. And indeed the number of copepods we are finding could be enough to support a small fish population.'

He speaks with passion, conveying his own excitement to his listeners. It is a mistake to suppose that scientists are necessarily cold-blooded people. Studying fresh-water lakes in the mountainous Antarctic – this is the stuff that dreams are made on.

Dave Rootes was also on board for dinner that last night in the South Orkneys. He is thirty-two years old, studied zoology and chemistry at the London Polytechnic before doing a teachers' training course in England, followed by two years in the Antarctic. He went back to the UK and then was offered the job of Base Commander at Signy. He was expected to stay just one summer but in fact has stayed six. He talks about counting penguins.

'The way we count penguins is to wander through the colony plopping bits of paint on birds and using a tally-counter. You count the birds on the nests. I counted 83,000 pairs of penguins once. Another method, which they use at Bird Island, is to string a cord across the colony and then to walk down counting every two or three metres. You can try photographs but you've got to be able to see the birds.'

He said he was off to climb in the Peruvian Andes on his way back to England at the end of this Antarctic summer.

A third guest from the base that night was Ray Cannon, a BAS scientist with a PhD from Cranfield Institute of Technology. His speciality then was the aphid wheat pest; now it is cold tolerance.

'You get absorbed in your work down here. Communication with the outside world is difficult, but most of the time you don't want to know anyway. I was coming down a couple of years ago on the *Biscoe* when we saw the Russian flag flying at half-mast at their Bellingshausen base on King George Island in the South Shetlands. The reason we were there', he added parenthetically, 'was that we were dropping off a spare Otter at the Chilean base, Rodolfo Marsh. We looked at the Russian flag and asked the Chileans, "*Qué pasa?*", and the Chileans replied that Brezhnev had died.'

Norman, the electrician, who has a knack of summing things up, says: 'It's not that one is against having the information. It's more that one doesn't care.'

After dinner, Dave Rootes and the other guests went back to the base. I went down to the Fids bar to find the second steward, David Tomaszewski, having a quiet drink. I am used to seeing him in the wardroom, spick and span in his white uniform, serving the meals in the roughest of weather.

'Cheers,' he says, raising his glass. 'Only thirty-eight days to go until we get back to the UK. I was married just a week before we sailed and that was in June last year. Now it's February. I'm looking forward to seeing her.'

He drains the glass and looks speculatively at my collar. 'Do you want a hair cut? I could probably fit you in before Rio.' One of Tomaszewski's skills, it turns out, is that of hairdresser. He is apparently much in demand.

We were meant to have left Signy on Sunday morning but Twecky, who was working on the computer programme, hadn't finished. Once he has got the thing going others will be able to take over but in this initial phase his expertise, his uncanny *rapport* with the machine, is essential. It was a glorious day so the delay was perfectly tolerable. Filling in time I climbed up to the wireless mast and sat there looking down at the *Biscoe* in the bay below, the red of her hull contrasting with the blue sheen of the water and the white of the snow. After a while, I trudged on up through the snow towards the cliff which overlooked the base and then made my way up through the rocks. This is where the Cape pigeons and the snow petrels nest. As I climbed I could hear, from every snow-covered nook and cranny, the cheeping of young birds. Some of the nests are numbered: BAS scientists are trying to find out if the same birds come back to the same nests year after year. It was so warm that the snow was melting and dripping off the rocks. In my pocket I had one of those little plastic film containers; I took it out and filled it with ice-cold Antarctic water to drink.

I finally reached the top of a small mountain and sat there, looking out at Coronation Island across the sea. The sun is shining on the glaciers over there and today, unlike yesterday, we can clearly see the tops of the mountains in the interior. Nearer at hand, from the direction of Gourlay Point, I feel certain I can hear the noise of the seals and penguins as it is borne inland on the wind. Another unmistakable sound, which occurs from time to time, is the thud and crash of icebergs breaking away from the shelf into the water.

I managed to lose a glove on the way up but the weather is so balmy today that this is not the tragedy it might otherwise have been.

As I walked back down to the ship I came under serious attack from a pair of skuas. I could see them high up on the cliff watching me flounder down through the snow. At a given moment they launched themselves into the air and came in, like Argentine fighter planes, low and fast. You have to hold up your hand, otherwise they will chip at the top of your head with feet or beak.

David Rootes came on board for a last lunch before we sailed. He presented BAS's guests with a complete set of British Antarctic Territory Stamps, which he had franked in his capacity as Antarctic sub-postmaster. It was a marvellous souvenir.

9

Leaving Signy

At 2 p.m. precisely on Sunday, 5 February, the ship's hooter sounded as we pulled out of Signy. The BAS scientists had all climbed up to the wireless mast, set up there on the hill behind the base. Their red shirts and orange anoraks made a bright blob of colour as they waved us off. The *Bransfield* would be in and out once or twice more before the end of the season but after that it would be a long lonely year.

We stopped a mile or two out to ditch the two old Rolls-Royce generating engines which we had taken on board at Signy (the base had recently been equipped with new generators). Disposal of waste is always a problem in the Antarctic. If you're an intelligent base commander you take advantage of visits by vessels to off-load your heavy rubbish and 'gash'.

By mid afternoon the day had turned into an absolute scorcher. I sat on the boat-deck in shirt-sleeves, watching as the glaciers and mountains of Coronation Island slid past. Penguins were popping up in the water all around, whereas the sea was dead calm, reflecting the full force of the sun. I found it terribly hard to believe how beautiful the place actually was.

By 5 p.m. the sun was finally about to disappear behind the clouds. Over to the right loomed the peaks of Laurie Island where the Argentines have a base. BAS people I have talked to say that the occupants are soldiers and doubt whether any serious science gets done. To the west was Frederickson Island and in the far distance, slipping away from us now beyond the horizon, I could still see the peaks of Coronation Island.

As we passed Powell Island to our left – named after a Briton who sailed with the American sealer Nathaniel Palmer – we saw a fleet of Russian ships. The mother ship – or factory vessel – was tucked into the shore. A dozen other vessels were spread out across a wide sweep of sea ahead of us. As I stare at them through binoculars, Martin White explains the pattern of Soviet operations.

'You see the mother vessel tucked right into the coast beneath the glacier. She'll stay down here the whole time. She'll travel around with the fleet. You can see a trawler alongside her now and another one the other side. The trawlers themselves probably have 400 tonnes' refrigeration capacity. That's hard freezing. They also have the capacity to make fishmeal.'

I keep my eyes glued to the binoculars, fascinated, while Martin continues: 'Those trawlers you're looking at now will be unloading frozen products on to the factory ship; a reefer will come down maybe once a month and take the cargo back home. The ships operate in groups of twenty or so. It's a highly organized operation. The fisheries around South Georgia have been quite considerably damaged. We've seen a change in the composition of the catches; and the total catch has declined as well. Of course, it's hard to be precise. The Poles and the Russians are apparently sending in statistics of a general kind now, but they don't really give an indication of what has been caught in what area.'

Looking at the radar, I can see that there are more vessels than we can actually notice ahead of us.

'The Russians probably know we are coming,' says Martin. 'Most of the skippers of the large trawlers speak good English and we're operating on the same wavelengths.'

I asked Jerry Burgan, the First Mate, who is on duty on the bridge, whether I can try to raise the Russians on the RT. I know a few words of Russian and I try them out.

'Hello, hello, this is the *John Biscoe*. Can you hear me? How are you? – *kak vui pazhevayete*? Good morning – *dobroe utro*; goodbye – *da svidanya*.'

We draw near enough to one of the vessels to see, with the aid of the binoculars, the hammer and sickle on the red funnel.

I flip through the channels listening for a Russian reply but there seems to be sudden radio silence. I try another tack, but this time in English.

'We will trade two bottles of whisky to one bottle of vodka,' I say. If that doesn't raise them, nothing will. It doesn't.

Colin, who is on the bridge with us, regards my efforts with mild amusement. 'What do the Russians do with the krill?' he asks Martin.

'They make it into fishmeal,' Martin replies. 'There's a technical problem. Krill doesn't peel if you boil it. The Japanese have a system of freezing the whole animal and then abrading the peel off. Another technique is to put the krill into a large drum with holes in it. The drum is then spun round and round, so that the protein juice is precipitated out. This can then be frozen once it coagulates. Or they make a kind of mince out of it. You can get potted krill tails at Harrods,' Martin adds. 'But you can't sell them in the United States because the Food and Drug Administration lays down rules about the fluoride content and the krill wouldn't meet it.'

Martin reckons that the total annual krill catch in the Antarctic is around 250,000 tonnes. Other estimates have put it as high as 1,000,000 tonnes.

'A managed resource is better than a free-for-all,' he states firmly. 'And here we do indeed have a free-for-all. We have the Antarctic Treaty, but they haven't begun to set catch limits yet, not even on a global basis, and certainly not on an area or species basis. The time to manage Antarctic resources was in the 1970s. If we had managed fish stocks off South Georgia from the very beginning we could have maintained high fish-yields. Now it may be too late. I've come down here for the last two years with OBP and we found very little krill. This could be just an oscillation, relating to meteorological and hydrographic conditions. Or it could be something else.'

Colin intervenes with all his magisterial authority. 'Did you know', he asks, 'that krill constitute the world's second largest biomass after human beings?'

'I hadn't thought of human beings as biomass.'

'Oh, but you must – 5,000,000,000 human beings with an average weight of forty kilograms is a very considerable biomass indeed.'

Since I was up on the bridge, I jotted our position down in my notebook: latitude 61.31S, longitude 41.51W. We had 447 miles to go to Bird Island off South Georgia. Leaving the Russians abeam, we changed course slightly and headed off on 030 degrees. The water in front of the ship was absolutely packed with penguins, most of which had their heads down and were feeding energetically. These waters are obviously rich in resources. No wonder the Russians are here.

'The pinkish tinge in the water means we're probably going through a krill patch,' Jerry explains. 'Or perhaps it's the old eyeballs. It was a late night last night.'

I stand there next to the First Mate thinking about penguins. Apparently the Americans once took twenty or thirty birds from a colony in Adélie Land, which is right the other side of the Antarctic Continent, brought them round to this side and then let them go again and they found their way back two thousand miles or so. And there's a colony of emperor penguins at Halley the position of which has been accurately charted by the *Bransfield* over the years. BAS scientists discovered that even though the ice had been shifting, the actual position of the penguins hadn't changed.

Talk about penguins often leads to talk about seals. Today is no exception.

'Almost every crab-eater has scars,' says Martin. 'I always used to assume they were caused by killer whales. But then Dr Laws came and looked at the crab-eaters and saw that the scarring corresponded to leopard seal jaws. Killer whales would have produced a different kind of scarring.'

'There was some trouble with leopard seals at Palmer Station. The Americans there wouldn't go in the water without a shark billy – that's a kind of stick which makes explosive sounds. I think they aggravated the seals, so the seals decided to knock them around a bit. A photographer from *Time/Life* came down and was diving. He found himself taking a picture of a grinning face and eyes like a locomotive rushing through the dark. He climbed out of the water so fast, carrying all his photographic equipment, that he actually threw his shoulder out. That shows what adrenalin can do for you.'

Next day around noon Stan, the Chief Engineer, came up on deck and complained about the movement of the ship. He says it bobs around like a bottle. On his last ship this kind of water would have just been a ripple. 'The problem is the length of the ship compared with the length between the tops of the waves. I was down there in the engine-room trying to mend a pipe and for the first time in years I broke a hacksaw, the ship was moving so much. This is a short swell; the sea comes up so fast there isn't time to build up a long swell.' He sighs. 'It looked so good last night when we were leaving Signy. I thought they were going to get a clear run up to Bird Island.'

When Stan has disappeared I go up to the bridge. Peter Kerry, the Second Officer, has been showing me how they do survey work. Sometimes they have to go into areas on which there is very little available information so they will run their own surveys using launches and echo-sounders. Apparently the *Biscoe* did a lot of survey work earlier this year when they were supporting some geological landings south of Deception Island.

While I am on the bridge Steve Stephenson arrives for a breath of air. We haven't seen much of Steve today or yesterday. He's been lying low in his cabin. Today he looks at the sea and wonders what these tremendous waves must have seemed like to Shackleton and his men going in their open boat from Elephant Island to South Georgia.

'How', Steve asks, 'could Worsley [Master of the *Endurance*] conceivably have managed to take bearings in this kind of weather. I'm not surprised that he thought the boat was going to be swamped when he looked at waves like these.'

Elephant Island is the most northerly of the South Orkney Islands, so we have in a very real sense been retracing Shackleton's historic journey over the last twenty hours or so. Steve says: 'We're doing at least nine knots at the moment. It took Shackleton sixteen days to cover 850 miles. That's an average speed of two knots.'

From the bridge, on the following afternoon, I could dimly see the outline of Willis Island and then, ahead of us, Bird Island and the mainland of South Georgia. It had been an extremely rough night. The ship was rolling frenetically and it was very hard to get to sleep. Stan, the Chief Engineer, tells me he spent seven years of his life in a hammock. 'What's more,' he adds, 'a hammock will float for twelve hours in the water if you roll it up.'

The crockery has been flying all over the place in the wardroom. Soup has been spilled in people's laps but still life goes on. Rough weather doesn't affect the albatross wheeling and soaring above the ship, together with the giant petrels and Cape pigeons.

Paul Copestake is up on the monkey-deck with me. Thousands of dove prions are flying past. Paul says: 'This is the breeding area. That's why you get these extraordinary concentrations. They nest in burrows and in the tussock grass. It's estimated that there are half a million pairs of prions just on Bird Island alone.'

As we approach Bird Island we pass the grim, forbidding mountains of South Georgia. I wonder how Shackleton could possibly have climbed them at the end of his epic journey.

The wind is coming from the south, which is the wrong direction for us to make a sheltered anchorage at Bird Island itself. The plan is for a party consisting of Tweeky and Paul to be put ashore, while the *Biscoe* goes on round South Georgia to Grytviken. We shall hope for calmer weather on the way back. Gentoo penguins, bigger than those we saw at Signy, bounce through the sea in front of the ship followed by a small posse of fur seals.

Quantities of albatross have settled on the water all round the ship, so that there are birds everywhere you look. The green hills ahead of us are covered with white specks. Paul explains that these too are albatross, nesting in the tussock grass.

'Look at the bald patches in the grass, fifty or a hundred feet up the hill. That's where the fur seals have been wearing it away.'

The *John Biscoe* is coming in as close as it can, carving a channel through the patches of kelp. The Zodiac is lowered and Tweeky and Paul set off over a choppy sea towards the base hut which we can see on the stony beach.

I stay there on the deck of the *Biscoe* after they have gone, trying to take in this extraordinary scene. Between the stern of the ship and the shore there is an outcrop of rocks. The waves are crashing over the rocks and the fur seals are playing in and out of the water. Martin, who stayed on deck when the others went off in the Zodiac, says: 'If you go into the water with them, they will play and roll around with you as well.'

I notice that, where there is kelp, the motion of the waves is less violent. The kelp seems to have a dampening effect.

'That band of giant kelp will extend sixty or a hundred yards out from shore,' Martin explains. 'It will go down to a depth of twenty metres, growing out of the seabed itself as it were. In the old days before they had complicated devices like echo-sounders, whalers and sealers used to rely on the kelp to know where they could bring their boats in. There's a gas-filled bubble or frond which keeps the head of the kelp floating on the surface. It looks like a bit of a tangle on the surface but underneath there are clear lines going down to the bottom. Kelp plays its role in the coastal marine ecology. It's a primary converter. Like algae, it's using sunlight to grow. It's a habitat for fish. Pieces of kelp drop off because of wind or wave action and are found on the sea-bottom where they act as a kind of compost. They did a study at Signy and discovered that kelp contributed probably 2% to the energy input of the ecosystem. That's quite considerable when you consider that 2% is right there on the shore as opposed to being miles out at sea. And kelp as you can see has a protective function too. You have the kelp-beds offshore here and in places like the Falklands where the presence of kelp helps diminish the action of the waves on the white sandy beaches. If you did not have the kelp barriers, then those sandy beaches would be worn right back to bedrock. The 'kelpers' in the Falklands use kelp as a kind of fertilizer, but there are other industrial uses. Lord Shackleton, in his report on the Falklands, spoke of the possibilities of extracting alginates from kelp. One of the uses would be for keeping the froth on the beer.'

Martin White must be one of a very few men who can talk for several minutes about kelp, without repetition and without sending the listener off into a deep sleep.

He turns his attention from the sea to the surrounding hills. 'The tussock grass is dark-green where the seals have been; the seals have fertilized the grass causing it to go darker. Whether or not the seals on Bird Island have as yet climbed back to their historic level, i.e. the level they were at in the pre-sealing days, is not quite clear. There are probably a million seals here now anyway. And their colonies are spreading out not only on Bird Island but also down both sides of South Georgia.'

As we stand there on the deck we can see the Zodiac coming back through the swell towards us. The little craft seems to be making quite heavy weather, the tide being contrary. The journey back to the *Biscoe*, even without Tweeky and Paul, takes twice as long as the journey to the base.

In mid afternoon we raised anchor and went round Bird Island before working our way along the north coast of South Georgia. The plan was to anchor somewhere for the night before continuing down to Grytviken. Norman, the electrician, comes up on deck. As we go round the first point after leaving the base on Bird Island, he indicates a large area of rock on the mountain opposite denuded of all vegetation. Looking more closely through binoculars I discover that I am observing a colony of macaroni penguins which extends from the water-line to the very top of the towering cliffs.

'There may be a million birds altogether there,' says Norman, 'and you'll have similar colonies on Willis Island and Trinity Island. There could be five or six million penguins altogether.'

That it seems to me, is a statistic to dwarf all others.

10

South Georgia

Next day I came up on deck at 8 a.m. to find that we were already steaming down the coast of South Georgia, having made an early start. I could see the snowcapped range of mountains in the middle of the island; nearer the coast the peaks were largely free of snow. It was a cloudy, grey day, but the sea was calmer than yesterday. The penguins in the water were having an easier time of it.

We come into Cumberland Bay ninety minutes later. Grytviken is just round the corner. What one has to realize as one takes in the scene is that in the past this bay would have been full of whales. Now, sad to say, there is not a whale in sight. Even without whales, the place is beautiful beyond description. Rocks rise out of the sea to the right as we reach the little cove where Grytviken is situated. I can see the tussock grass clinging to the cliffs wherever it can find a toehold. As the *Biscoe* noses its way in, it's not difficult to imagine how this scene must have looked to the first sealers and whalers – or even to Captain James Cook, who was the first to discover South Georgia, claiming it for the Crown.

Mike, the Third Mate, comes out to the wing of the bridge where I'm standing and says that we will see the Shackleton Memorial as we go round the point. 'He actually died in South Georgia, you know, and is buried in the cemetery in Grytviken.'

At breakfast this morning Jerry said they had already been in touch with the army garrison on South Georgia. 'Apparently the army were listening in on one of the frequencies we use; anyway they're waiting for us. They seemed particularly chuffed that we're bringing some of their mail.'

Jerry said he could understand what the Army were saying but he wasn't sure that the Army could understand what he was saying. That isn't surprising because Jerry, for all his qualities, simply does not open his mouth when he talks. Words stream forth in a virtually unintelligible mumble. Added to that he's usually smoking a cigarette or two.

As we draw closer, the Shackleton Memorial – across above the bay – comes into sight and beyond that, in the curve of the cove, I can see the whaling station of Grytviken, the little white church clearly visible against the background of rusting tanks, buildings and machinery.

'That's where the BAS people took refuge when the Argies came in,' says Mike. And he adds, gesturing with his hand, 'On the right here is Shackleton House which was the main BAS building; now the army have taken it over. That's a wire-guided missile site up there next to the Shackleton Memorial. Those buoys in the harbour mark the place where the Argentine submarine sank. And over on the hill there, just out of sight, are the remains of an Argentine helicopter.'

'Didn't we lose a couple of helicopters ourselves?'

'Yes, but they are in the interior and pretty much inaccessible.'

Shortly before 10 a.m. the *Biscoe*'s anchors went down at Grytviken. We tied up alongside the jetty. The army was there in force to greet us. At least half a dozen men – squaddies, as they are called – seemed to be making quite heavy weather of getting the warps attached to the bollards on the shore. Finally they managed it. Immediately across from the ship at the end of the jetty there was a sign saying 'Post Office – South Georgia platoon', and an EIIR red mailbox. A reassuring sight; home from home as it were. Near by the Union Jack flies over Grytviken. Indeed, since this was the first place to be retaken during the Falklands War, the flag was flying here even before Port Stanley was restored to British rule.

Two of the soldiers on the dock below have flowers in their hats. They are walking around without actually doing anything, so they are probably officers.

It was mid morning before we finally went ashore. I decide to walk up through the groups of houses towards the Shackleton Memorial on the point. The road runs past a building with a red cross outside which I presume is the sick bay. A sign says: '39 Field Squadron, South Georgia detachment'. A harpoon gun has been mounted on the front of the building. It points out into the bay, looking ugly and menacing. Behind the head of the harpoon comes a shaft with flukes – the flukes open out, like a parachute being towed behind a plane, when the harpoon hits its target. The tip of the harpoon is a hard triangular piece of iron with an explosive charge behind it. You see great piles of these old harpoon tips at Grytviken. Tourists (if visitors to South Georgia can be called tourists) sometimes take them away as souvenirs.

There is a new kind of harpoon, with a circular tip to it. They found that the old pointed tips had a tendency to fly off if they hit the whale at an angle. The circular version for some reason had better grip.

Next to the harpoon gun is a flagpole, flying the Union Jack. A seagull perches on top. A few yards further on is an open tarmacked area, where a large red circle with an H in the middle has been painted – presumably a helicopter landing pad. It makes a strange contrast with the distant mountains across Cumberland Bay, the congregation of birds, the kelp-beds in the water and the tussock grass all around. (Tussock grass is very much the dominant vegetation here. It stands three or four feet tall, dark-green and stringy.)

There are bunkers all over the place, heavily disguised with tussock grass. Only when you look carefully do you see the slots in the ground. Two soldiers emerge from one of them. 'Pretty miserable weather,' one of them says to me as though we were both strolling down to the shop to buy the newspapers. 'Normally you can see the mountains.'

I'm not sure what mountains he means. There seemed to be plenty of them around. I think it's a pretty good day, actually. As we talk I hear the roar of elephant seals.

The cross on top of the Shackleton Memorial has been decorated with an aerial. A bunker surrounds the memorial. A squad of soldiers is on duty, waiting for the first sight of the Hercules which is flying down from Stanley and will be making an air-drop. The *Biscoe* has brought some mail today, but that was Christmas mail. The Hercules, with any luck, will be bringing fresher news.

While we are waiting I examine the memorial. The inscription reads 'Ernest Shackleton, Explorer, died here January 5th, 1922. Erected by his comrades.' Shackleton never gave up. He was on his way south again, for yet another polar expedition, when he died.

Activity in and around the bunker increases. A soldier has his earphones on and is talking on the radio to the plane. 'Commencing dummy run now,' I hear the pilot say.

Another soldier says to me: 'It's a 1,600-mile round trip from Stanley to South Georgia and back. The Hercules will probably be refuelled once in mid-air because they don't want to find they can't get into Stanley and they've no fuel left to go anywhere else.'

Suddenly the Hercules lumbers into view, heading straight across the bay, then banking and climbing at the end of the run. It disappears from sight. Two Zodiacs skim out into the middle of the water ready to pick up whatever is dropped. A few minutes later the Hercules appears again. This time two pink parachutes float down as it passes, landing in the sea a few yards from the waiting boats. It seems an expensive way of bringing the mail but then I remember that the defence of liberty always has a price.

Shackleton House, which used to be the home of the British Antarctic Survey on South Georgia, is now the headquarters of the army. The non-commissioned ranks were having their lunch in the large room to the left of the main entrance. The officers had organized their own mess in the small room on the right which used to be the bar. All the accoutrements of the BAS period had been faithfully retained: the medallions and shields of the different ships which over the years had called at Grytviken; photographs of Antarctic heroes; the billiards score-board mounted on the wall behind the table. (The billiard table itself had disappeared.)

Captain Marius Coulon, Commanding Officer of the South Georgia detachment, Harbour Master, Customs Officer and Magistrate all rolled into one, welcomed me with a cup of coffee.

'There are fifty-three men on the island altogether,' he says. 'Most of them are from the Royal Regiment of Fusiliers. We're doing our best to maintain the place, though it's an uphill task. The whaling station is a fine example of industrial archaeology. My men are trying to restore the church. And it's not just Grytviken which is suffering – you've got whaling stations at Leith, Stromness and Husvik.'

'Why is it all disintegrating?' I ask.

'Vandalism,' Coulon replies. 'It's hard to say who is responsible. Ships come in and ships go out; there always seems to be vandalism of some kind. We try to keep an eye on things but what can you do with a handful of men? Besides, that's not our main task.'

'How long are you down here?'

'About four months. We came straight down from Stanley after a week in the Falklands. We'll go straight home after our tour in South Georgia.'

'Isn't four months a rather short period?' I'm not a logistics expert but it seems a long way to bring people and then whisk them back again.

Captain Coulon takes the point. 'We're abroad a great deal of the time anyway – Cyprus, Kenya, Northern Ireland, the commitment to BAOR and so on. We have to think of the home and family situation.'

Elephant seals are grouped in a bundle outside the little cemetery which lies beyond the whaling station. I step around them, open the wooden gate in the white railings, and walk among the graves. There is one new grave among the old. The inscription reads: 'Felix Artuso 26 April 1982'. I remember the story. The British, when they retook South Georgia, found and crippled an Argentine submarine at Grytviken. By some misunderstanding (he was wrongly suspected of being about to scuttle the damaged vessel) Artuso was shot and killed.

Near the middle of the little cemetery is Shackleton's grave. Here again I pause to read the inscription: 'To the dear memory of Ernest Henry Shackleton, Explorer, born 15th February 1874, entered life eternal 5th January 1922'.

On the grave itself there are various memorial offerings. One plaque, carefully placed, says 'A Sir Ernest Shackleton: El Yacht Club Argentino, Enero 1923'. Other medals and plaques come from various ships and expeditions which visited South Georgia in the past. On the back of the memorial is a quotation from Robert Browning: 'I hold that a man should strive to the uttermost for his life's set prize.' I think I agree with that.

Shackleton is surrounded in death, if not in life, by Norwegians. Among the Trygves and the Gunnars lies one William Pailess, Magistrate South Georgia, 'killed by avalanche in the course of his duty, 17th September 1941'.

Norman, the electrician, who is with me for this afternoon's trek around the edge of Cumberland Bay says: 'Apparently he was just walking along the road between the whaling station at Grytviken and King Edward Point, where the BAS base is, when the rocks fell on him.'

We walk on. The shore is littered with whalebone, relics of the unbelievable carnage which took place here in the first part of the century. We thread our way through clumps of elephant seals; the beach is narrow and there are times when, to pass by, one almost has to walk over them.

Up on the hill above the beach lie the remains of a crashed Argentine helicopter. It was not hard to find. A soldier had pointed out the spot to me that morning. 'Just follow that re-entrant,' he had said, waving at the hills across the bay.

I hadn't consciously followed a re-entrant since the days when, as a schoolboy in the cadet corps, I had leopard-crawled over the Dorset hills. What was a re-entrant to him, was – to me – a gully or a gulch which led as the man indicated to a dead helicopter lying on its side on a boggy saddle of land between sea and mountain. It was a surreal sight, made the more so by the graffiti which had already been scratched in the khaki paint of the fuselage. The legends were harmless enough: Kilroy was here, Arsenal for ever. There were even some signatures in Russian, not surprising when one considered the extent of the Russian presence in the South Atlantic. Captain Marius Coulon had told me – and I had no reason to doubt him – that a recent survey made by RAF Nimrod aircraft had revealed the presence of no less than 180 foreign vessels around South Georgia and many – if not most – of those ships would have been Russian. South Georgia is not out of bounds.

The helicopter itself seemed to be of French manufacture, but I am no helicopter buff. One thing seemed certain; that machine would never fly again.

A group of king penguins stand on the beach when we return from the wrecked helicopter. This is my first sight of these birds. They stand much larger than any other penguins we have seen so far, with yellow chests and upward-pointing feet. The shape of that group of penguins on the shore echoes the shape of the mountains across the bay.

We walked at least a couple of miles along this beach and there wasn't a yard of it which wasn't covered in whalebone. The same probably goes for every other beach around Cumberland Bay.

'The incredible fact is', says Norman, 'that when they started whaling here, they operated for several seasons without ever having to go outside Cumberland Bay.'

At the far end of the beach we come to Penguin River, which runs down off the mountains, through the rafts of tussock grass and into the sea. We walk upstream for a few hundred yards and come across a group of about thirty king penguins who are dabbling their feet in the shallow river. They don't seem at all surprised to see us. I suppose to them we ourselves look like penguins, only rather larger. Kneel down in the grass and they will come right up to you, curious to investigate who you are and what you are doing. Some of the young ones are still covered in down and have yet to achieve the sleek charcoal-grey coat with the brilliant splash of yellow on throat and chest which characterizes the species; some of the adults are still in the process of moulting. Most of the birds are busy preening themselves, pecking and pushing at their feathers, probably to clear the moult.

'You can see the flap which they use to incubate the egg' – Norman points it out to me. 'They balance the egg on their feet and they pull the flap over it. The emperor penguin does that too.'

We walk back the way we came. Two sooty albatross wheel above us and swing into the cliffs where they are nesting.

'The light-mantled sooty albatross has a velvety-textured plumage and a fine white ring around its eye,' says Norman the electrician. Antarctica makes naturalists of us all.

The fur seals seem to be everywhere; the pups are slithering in and out of the water. 'A couple of seasons ago', says Norman, 'I came out here and sat and watched them for an hour, just playing in and out of the water.'

We visited the whaling station itself on the way back. As Captain Coulon had warned, Grytviken whaling station is enduring a process of steady disintegration. The power-house has broken down; water was pouring through it and there was a strong smell of fuel-oil from ruptured tanks. Debris was everywhere. Rusty rotting machinery, cogs, wheels, axles – a scrap-dealer's paradise. Indeed it was the arrival of unauthorized Argentine scrap-dealers intending to dismantle the whaling stations on South Georgia which sparked the Falklands conflict. Vandalism has clearly played a part in this process, but neglect has helped as well.

We walked up towards the church. Just in front of it a white wooden building BAS used to use as a badminton hall has collapsed. The sign KINO still hangs outside. The Norwegians obviously preferred films to badminton. The church itself is a pretty structure; again made of wood and painted white. For some reason there's a cardboard box outside the door which says: QUICK FROZEN GLAZED HUSVIK WHALE MEAT PRODUCED IN SOUTH GEORGIA. Then on the door of the church itself there's a notice signed by Captain Coulon which says: 'This church is being renovated by 20FDSQN and 42FDSQNRE and 2RRF. Visitors are invited to get the key from either the REDET at King Edward Point or from the OPS room at Shackleton House. The Church is inspected after each visit for damage and HQBFFI informed.'

I had the key with me because I had asked for it earlier in the day. We removed the padlock and the heavy wooden bar across the door to get in. Inside it is a beautifully quiet plain simple little church. Somehow it is difficult to reconcile the thought of those God-fearing Lutheran Norwegians sitting in that church on a Sunday and the dreadful trade being carried on outside on every other day of the week. I suppose the conventional answer is that these people were 'just doing their jobs'. But I wonder if that is good enough any longer.

I went up into the organ loft. There was a small pedal organ made by Ostlund and Almquist. On top of it was a copy of HMS *Yarmouth*'s Holy Communion service. Someone had written on the sheet: 'This organ was played on Sunday 19th January 1984 by sub-lieutenant Peter Snoxall Royal Navy HMS *Yarmouth* during a service conducted by the Reverend Marcus W. Robinson Royal Navy HMS *Yarmouth*.' I admired Sub-Lieutenant Peter Snoxall's powers of improvisation because when I tried out the instrument I found that there were several notes which weren't sounding at all; there were also several missing stops. As I sat there, I felt confident that Captain Coulon and his men would soon set matters to rights.

In the body of the church itself, one feature of the greatest interest was a tall enamelled wood-burning stove at least twelve foot high. How many bodies and souls had that stove warmed over the years? And then, on the altar itself, perhaps most moving of all, was a cross and under it a panel bearing the words:

Kom Til Mig
Alle i Som Straever
Og Har Det Tungt
Og Jeg Vil Give Eder Hvile. Matt. 11.28

I did not need to look up the Gospel according to St Matthew to know what those words meant. Come unto me all ye that labour . . . Something of the rage I had felt earlier in the day as I walked along the whalebone strewn beach evaporated. Hear what comfortable words our Saviour saith! That little church was not a place for anger.

On the table near the altar was a pile of Norwegian hymn books bearing the inscription SYNG MIG HJEM, while on the other side of the church was a small room with empty bookshelves in it. Norman says: 'There used to be a lot of Norwegian books in here. Maybe the army has taken them out for cataloguing or renovating or whatever.'

At the end of our long afternoon we went round the whaling station itself. There were enormous piles of chains on the flensing area, the area they called the Plan. They used the chains to lash the whales to the capture-vessels and also to pull the whales up on to the Plan. 'Whales were pulled up by their tails or flukes', Norman tells me. 'If you look carefully at the wooden planks on the floor of the Plan you can see lots of little stud marks. This is because the whalers wore studded shoes.' To the right-hand side of the Plan as one faces the mountain behind, is the shed where they boiled down the blubber. We go inside and see three enormous vats. The blubber came down a chute into a machine just inside the building which chopped it up. It then went on a bucket-type conveyor belt up into the vats. The vats themselves were fired by fuel-oil, not whale-oil, the latter being much too expensive.

Not long after whaling operations started, the British who controlled South Georgia from the Falklands insisted that the whole carcass should be used. (This was a far-sighted conservation measure first introduced by Governor Allardyce – indeed if whaling had not become largely pelagic, i.e. an operation conducted mainly or entirely at sea, it is possible that some of the worst forms of over-exploitation might have been avoided.) On the other side of the Plan Norman showed me the sheds where the whale meat was ground up along with the bone into whale meal. He also showed me an area where they used to get the bits of harpoon out of meat and the piles of metal consisting of thousands of fragments and shards and splinters which they would extract from the whale as they processed it. We also saw the foundations and outer walls of the new building which was actually being built at the time the Norwegians left Grytviken, in the middle 1960s. The building would have housed a refrigeration plant for freezing whale meat for export.

Half submerged in Grytviken harbour, not far from the ramp where they used to pull the whales up on to the Plan, are two whale-catchers. The name on one of the boats, the *Petrel*, rings a bell. I remember that Captain Peter Erskine, Senior Naval Officer in the Falkland Islands, had spoken of the efforts being made to raise money to take her back to Norway and I look at her with interest.

It is not hard to envisage this vessel ploughing through the water with, say, two or three whales at either side. Apparently when they found one whale and harpooned and killed it, they would blow it up with compressed air, plug the hole made by the harpoon with tow, then stick a flag in it on a pole and go off again to look for other whales. When they had caught enough, they would come back and lash the whales to the ship's side.

'One of the problems,' Norman tells me, 'was that giant petrels would come and peck away at the tow and finally open up the hole again so that the whale would sink. Well, they got round this by impregnating the tow with blubber and paraffin so that the petrels didn't wish to eat it. You wouldn't go off looking for new whales with one whale already tied alongside you because that would slow you down too much.'

We walked back from the whaling station towards the little wooden jetty at King Edward Point where the *Biscoe* is tied up. The road runs under the cliff. This, I recall, is the spot where Mr Pailess was killed by an avalanche. I keep a watchful eye on the mountain behind.

Norman tells me more about what happened to the BAS people when the Argentines invaded. 'Some of them had gone over to St Andrews Bay to be with Cindy Buxton and Anny Price. Others were at Lyell Hut in the interior and the rest of them were in the church.'

We came back in time for drinks in the wardroom before dinner. We were sailing at 8 p.m. Marius Coulon comes on board with his second-in-command, Andrew Barker, and Sergeant John Asprey, one of the two constables who serve the CO in his Magistrate's capacity. Our military guests are invited to dinner and sit at the Captain's table.

It is a good evening, made memorable for me by a conversation I had with Colin who tells me about his own visit to Grytviken in 1937 when the British Graham Land Expedition was on its way back from Antarctica.

'They were pulling up a dozen whales a day. The catchers brought them in with three or four lashed to each side, like a bundle of carrots, and then they pulled them up one by one by the tail. They separated out the blubber and the meat and the bones. When the whole station was working, it was steaming and smoking and smelling and you heard the clatter of engines and chains and shouting. Up to 1,000 people might work here in the summer. You saw those enormous chains, didn't you? Well, they were used not only to pull the whale up off the catcher, but also to roll it over. The men stood there with their flensing knives and the whale was pulled on to the knives rather than their working down the whale. In fact, the skin came off rather like peeling a banana. You stayed there and the whale was pulled past you. Maybe four or five huge strips of it and you got the skin and blubber off. On your hip you had a whaling stone which you used to sharpen your knife as you worked.

'Whaling went on at Grytviken from the shore even after pelagic whaling had begun. When it finished, the company kept a caretaker here and everything was in apple-pie order. There were stores full of everything you could need, including for example bottles of HP sauce costing sixpence, the old sixpence. The beds were made in the houses, the equipment in the workshops and the repair shops was all in order. They had a huge engineering workshop as well, and ship repairing facilities. In fact you could build a ship here.

'The caretaker, who was called Thorsson, went back to Stanley in 1972. It was after that that the place began to disintegrate.'

Martin White says that, while it lasted, this was one of the most efficient whaling stations as far as the quality of oil was concerned. And they also squeezed out every last drop.

I tell Colin and Martin about our visit that afternoon to the little church at Grytviken whaling station. Colin recalls how the Reverend Launcelot Fleming, who was with them on the British Graham Land Expedition, conducted a service here in 1937 attended by both the Norwegian families at Grytviken and by the men of the BGLE. Fleming went on to become Dean of Windsor, and has now retired to live in Dorset.

While we were out on our walk a football match had taken place between the army and the men of the *John Biscoe*. They played for forty-five minutes each way and the army won 7-0. At half time, apparently, the score was only one-love to the army, but over the long run the superior fitness of the home team told. Barry Short, the *Biscoe*'s fourth engineer, tells me: 'We had no chance; they've been running up and down these hills with a sixty-pound pack on their backs. One half of the country is a swamp; the other is a quarry. No wonder they're fit.'

Barry Short is a Geordie, his definition of a Geordie being someone who can see the Tyne.

Sergeant Asprey sits at our table at dinner. The heaviest item in the morning's air-drop, he tells me, was one hundred tins of black boot-polish. While I am busy reflecting what a field-day a hostile MP might have in the House of Commons with that kind of information, Sergeant Asprey hastens to add: 'Of course, the Hercules isn't just making an air-drop; that is only an incidental part of its task. Its real task is surveillance.'

Asprey says that the Royal Regiment of Fusiliers, a detachment of which is now on duty in South Georgia, was the result of the amalgamation of the Lancashire, the Royal Fusiliers, the Warwick and the Northumberland Regiments. They now have three battalions, with 650 men per battalion. Asprey has also been in the Falklands. 'The islanders are not always so keen on the troops. The fact is that there are only twenty or thirty unmarried women of marriageable age there and a lot of kelpers are looking for a wife. But then our unmarried soldiers come in and sweep them off their feet and back to Britain. That's why the Falkland Islanders want the army to bring in so-called accompanied troops.'

Martin White is also at our table that evening. While I was out walking, he had been looking at the installations of the BAS former base on South Georgia, now under the tender loving care of the army.

'One of the key questions', says Martin, 'is: should BAS come back to South Georgia? Should BAS wait till the army has left or should it come back now? If the latter, in what building? My own view is that it is essential for BAS to come back if we're to control any kind of economic zone around these islands. And there's the research element of the Offshore Biological Programme which I was involved in, as well as the terrestrial work and some atmospherics.'

Later, on the long haul up to Rio, Martin White talked to me in greater detail about these ideas.

11

Bird Island

It took us five hours to get into Bird Island. We plied up and down outside the base waiting for an opportunity. The sea was too heavy to launch a boat. As the Captain explained at breakfast, this was a place where you just had to seize your window of opportunity. Sometimes they had to hang around two or three days. We hoped that wouldn't happen to us. We could see the base in the distance through the mist. A nasty day, though not any nastier than it was two days earlier when we landed our party here before going on to South Georgia. The water between the *Biscoe* and the island was thick with albatross and the waves were crashing against the shore.

Up on the bridge, the Captain was talking over the radio to the base about the state of the sea. He had his windscreen wipers going and was peering intently ahead through the spray and spume gauging – I supposed – the lie of the water. This was the kind of moment when captains or masters really came into their own. They had to take the tricky bits. If they didn't, they would find quite soon they weren't captain for much longer.

A group of fur seals was 'porpoising' to port, keeping a course parallel to our own between ship and shore. We head them off at the pass, turning at last into the mouth of the harbour as Chris Elliott decides to make a run for it. The wind is backing to the north-west which is good. Over the radio the base on Bird Island confirms that conditions inshore are calmer. The launch and scow will both be going over since we have to pick up some rubbish from the base. On the after boat-deck, two Geminis – which will go over ahead of the scow and the launch – are being got ready. They've had their air checked and replenished from the pressure-hose, and Mike Jenkins tests the engines before the craft are lowered to the water. 'There's nothing worse', he explains, 'than trying to pull the cord on an engine which won't start when you're tossing about in ten-foot waves.'

We had lunch on board while waiting.

Peter Prince, Station Commander, comes over in the base's own Zodiac. With him is an American called Dan Coster – a young man of about twenty-five.

'What are you working on?' I ask.

'We're looking at the reproductive energetics in seals. Different rates of material and energy transfer. That kind of thing.' More illuminatingly, he goes on to explain: 'We are using radio-tagged females. We've discovered that even though the normal trip length, i.e. the length of time the female goes out to sea, is four or five days, this year they were averaging ten or twelve days and one female has gone out for eighteen days. They're working harder to find the food.'

Coster comes from the University of California at Santa Cruz. He says he's working on a programme organized by the National Science Foundation in the United States in collaboration with BAS.

For a change we are eating in the Fiddery rather than the wardroom. Tweeky, our unsung hero, who is back on board after his spell on Bird Island, comes down to join us. Once again he had had a sleepless night. 'Thirty hours on the trot fiddling with the programme,' he says. If that wasn't enough, as soon as he has grabbed a mouthful to eat he goes off to talk to Signy over the radio. 'They're still having some problems. May as well help sort them out while we're within range.'

It is much calmer now. After backing to the north-west, the wind has dropped and died away. 'That's been the weather pattern for the last five days,' says Prince. 'While you were off at Grytviken yesterday there was brilliant sunshine here at Bird Island. On the whole, though,' he adds, 'the weather has been colder than usual. This could have something to do with the disappearance of krill.'

'What's life like?' I ask – a banal question, but Prince takes it at face value.

'It has perked up a lot recently. We've been having a visit every two weeks from one ship or another and mail drops every fortnight. In fact,' he laughs, 'we're having to increase the rate of letter writing. The other day we saw a fifty-million-pound battleship out there in the bay. The Commander helicopters in and says, "We are here to protect you." That's the kind of treatment we're getting nowadays. I've asked them to avoid flying their helicopters over the beaches when the cows are pupping.'

After lunch we boarded the launch. As we came in through the kelp-beds the fur seals were poking their heads up like otters or little dogs begging; the albatross on the water were gliding in and out among the seals. A giant petrel flopped up and down in the water in front of us as we waited to disembark. Colin explained that the bird was probably washing.

Cat-walks make it possible to move around the base at Bird Island without treading on the seals though I notice that the seals have started lying on the cat-walks too. One or two of them are white – apparently the incidence of white fur seal pups is one-tenth of one per cent or one in a thousand. Inside the hut on the beach we kit ourselves out in 'hunter' gum-boots, which have studded non-slip soles (our Antarctic boots would probably slip on the wet surfaces of the hills on Bird Island). Then we go outside again to walk around. It's a grey murky day. I've put a 400 ASA film in my camera.

Our guide for the day is one of the Bird Island scientists, a young man called Ben Osborne. As we head on up the hill, he explains that the seal pups congregate on the duck-boards of the cat-walks because it is warmer on a cold day like today. Ben carries a stick and advises us to do the same.

'The seals are all up in the tussock at the moment. They tend to jump out at you and it can be quite alarming. They get more and more nervous when they see large parties. One person is all right or even two but when several people walk past them they get quite agitated. Basically, we'll try to avoid them.'

Ben has a scar across his hand which he says was caused by a wandering albatross.

We climb up the rocky track which, through erosion, has become a stream-bed carrying the rain off the hill and down through the tussock grass. Two hundred feet above the beach we pause to take in the scenery – the *Biscoe* out there at anchor in the bay, the kelp-beds stretching out from the shore, and down below crowding the beaches like the troops at Dunkirk the army of fur seals, keening and howling, so that the sound carries up the hill towards us.

'The grass is greener and "tussockier" than it was last year,' says Ben. 'That's because it has been drier. When it is dry, seals can stay down near the beach. When it is wet they climb up the hill to get away from the mud and damage the grass in the process. This year there has been a dearth of krill which is one of the reasons why we don't see so many cow seals around. They are spending longer and longer out at sea before they come back to suckle their pups. But this has been a good year for the South Georgia pippit – that's a little songbird. They've had two or three broods this year. They've been singing all over the place. They sit around the ponds. Absolutely beautiful.'

Ben has been out here for fourteen months. He goes back on the *Bransfield* at the end of the season, i.e. in March. 'It has been a fascinating year; wouldn't have missed it. It's the first time Bird Island has been wintered on for about twenty years.'

Once we've climbed up the hill we head west across the island. Ben sees a young skua and runs after it crying 'mu-mu' which seems to do the trick. He catches the bird with his stick which has a hook on the end like a shepherd's crook. The skua parents run up screeching.

'I tend to wear a crash helmet when I'm working with the skuas. They can dive-bomb pretty effectively. This one's tamer, since I pass him every day as I cross the island.'

The skua is an exception. This part of the island is albatross territory. The plateau is covered with nesting birds.

'Every breeding albatross on the island has red paint on it at the moment',

Ben explains, 'because it's the only way you can be sure that you have actually marked them. They hatch now and up until the end of March. The adult bird weighs about ten kilos, but its chicks can go up to sixteen or seventeen. They put on so much weight that they become great swollen balls of fat. Add Bird Island and South Georgia together and you've got maybe 10% of the whole world population of wandering albatross – *Diomedea exulans*.'

To stand there on that grey blowy day looking across the plateau at the mass of nesting albatross was another of the high points of my Antarctic trip. I have seldom in my life felt more privileged than at that moment when I was able to observe the great white birds on their nests, almost mythical creatures, which – unlike the more aggressive skuas – seemed not the least bit disturbed by our presence. This was their world, not ours. Some birds weren't nesting, but strutting around – singly or in groups.

'Over there', says Ben, 'is a display group. There are some males and females who simply don't seem to pair up. They go along in an unmarried state for quite a long time. Display is all part of the pairing-up business when they're ready for it. The youngest breeding birds are about nine and they live till well over forty.'

Ben catches a wanderer with his hook and holds it by the beak to demonstrate the bird's extraordinary wingspan. 'Ten to twelve feet for a big male. White tail feathers. The older they get, the whiter they get. Look at the tubes, the nostrils at either side. The giant petrel has its tube on top.'

We had more or less reached the most westerly point of Bird Island. I could see Willis Island looming up in the mist across the water. This must surely be one of the most beautiful places on earth. Wherever I looked I could see birds, wanderers on their nests or displaying on the green sward of the plateau. Now, as we walked on, we passed a cliff on the left which is the breeding area for a different kind of albatross – the black-browed variety. I watched them whirling and wheeling above us, while the face of the cliff is itself dotted with the white blobs of nesting birds.

Ten minutes later we walked through a colony of yet a third variety of albatross, the grey-headed variety, to look down on a sweep of cliffs – over fifty hectares in extent – which has been occupied by some 45,000 macaroni penguins, pretty little birds with striking gold crowns. The noise was unbelievable. Twickenham on a spring afternoon with England playing France for the Triple Crown has nothing on a rookery of macaroni penguins. The sound of the birds blended with the sound of the waves crashing on the rocks below.

'And this is only a tiny part of it,' says Ben. 'There are probably five million penguins over there on Willis Island.'

Looking at those penguin cliffs I realized what a colossal effort it must be for the topmost birds to get where they are. To find their little patch of living-room, they have to scramble all the way up. What a performance that must be. At the beginning when the chick is young, one or other parent may be able to stay at home. But later when the chick's demands are greater, they will both have to go off to get food.

It's hard to imagine that in the not-so-olden not-so-golden days at other similar sub-Antarctic islands, like Kerguelen or Macquarie, men used to force-march penguins into the boiling vats and then simmer them down for oil.

It was time to go. Even in Antarctica time presses. We slithered down to the beach, the little fur seal pups growling and yapping at us in brave imitation of their parents. Some of them have already moulted and are now a shiny silver-grey. One little gentoo penguin hops about among the seals.

Peter Prince came out as we were taking our boots off and said that the launch had broken down so we have time for a cup of tea.

We haven't been particularly heroic – just a brisk walk over the hills to paradise and back – but the hot sweet liquid is very welcome. While we are waiting for the launch to be fixed, Paul Copestake shows me round.

'The original base was open-plan. When there are only three of you, it's better to have a sense of all being together. They had to redesign the base to accommodate more people; by then, UK building regulations applied which said that the kitchen had to be separate. So they hit on the idea of having a glass partition between the kitchen and the main living and working areas. They take it in turns to cook. They're all pretty expert.'

Next stop was the bathroom. 'Frankly', says Paul, 'we had the option of a toilet or a shower and we opted for the shower. We use the beach as the toilet.' Colin, who has joined us for the little tour, says, 'That's what we did in our day.' Well, I guess it's what the seals do too.

On to the drying-room. 'One of the things which is essential', Paul says, 'is a really good drying-room. And this year they built a porch outside the hut. That has made a huge difference because it means that they have been able to store their boots and their clothes. Also it means that the wind doesn't blow in every time you open the front door.'

Our last stop is the bedroom. 'You've got four bunks one side of the house; four bunks the other. But they're all pretty close together. Again, it's the proximity principle.'

Paul has been here four summers and one winter. He should know what he is talking about. Peter Prince has been here nine summers.

Outside the hut there is an array of weapons. 'These are seal bodgers,' says Paul, 'for fending the seals off. There are two theories about fending seals off. One is that you kind of tickle their noses; another is that you give them a sharp thwack. My usual practice is to carry a long thin bamboo in my right hand and a stout axe handle in my left hand. But if you are dealing with an irate bull seal, you simply can't rely on the tickling technique. Furckling hooks – that's what we use for catching the albatross – can double as bodgers of course.' Of course.

Outside, round beyond the back of the house, we encountered a strange sight. There are seal carcasses everywhere, almost as plentiful in death as they are in life. 'These are bulls which have died from the stress of the breeding season,' explains Paul. 'The cow comes up out of the sea and after it has pupped it immediately comes into oestrus. Mating takes place but there's delayed implantation of the embryo.' Colin nods as Paul speaks. Colin is the man who first demonstrated delayed implantation in seals, although it had been known for badgers and roe-deer.

'Delayed implantation', continues Paul, 'enables a seal cow to have an annual pregnancy even though they only come up once a year out of the sea.' He points to the bull-carcasses which are lying around. 'We cut them open so that the birds can get at them. They don't smell so much that way too.'

On the way down to the beach we passed a hut no bigger than a garden shed. 'This is Bonner's bothy. It's now used as the bio-store. Nigel came here in 1958. This is where he lived.'

I have met Nigel Bonner and remember him as quite a large man, so I rather wonder how he managed to fit in. Bonner's original decorations are still up on the wall inside the hut, as memorable in their way as the cave-man drawings in the Pyrenees. Outside Bonner's bothy is a cement-mixer.

'They brought it down from an old whaling station,' says Paul. 'It still works. In fact we used it this summer. It's called Boris.'

Word came that the launch had been fixed. Ben and I walked down to the beach together. 'What will you do when we've gone?' I ask.

'Sleep, I expect.' Ben explains that Bird Island has its own peculiar system of time. 'We actually get up at half-past five in the morning but we call it half-past eight because if we were to call it half-past five no one would get up. It's a purely local decision.'

We talk about the noise. This is one of the extraordinary features of being in the Antarctic. You're hearing noises which you simply don't hear elsewhere, other because they don't exist elsewhere, or because they're drowned out by other noises.

'Noise', says Ben, 'builds up in September onwards when the albatross come back and all the burrowing petrels which you don't see at the moment because they come in with the night. They make an incredible row. Especially the white-chinned petrels, but also the diving petrels and the dove prions. In fact,' says Ben, 'petrels of one kind or another probably constitute the biggest biomass of birds on the island.'

He looks out to sea. 'We saw a Russian trawler right up close to the shore the other day, putting a trawl down. Close enough for us to see the hammer and sickle on the funnel. It would be tragic if man's intervention upset the balance of the system. Take too much out and you could have a massive die-off.'

12

North to Rio

I think that all of us felt a deep-down sadness as we weighed anchor and left Bird Island. This was the last land within the Antarctic region which we would see, unless anything went wildly wrong and we became shipwrecked. It had been a marvellous afternoon, an almost unreal experience which made the parting that much more poignant.

Soon after six we steamed round the island to the west, the way we had walked that afternoon. We could still see the great white albatross perched on the cliff, and others wheeling below them. The dove prions were there too, hundreds of them. As I stood, waving goodbye, a black-browed albatross swooped around the boat. The ship's hooter sounded and the base disappeared from view.

'At Bird Island, early in the spring,' says Martin White, who is up on deck with me observing our departure, 'there can be the most extraordinary cacophony as most of the breeding populations start returning. A riot of sound and colour. By now, most of the species are already thinking of migrating. The penguins and seals go back to sea. You start seeing leopard seals as they come north and the whales around South Georgia will themselves go even further north.'

He put it so simply. Yet there was a poetry in this description of the vast seasonal movement of wildlife in the world's southern regions that touched me – and still touches me – to the core. In this context man is an irrelevance – and that is the way it ought to be.

At dinner that night Martin says that he looked closely at the macaroni penguins this afternoon and thought they were very thin on the ground. 'Normally, at this time of year, you'd hardly be able to see any space between one bird and another. And there were very few chicks in the macaroni colony. This may be the krill problem again. The macaroni feed exclusively on krill. The black-browed albatross too is having a very poor hatching rate, the grey-head chicks on the other hand seem to be fine, but they grow more slowly and in any case the grey-heads have a different diet and they don't feed locally to the same extent. In the end of course there are the knock-on effects even for those birds that eat squid and fish.'

Martin talks about Russian fishing tactics. 'During the early 1970s they would catch white fish if they could. If they couldn't they would switch to krill. We have the impression they were using their research vessels to locate the potential catches. Then something happened two years ago to affect the survival status of krill which is being shown up in this year's catches. Something has probably happened this year as well, but the cause could be more hydrological than biological. Krill seem to move with the currents and congregate in certain areas. Well, this year they simply didn't arrive in the traditional areas. There was such a global absence of krill that this simply couldn't be put down to Soviet trawling. I mean, all the trawlers in the world would have had to be down here to achieve the kind of absence of krill which our OBP noted. But the Russian trawlers may have been exacerbating the effects of krill decline.

'Large fluctuations have a dramatic effect; but only one season now and then doesn't make a difference to the overall levels of mortality given the long life of the species we are talking about, seals and penguins and so on. But if you have an artificial harvesting coinciding with these periods of shortage, then you may have a serious effect. The scientists at Bird Island have noted 30% mortality already in this year's seal pups and we've still got two months to go before they are weaned. That's in excess of normal levels of mortality. One of our big problems is simply the lack of knowledge. That is another reason for having a licensing system for fisheries. The history of fisheries all over the world is that when they are not managed they collapse within a ten-year period and other parts of the marine ecosystem collapse with them.

'What we need is a trawler at Grytviken,' Martin continued. 'This could perhaps be linked with the monitoring obligation we have accepted as signatories to the Convention on the Conservation of Antarctic Marine Living Resources. A permanent vessel based on South Georgia, half the size of the *Biscoe*, would do the trick. The *Biscoe* at the moment is studying phytoplankton and zooplankton, small fish and the larger crustaceans. But it's not really good at catching the larger fish which can simply swim round the net. We have a problem of net avoidance. Basically we need a large net, one which can be spread out from the stern of the boat.' Martin points out that in the 1920s research carried out by the *Discovery* in the South Atlantic was actually paid for out of the revenues of the whaling industry. A fishing regime controlled from South Georgia should be able to pay for an extra vessel.

'Actually', he adds, 'we need a little coaster as well to replace the BAS boat, the *Albatross*, which was wrecked in a storm after the army took over. Mike Burchett, one of the BAS scientists, wanted to see how the fish were distributed around the coasts of South Georgia. He was using a classic tag and recapture method. Well, the fact is we didn't have the transport. Our little rubber boats couldn't do the job safely. In any case BAS wouldn't allow it.'

We linger over the dinner-table talking about fish in the Antarctic. 'One of the commonest groups', says Martin, 'is *Notathenia rossii*, which is a big black rock cod. It spends four or five years growing until it reaches the sub-adult stage in the kelp-beds. Then it goes to sea. People were sending back our tags including Russians and Poles even though we weren't paying a bounty on them. We didn't have the funds to make this kind of bounty payment. Instead when people return the tags we tend to send them piles of BAS postcards or T-shirts or plaques or whatever.

'One of the problems about Antarctic fish is that they mature slowly and recruitment rates are low, so you can quite easily damage a stock. The median age in an exploited stock is about nine years, with fish living up to sixteen or seventeen years. In an unexploited stock this could go well over twenty. If you reduce the median age, you can in fact get a larger stock because you are removing the older fish and probably leaving more food for the actively breeding population. But you can go over the top. You can get under-age fish, i.e. fish which haven't had time to breed. There are no net-size restrictions down here. The Russians probably utilize everything that comes over the side of the boat, so they could in fact easily be damaging the stocks.

'Ninety-five per cent of the fish found in the Antarctic are notathenians. There are four main families: ice-fish, rock cods, plunder-fish and dragon-fish. There are a hundred and twenty species of fish in the Antarctic, of which seventy per cent are notathenians.

'Like whales and seals, fish form part of an interlocking pattern of trophic levels. Not all of them, of course, are top predators. Some fish are eaten by other fish. The ice-fish, for example, feeds on other fish. It is known as the engulfer.

'The marine systems seem simple here because the ice comes on to the foreshore. You don't have the productive diverse system which you have elsewhere where there is an ice-free foreshore. But below the scour level there is a mass of invertebrates colonizing the rocks and the bottom.'

We talked about the problems of getting Antarctic fish back to the markets. 'The Russians', says Martin, 'probably have a food technologist on their boats studying the best way of stabilizing fish. If you take fish out of the water at 15°C and shove it in a freezer at −20°C you've reduced its temperature by 35°, but Antarctic fish are being caught at temperatures around −2° to +3°C, so what you're gaining by putting it into a freezer is much less. The freezing point of normal seawater is about −1.8°C although', says Martin, 'there are some lakes in the eastern part of the Antarctic which were formerly part of the sea where the water is so salty that it never freezes. The salt level might be five or ten parts above normal.'

We talked about the effect of oil-spills. 'Yes,' says Martin, 'an oil-spill could affect marine life, but will the spill be confined to the surface or will it penetrate the water column? If you put oil on the surface it basically acts like a sunshade.

It stops light getting through. Or the oil could have a toxic effect with the hydrocarbons, particularly the lighter fractions, poisoning organisms. Another effect could be simply the clogging of alimentary tracts with oil and tar.' He believed that oil-spills around the Antarctic islands could be disastrous. 'And one of the extra problems is that oil spilled in Arctic or Antarctic regions may take longer to degrade because of the cold factor and therefore could have an additional impact on the ocean or the tundra.'

The following morning there was a hint of warmth in the air as we steamed north. A young wandering albatross, the upper part of its wings still black, followed the boat, along with several giant petrels and a great shearwater. Paul stared through his binoculars, keeping me informed about any new actors on the scene. 'Sea temperature today is 5.3°c which is definitely warm,' says Paul, 'so we are probably out of the Antarctic convergence. South of the convergence the temperature is probably 2° to 3°c.' As he speaks I see two white-headed petrels far out towards the horizon.

A moment later Ray, one of our stewards, comes up and asks me whether I know of cheap flights to the US and Canada. One of the problems these people have is that if they want to be rebated on UK tax, they can't spend more than sixty-two days a year in England. They are out of England a lot on these Antarctic voyages, but not quite that much. Hence the enquiry. Another little fact of life.

The day turned into a murky evening, but in the mist I could see the wandering albatross I had first spotted that morning. It was still with us, a magnificent sight, swooping around the ship just above the water, then soaring away from us with two beats of its giant wings. I wondered how long it would stay with us and whether it enjoyed flying as much as I enjoyed watching it.

Our last Sunday on board the *Biscoe* was a beautiful, semi-tropical day. I spent most of it sitting on deck. The albatross was still with us; in fact, there were now two of them. They had followed the *Biscoe* all the way from Bird Island. The memory of those birds would, I was sure, follow me for the rest of my life.

In the course of that Sunday I paid a visit to the engine room. Sakti Chaudhuri showed me around. 'The engines are as old as the ship,' he told me, 'but in a major refit in 1979 a lot of the equipment was updated, so you now have a fairly computerized system.' We had to wear ear-muffs at first but once we were inside the control-room the noise level was tolerable even without muffs and we could hear each other speak. Sakti explained: 'You can vary the speed of the ship not just by varying the revolutions of the engine but also by varying the pitch of the propellers'. That was something I didn't know. We went through the tunnel and had a look at the propeller shaft. You have to be careful when you are down in the engine area not to bang your head on various hard protruding objects. There isn't much room to make sudden extravagant movements.

Two days later I was talking to Peter Kerry, the Second Mate, who explained how the *Biscoe*, as a research vessel, takes soundings wherever it goes or at least wherever the water isn't particularly well charted. They have an echo-sounder which can go down to about 15,000 metres. Also they know their position very accurately from the satellite navigation system. So they take the soundings and make a note of the depth and the position and then send the results in to the Admiralty who will probably use them in their own compilations. Peter showed me some beautiful old charts which had been done by the *Biscoe* twenty-five or thirty years ago. He also showed me some done by HMS *Endurance*. These are really works of art. Peter explained that there is the deep ocean survey work and also the inshore work. At Pitt Island, earlier this year, they couldn't get the *Biscoe* right into where they wanted it so they used the launch to do echo-soundings and produced a map as a result of that.

Last night Martin gave us a slide show. We saw some of the pictures taken during the *Biscoe*'s last OBP cruise. He also showed some fascinating underwater slides which he had taken. It is clear, as Martin told me the other day, that below the scour line life on the ocean floor is really extremely interesting. We saw starfish, anemones, underwater seals, and close-ups of krill. He told us how, when they are looking for krill, the ship sails in a geometric pattern taking echo-soundings at regular intervals.

While we were waiting for the dinner-gong, Paul came up and reported that three wandering albatross were still with us, and at least one of them came from Bird Island itself. When he points it out to me, I too can see from the paint on the wanderer's chest that it is one of this year's breeders. I am absolutely thrilled. That bird is still within its forage range.

'About 1,000 miles from Bird Island to here, and 1,000 miles back', says Paul. 'That's 2,000 miles, and of course it is swinging and swooping around all the time. It's not flying in a straight line, so it is much more than 2,000 miles. If you do see an albatross fly in a straight line, it fairly moves! It will go two or three times the speed of the ship.'

In the event, the albatross stayed with us for two full days more, until some hormonal balance in its blood told it that it was time to turn and fly back.

Two days after that – to be precise at 9 p.m. on 16 February – I was standing looking at the lights of Rio de Janeiro. We were about eight miles off. Through the binoculars I could see the statue of Christ the Redeemer ahead of us, arms outstretched over the city. Over to the right was the Sugar Loaf mountain, with the great sweep of Rio's famous beaches – Ipanema and Copacabana – lying between the two points.

Watching that unique panorama I couldn't help thinking of the time I first came to Rio, twenty-five years ago. I had left school and was waiting to go up to university. I have been to Brazil many times since then, but this particular

South American landfall remained as spectacular as ever.

At dinner, Chris Elliott gave a small speech. He told us that when we got back home he would be sending us all a group photo set in the middle of a photo of the *John Biscoe* in ice. And then Colin made another little speech and Steve toasted the *Biscoe* and the crew. We all drank to that.

There was a party that night on the poop-deck. It was a good time to say goodbye. This Antarctic trip was about people, as well as the landscape and the wildlife. The people of the bases. The people of the ship. The people, wherever and whoever they are, who care about Antarctica.

Paul, glass in hand, looked out over the water at the great city and exclaimed: 'I just can't get over the lights. After two and a half years in the Antarctic, these are the first I have seen.'

Next morning we went on in to Rio. I could see the rising sun reflected in the glass of the tall buildings on the shoreline a mile or two away. A plane flew overhead, coming in to land at the airport to the north of the city. It was the first plane I had seen in weeks, apart from the BAS Otters down in the Deep South. The giant statue of Christ became more visible with each passing moment. The hillsides beneath it are crowded with Rio's slums and *favelas* which must take what comfort they may from their privileged location. You couldn't have a greater contrast with Antarctica.

We flew the Brazilian flag as we came into harbour and all kinds of other flags as well. Colin, who to the last remains a fount of information, tells me that the flags represent the radio call-sign of the *Biscoe*, except for the yellow flag requesting the port's quarantine authorities to take note of the ship's arrival. I wonder what diseases we could have picked up in Antarctica.

We docked in good time to catch the flight to London. Several of the BAS scientists were flying back with me, since the *Biscoe* herself would not be returning to the United Kingdom until mid March. Just across from the *Biscoe* a glorious four-masted sailing ship was moored. Apparently the vessel belonged to the Spanish Navy and was on a goodwill visit. In the old days they used to sail down to the Antarctic – and a tough time they had of it. This voyage of the *John Biscoe* could hardly compare with the epic journeys of, say, the *Belgica*, *Discovery*, *Endurance* or *Penola*. But I would not have missed the experience for the world.

The full complement of the *Biscoe*'s officers came to the ship's side to see us off. (Most of the crew were either still sleeping off the previous night's party or had already gone into town to sample Rio's various attractions.) We piled into a couple of taxis which were waiting on the quayside and headed for home.

13

The Last Great Wilderness

What is it that makes Antarctica unique? For me, it is above all the fact that Antarctica remains a wilderness, a tenth of the earth's land surface which so far remains relatively untouched by the ravages of man. How can one put a price on wilderness? How much wilderness is enough? These are not easy questions but I am convinced that in a shrinking world we have to hold fast to that which we have. That is one essential reason for conserving Antarctica.

Can a wilderness by valuable if no one visits it? Or if no one even knows it exists, as was indeed the case with Antarctica two or three centuries ago? I have no doubt myself about the answer to those questions. No world, microcosm or macrocosm, needs to be observed or enjoyed by man to have a right to exist. The myriad species of fauna and flora which inhabit the Brazilian rain-forest do not, it seems to me, have to demonstrate their existence or their utility to man in order to be able to continue. They are there and that should be enough. The aesthetic and moral considerations involved in the conservation of Antarctica are of a similar order. It is there and that too should be enough. Humanity has laid its mark hard upon the earth. Most of what we have touched we have altered or destroyed. Amazingly, Antarctica has been preserved as a gigantic model of what one part of the world was like before the coming of man. We may not have planned it that way but at least we should be prepared to recognize what we have.

But, of course, the continent is much more than a museum piece. Apart from the spectacular scenery – iceberg and cliff, mountain and sky – which no one who has seen it could ever forget, that voyage through the Antarctic revealed to me a world of unbelievable biological abundance. The crab-eater seals in Antarctica alone account for close to half of the world's population of seals – some thirty million of them. There are probably 1,000,000 Weddell seals, 200,000 leopard and Ross seals; 600,000 southern elephant seals and over 500,000 fur seals. The bird life, particularly around the sub-Antarctic islands, is extraordinary. I have never seen such a profusion of birds as I did as the *Biscoe* swung across to the Falklands from the tip of the Antarctic Peninsula or again when we visited South Georgia and Bird Island. Biological wealth of this order of magnitude does not occur in many parts of the world. Perhaps you have to look to the mature canopy of the tropical rain-forest (now fast diminishing) or the plains of Serengeti when the wildebeest are migrating to find similar examples of sheer unadulterated biomass.

Why, someone may ask, do we need 30,000,000 crab-eater seals, if 1,000,000 will do? Why 1,000,000, if 10,000 will do? This approach reminds me of the way Lear's unkind daughters treated the old King when discussing the size of his retinue ('What need you five-and-twenty? ten? or five? . . . What need one?'). Nature is more than a postage-stamp collection of animals and plants – in zoos, in reserves, or in national parks. When we have an example of wildlife – fauna and flora – at its most superabundant, we should not seek to apply the collector's mentality. In any case, if we do not preserve the Antarctic ecosystem in its entirety, we may not preserve it at all. And it is quite clear that major threats to that ecosystem exist today.

When we visited the South Orkneys and South Georgia we saw the sad relics of the whaling industry: beach after beach strewn with whalebone; giant skulls on the foreshore; industrial artefacts which were the tools of this trade. A few years ago the International Whaling Commission, meeting in Brighton, voted in favour of a moratorium on commercial whaling beginning in 1985. Conservationists around the world thought that a great victory had been won. Even though the principal whaling nations, Japan, Norway and the Soviet Union, filed objections and announced their intention to continue whaling as long as they wanted, many people felt that whaling was at last on the way out – and none too soon. Whale populations in almost every region had been drastically reduced. Some species, such as the blue whale, were virtually extinct. The moratorium could just possibly give some of the threatened species a chance to begin the long climb back towards a viable population size. The optimism was in part based on the fact that the US Senate had voted the Packwood–Magnuson Amendment to the 1976 Fisheries Conservation and Management Act which required the US President to invoke sanctions against those countries that 'diminish the effectiveness' of the IWC Convention.

I was present in Buenos Aires in May 1984 when the International Whaling Commission held its last meeting before the moratorium was due to take effect. Final quotas were set for the various whale species including the southern minke whale (found in Antarctic waters). Hard bargaining took place between the commissioners of the non-whaling nations represented in the IWC (often led by the tiny Seychelles which has consistently fought on the side of the whale) and the whaling nations dominated as always by Japan. If the quotas finally agreed for this supposedly last whaling season were on the generous side, the hope seemed to be that this might somehow make it easier for the whaling nations finally to accept the 1985 moratorium. So four thousand southern minke whales were consigned to oblivion in a last 'hurrah!' and several hundred other whales as well. Some conservationists came back from

Buenos Aires convinced that the bartering, the whale-trading, was all too cynical and did nothing to reflect the moral and ethical realities of the situation.

Worse was to follow. In November 1984 the United States Secretary of Commerce, Malcolm Baldrige, announced that so far from invoking the Packwood–Magnuson Amendment if the Japanese continued whaling after the moratorium came into effect (which would have entailed cutting by 50% the amount of fish caught by the Japanese in US territorial waters), he had struck a private deal with Japan which in effect drove a coach-and-horses through the IWC moratorium. In effect the two countries had bilaterally worked out a new quota system whereby Japan would be able to continue whaling at least until 1988. Shigeru Hasui, managing director of the Japan Whaling Association, declared that 'we do not intend to stop whaling after 1988 because there is no reason to do so'.

All this of course has a direct bearing on Antarctica and on the prospects for a whale recovery in the southern hemisphere. If Japan can evade the terms of the moratorium, other nations, like Peru and Brazil, may follow. If whaling resumes in force in the oceans of the world, including the southern oceans, the seas may once more flow red with the blood of those last whales which have so far miraculously escaped the depredations of the industry.

Even if large-scale whaling does not resume, there are other threats which in Antarctica at least could be just as serious and which could affect not just whales but the whole marine ecosystem, that marvellous nexus of biological productivity which we on board the *John Biscoe* had been so privileged to observe as we made our way around the coasts of Antarctica.

Chief of these threats is by all accounts the damage to the ecosystem which could be wrought through the indiscriminate harvesting of krill. Hard figures are difficult to come by. Serious fishing operations for krill began in 1972–73 and the yield is now believed to total over 700,000 tonnes per year. The main fishing nations are the USSR and Japan, with other countries taking experimental catches. Undoubtedly some of the Soviet and Eastern European vessels which we saw as we made our way up from the South Orkneys were involved in krill-fishing. Some scientists believe that even a 'small' harvest of krill – between 1,000,000 and 2,000,000 tonnes – could jeopardize the tenuous position of the great whales, specially if fishing is concentrated in just a few areas. And, of course, it is not just the whales which depend on krill. This tiny crustacean is at the basis of the whole food chain. Directly or indirectly it nourishes all the higher species – seals, penguins, seabirds, fish and squid – as well as whales.

The Convention on the Conservation of Antarctic Marine Living Resources (CCAMLR) came into force in 1982. The Convention is supposed to regulate the harvesting of krill, fish, squid and birds in the Southern Ocean. An innovative approach required that harvesting decisions should take account not just of individual species but also of the interaction between species. This sounded fine in theory and was greeted as an advance by conservationists. Unfortunately, however, the Convention also required that decisions should be taken by consensus, which has meant that a single fishing nation can block any actions with which it disagrees. In practice CCAMLR has been unable so far to set any global catch limits, let alone limits by region, which is what would be needed for an effective regime. Even more important, the Convention makes no provision for the allocation of catches between nations. The likelihood is, therefore, that the free-for-all will continue as each nation, in a classic illustration of the 'tragedy of the commons', seeks to justify its own capital investment by intensifying its fishing effort until the resource itself is exhausted. It happened with the whales and I see no reason why, given the present limitations of CCAMLR, it should not happen with krill and fin fish as well – with horrendous consequences for the whole ecosystem.

Destroy the krill and the fin fish and you destroy Antarctica. It is as simple as that. The existence of institutional machinery like the CCAMLR is no guarantee that the unthinkable will not happen. On the contrary, the very fact that mechanisms such as CCAMLR have been created may lull us with a false sense of security. 'No need to worry about Antarctic krill,' we may say. 'The Convention will look after krill.' The reality is that it will almost certainly do nothing of the kind.

It is, I am afraid, a case of piling Pelion on Ossa. Even if the krill and the fin fish survived over-fishing, there could be other dangers in store for them and for the marine ecosystem as a whole. Ever since the *Glomar Challenger* in 1972-3 drilled four holes in the Ross Sea continental shelf, finding traces of hydrocarbons, governments and oil companies have been interested in the possibility of finding oil in the Antarctic. The most promising areas are thought to be the continental shelves of the Ross, Amundsen and Bellingshausen Seas and the continental shelf under the Weddell Sea. Experts have estimated that the accessible continental shelves could contain 50,000,000,000 barrels of oil or more. But extracting this oil could cause major problems. One oil company representative has described the risks this way:

Ice-choked and stormy seas hinder access to the continent. Great cyclonic storms circle Antarctica in endless west to east procession. Moist maritime air interacting with cold polar air makes the Antarctic Ocean in the vicinity of the Polar Front one of the world's stormiest. The seas around Antarctica have often been likened to the moat surrounding a fortress. The turbulent 'roaring forties', 'furious fifties' and 'shrieking sixties' lie in a circumpolar storm track and a westerly oceanic current zone known commonly as West Wind Drift or Circumpolar Current. No lands break the relentless force of the prevailing west winds as they race clockwise around the continent, dragging westerly ocean currents along beneath. Superstructure icing can be expected offshore in all seasons.

The world's worst oil-spill so far was in 1978 when the *Amoco Cadiz* foundered off the coast of France losing 150,000 tonnes of oil. Antarctic tankers are likely to be three times as large and will, as the above quotation makes clear, be exposed to the roughest seas in the world. The circumpolar current will help spread pollution to the whole continent. Even if the technology to 'clear up' oil-spills in these turbulent and frozen regions existed (and it doesn't), the low temperatures themselves will hinder the processes of degradation and ensure that harmful effects on Antarctic wildlife and marine resources persist for a very long time.

Anyone who has seen, as those of us who were with the *Biscoe* have seen, those vast colonies of breeding penguins, those beaches crowded with fur seals and elephant seals, the albatross on the water in the great krill-swarming areas of the Scotia Sea, must shudder at the prospect of a major oil-spill in the Antarctic. It is the kind of incident from which the system might never fully recover. Because the ice-free areas are so limited in extent, wildlife concentrates in those areas in all its unbelievable abundance. But the greater the concentrations that exist, the greater inevitably must be their vulnerability.

Are 50 billion barrels of oil (which is, after all, only a few years' consumption at present rates) worth the risks that would have to be run if hydrocarbons are to be extracted from the seas which surround Antarctica? The answer, as far as I am concerned, is a clear and unequivocal 'no'. I cannot imagine any circumstances in which the benefits could outweigh the dangers. If the thermostats in most of our overheated homes were turned down just one degree, we should very soon have 'saved' a significant proportion of those 50 billion barrels of oil.

What about the exploration and exploitation of other minerals? Could the dangers be less and the rewards greater? It is possible, I suppose, that some treasure of valuable minerals is still to be found in Antarctica. Certainly copper, molybdenum, chromium, uranium, lead, zinc, silver, tin, gold, coal and iron are known to exist on the continent. But the commercial viability of any deposits of these minerals is far from being established – and the technical difficulties, for example in drilling or mining beneath the moving ice-cap, may be insurmountable. What is certain, however, is that the impact on the environment would be considerable, including, of course, the visual impact.

If there was one abiding impression that I brought home with me after those weeks on the *John Biscoe*, it was of Antarctica's unsurpassed beauty. Day after day we moved in a world whose landscapes and seascapes were like none other on the surface of this planet. The shape and colours of the icebergs, the sheen of the glaciers, the blue of the sky which was as pure as any I have seen (no contrails even, since the airlines of the world are not yet prepared to risk the South Polar route) – all this adds immeasurably to the uniqueness of Antarctica. Bring in the derricks and the dumps, the heavy machinery and equipment, the personnel to operate and supervise the process of commercial exploitation of Antarctic minerals and you could quite soon turn Antarctica into a garbage heap – a garbage heap moreover where the garbage would remain long after the commercial ventures which gave rise to it had ceased. Even now, when only 'scientific research' (as opposed to exploitation) is permitted under the terms of the Antarctic Treaty, the operations of the stations run by the treaty powers can have a considerable impact on the environment. Activities on any larger scale are bound to cause harm. With the best will in the world (and that commodity is not invariably present), scars would be left on the surface of Antarctica which to my mind would represent an unacceptably heavy price to pay for whatever minerals the continent may contain.

Much play is being made at this present time of a 'minerals regime' to be added to the existing framework on the Antarctic Treaty. Ambassador Beeby of New Zealand, his country's representative in the Antarctic Club, has produced several drafts of an 'informal' text which has yet to see the light of day as an official document. This text is now believed to contain one or more articles dealing with the necessities of environmental protection and proclaiming the need for appropriate forms of 'environmental assessment'. But will such texts, however cunningly drafted, ever be proof against the harsh realities of an Antarctic storm or a blow-out in sub-zero conditions? I doubt it.

And it is not only the physical impact on the environment which has to be considered. We must take into account also the damage done to the concept of wilderness, to notions of remoteness and inviolability which may be just as important, even though these ideas are not much ventilated.

What I am leading up to – it must be obvious – is the notion that Antarctica and the seas and islands that surround it should be declared 'off-limits to mankind' for the foreseeable future except for certain very restricted purposes, which would include science and tourism. But even where science and tourism are concerned there would need to be certain important caveats. Already, it seems to me, there are about as many scientists down in Antarctica as the continent can properly absorb. People who plan and construct scientific stations prefer the ice-free areas, just as the penguins and the seals do. The fact that the continent covers one-tenth of the land surface of the globe does not mean that there isn't, in certain key areas, real competition for *Lebensraum*.

The Antarctic Treaty authorizes scientific research. This is right and proper. No one who has spent six weeks as the guest of the British Antarctic Survey could or should believe otherwise. Earth sciences at Rothera; atmospheric sciences at Faraday; biology at Signy and Bird Island – we were able to get a glimpse, however fleeting, of the vast range of Antarctic science. As John Heap put it even before I set out to join the *Biscoe*, there are sound reasons for allowing scientific work to continue, and these reasons include, by the way, the value in human terms to the hundreds of young people who have 'gone south' of their Antarctic experience. As must be clear from this account,

I was deeply impressed by the quality of the personnel both on the ships and on the bases. But scientific research should never, to my mind, be used as a cover for exploitation. If that were to happen, then I believe it would be better for there to be no scientists in Antarctica rather than to have misguided scientists or scientists who are really businessmen in disguise.

By the same token, the presence of scientific research stations in Antarctica should never be used as a cover for 'colonization'. When I was flying down from Santiago to Punta Arenas, I read the Chilean Ambassador Zegers' article advocating the 'visionary programme of human settlement' in Antarctica. Though the *Biscoe* did not visit any Chilean base, it seems clear that the Chilean (and Argentine) concept of scientific research is somewhat elastic. Colonization of Antarctica, quite apart from its obvious environmental impacts, would lead inevitably to the consolidation of national claims and the breakdown of the Antarctic Treaty mechanism which has so far managed to finesse the issue of sovereignty. To reinforce national claims in Antarctica is, sooner or later, to run the risk of war in the Deep South. So far the Treaty has (more or less) managed to preclude all military activity in Antarctica and that is one of its great strengths. But any substantial programme of colonization would threaten, and almost certainly destroy, the delicate balance on which the Treaty is built.

War anywhere is nasty. War in the Antarctic could be especially nasty, both for the forces involved and for the environment. There could moreover be unforeseen global consequences, apart from the spread of radioactivity involved in any nuclear exchange. We hear a lot nowadays about the build-up of carbon dioxide in the atmosphere and the risk that the consequent rise in temperature will cause a melting of the polar ice-caps. But perhaps there are even quicker ways of going about it.

Apart from legitimate (and limited) scientific research, I think there is a case for legitimate (and limited) tourism. The notion that Antarctica, like the deep seabed and outer space, is somehow the 'common heritage of mankind' has taken root at least in the United Nations. If that notion means that every nation has a right to exploit Antarctica, then I am dead against it. If, however, it is taken to mean that the fruits of any legitimate activity undertaken there should somehow be shared among nations (in proportion perhaps to the extent of their disadvantages), then I am not so opposed.

Tourism is a case in point. Very modest, very carefully controlled tourist activities (not more, say, than a handful of ships a year) might not only increase the constituency of informed intelligent men and women dedicated to the conservation of Antarctica; it might also help to divert the pressures for other and far worse forms of exploitation. For Antarctica, as for the Galápagos, the central point must be the scale and nature of the tourist activities. So many of the animals – the birds and the beasts – have never yet learned to fear man. We have to keep it that way.

Wildlife tourism, landscape and seascape tourism, within the context of a 'hands off Antarctica' policy, seems to me to be an effective riposte to those who argue that in a world where 'millions are starving', it is wrong to let any resources which are available remain unused. Personally, I don't think we *need* to encourage tourism in Antarctica. But if a gesture towards 'internationalization' has to be made, this is probably the best – or least harmful one – to make.

What then should the future of Antarctica be? Given the conflicting pressures, the status quo is not likely to endure for very long. However much the Antarctic Treaty powers would have liked to keep the discussions 'in the family', the debate has already widened in scope. The United Nations will sooner or later adopt or promote a policy towards Antarctica. It should be a matter of concern to all of us to ensure that such a policy makes sense.

Back in 1972 representatives from over eighty countries met at Grand Teton National Park in the United States and first proposed that Antarctica should be declared the first World Park.

New Zealand took up the idea in 1975 when it suggested that the Antarctic Treaty consultative parties should give Antarctica international park status. New Zealand indicated its willingness to drop its own territorial claims if the other Treaty partners would follow suit. They didn't. The Third World National Parks' proposal was renewed in 1982 at the AZA conference in Bali and again on the tenth anniversary of the Stockholm Conference (also in 1982) when environmentalists and conservationists from all over the world gathered in Nairobi. They passed a resolution on that occasion which: 'requested the Antarctic Treaty powers and the United Nations General Assembly to give serious consideration to declaring Antarctica a World Park, in recognition of its inestimable value to humankind, and its status as a global commons'.

Is this all pie-in-the-sky? Will the Antarctic Treaty powers ever give up their privileged position and throw their weight behind the World Park concept? Will the United States, for example, with its massive lead in the technology of exploitation, be prepared to forgo this advantage in the interest of the 'wilderness option'? (The United States, along with Britain and West Germany, has so far resolutely refused to sign the Law of the Sea Treaty because it dislikes the provisions governing seabed mining – so the omens are bad.) Will Britain, with its now colossal investment in the Falklands (which I was able to see at first hand) turn its back on the possibility of exploiting 'British Antarctic Territory' – a slice of the Antarctic pie which may, because of its geological configuration, turn out to be one of the most mineral-rich areas of the continent? (One of my most vivid memories is of the time we landed on the glacier south of Rothera to talk to the two geologists working among the mountains and nunataks.) Will Australia, whose great pioneers like Sir Douglas Mawson did so much to earn that country its seat at the Antarctic table, lightly throw away the prospect of capitalizing on the fruits of those efforts?

And will nations who are *not* members of the Antarctic Club but who now cast longing eyes on the supposed 'riches' of Antarctica accept the notion that Antarctica should be off-limits except for certain restricted purposes? With the pressure of their own growing populations and their low living standards, it will be hard indeed for the developing nations of Asia, Africa and Latin America to content themselves with a few crumbs from the table of environmentally-benign Antarctic tourism or from licensed activities of scientific research conducted by the wealthier countries, when they have a sense that there is some wonderful windfall in the offing, some Antarctic bonanza which, if only they could get their hands on it, might buy them at least a week or two's respite from their horrendous problems. If you are a developing country, teetering on the brink of famine, even a week can be a long time. I recognize that it would be hard to persuade the countries of the Third World, and therefore the United Nations, to agree to the self-denying ordinances which would be implicit in the 'World Park' solution.

Yet still I think the goal is worth striving for. Even Third World nations may in the end be ready to appreciate the ecological hazards involved in the exploitation of Antarctica, particularly since most of them ('the poor south') are a good deal nearer the Antarctic in geographical terms than we are. And Asia, Africa and Latin America will be just as affected by the threat to world peace which would in my judgement necessarily be involved if, having moved once from the 'heroic' era of Antarctic exploration into the era of scientific research, we were now to take the fateful step towards full-scale commercial exploitation.

I do not myself believe that any regime can be devised under whatever auspices which will permit or encourage the commercial exploitation of Antarctica without there being posed quite unacceptable risks both for the environment (including fauna and flora) and for world peace. The World Park concept seems to me to be the best, indeed the only way out, short of going back in time in some reverse Rip Van Winkle manoeuvre and finding ourselves once more in those pre-Captain Cook days when tall sailing ships beat around the southern hemisphere without being aware that Antarctica even existed.

Could Antarctica ever be declared a World Park? Would the politicians ever agree? At the moment I suppose the odds are against it. There has been a 'greening' of opinion in some countries of Europe's heartland (largely as a reaction to the death of forests as a result of air pollution); but the process in much of the industrialized world (including most of the industrial countries with a major stake in Antarctica) has not gone very far. And in the developing world the environmental movement is in its infancy. Nor, on the whole, are the political systems there such as to respond to a 'green' movement even if one were to be born. There is certainly a long way to go before the necessary awareness is created.

Yet these are early days. Antarctica has been around already for about two thousand million years and, even though the threats are both immediate and pressing (especially the threat posed by over-fishing), the continent is not going to disappear or be radically and irreversibly altered between now and Christmas. There is a growing body of opinion today which believes that the future of Antarctica is too important to be left to governments, whether we are talking about a mere handful of governments as in the case of the Antarctic Club, or the whole comity of nations, as represented by the UN. That body of opinion is not to be ignored. Men like Jim Barnes have already devoted years of their lives to the goal of 'saving Antarctica'. There are many others like him all around the world – and they are not about to give up. They believe what Ernest Shackleton believed (I read the inscription on the grave in that little cemetery in Grytviken) that 'a man should strive to the uttermost for his life's set prize'. Such men have a habit of winning through in the end.

There are many different kinds of adventure. Historically, Antarctica has been a place where heroic deeds have been performed – and whole nations have thrilled to the tale of those deeds. Today, as I was able to see from my time there with the *John Biscoe*, Antarctica still poses many rugged physical challenges as well as the newer intellectual challenges having to do with science and man's acquisition of knowledge about the world in which he lives.

But Antarctica also poses another kind of challenge – the challenge of being able to look at the world differently. We shouldn't feel we have to exploit something just 'because it's there', however tempting it may seem. We should pause and take a deep breath and ask ourselves: do we really need Antarctic resources if this means the destruction of other values, both moral and material? After all, how many wildernesses do we have left? Where is there another wilderness like this? Do we want to live in a world without wilderness? And even if present generations decide they can survive quite well in such a world, will future generations of humanity feel the same? (And what about the animals, the plants, the icebergs, I hear a small voice cry at the back of the hall. Who speaks for them and for *their* future generations?)

My own belief is that there is no need now – and there will never be a need – to develop or exploit Antarctica. In the words of the Beatles' song, the best thing we can do is to 'let it be', to let it be what in fact it is: the world's last great wilderness.

Initials

BAS	British Antarctic Survey
IGY	International Geophysical Year
UN	United Nations
EEC	European Economic Community
IUCN	International Union for the Conservation of Nature and Natural Resources
SPRI	Scott Polar Research Institute
IATA	International Air Transport Association
FCO	Foreign & Commonwealth Office
NGO	Non-governmental Organization
CITES	Convention for International Trade in Endangered Species of Fauna and Flora
ASOC	Antarctica and Southern Oceans Coalition
PSNC	Pacific Steam Navigation Company
USARP	United States Antarctic Research Programme
AIS	Advanced Ionospheric Sounder
IH	International Harvester
VLF	Very Low Frequency
PI	Photo Interpretation
NOAA	National Ocean and Atmospheric Administration
WMO	World Meteorological Office
BTO	British Trust for Ornithology
INMASAT	International Maritime Satellite
FIC	Falkland Islands Company
NAAFI	Navy, Army and Air Force Institute
ODA	Overseas Development Administration
FIDS (Fids)	Falkland Islands Development Corporation, also its personnel
SNOFI	Senior Naval Officer Falkland Islands
FAO	Food and Agriculture Organization
NERC	National Environment Research Council
BAOR	British Army of the Rhine

BGLE	British Graham Land Expedition
IWC	International Whaling Commission
CCAMLR	Convention on the Conservation of Antarctic Marine Living Resources

Bibliography

Adams, Richard, and Lockley, Ronald, *Voyage through the Antarctic* (Allen Lane, 1982)

Barnes, James N., *Let's Save Antarctica* (Greenhouse Publications, Richmond, Australia, 1982)

Bonner, W. Nigel, *Whales* (Blandford, 1980)

Brewster, B., *Antarctica: Wilderness at Risk* (Friends of the Earth, New Zealand and Australia, 1982)

Byrd, Richard, *Discovery* (Putnam, New York, 1935); *Antarctic Discovery* (Putnam, London, 1936)

Cherry-Garrard, A., *The Worst Journey in the World* (Penguin, 1983)

Christie, E. W. H., *The Antarctic Problem: an historical and political study* (Allen & Unwin, 1951)

Cook, Captain James, *Voyages of Discovery* (Dent, Everyman Library, 1906; reissued 1976)

Fuchs, Sir V., *Of Ice and Men* (Nelson, 1982)

Fuchs, Sir V., and Hillary, Sir E., *The Crossing of Antarctica: Transantarctic Expedition 1957/58* (Cassell, 1958)

Hastings, M., and Jenkins, S., *Battle for the Falklands* (Pan, 1983)

Headland, R. K., *The Island of South Georgia* (CUP, 1984)

Holdgate, M. W., and Tinker, J., *Oil and Other Minerals in the Antarctic: the Environment Implications of Possible Mineral Exploration or Exploitation in Antarctica* (Scientific Committee on Antarctic Research, 1979)

Honnywill, E., *The Challenge of Antarctica* (Nelson, 1984)

Hosking, Eric, *Antarctic Wildlife* (Croom Helm, London and Canberra, 1982)

Huntford, Roland, *Scott and Amundsen* (Pan, 1983)

King, H. G. R., *The Antarctic* (Blandford, 1969)

Lansing, A., *Endurance* (Hodder, 1959)

Law, Phillip, *Antarctic Odyssey* (Heinemann, Australia, 1983)

Martin, Vance (ed.), *Wilderness* (Findhorn, 1982)

Mitchell, Barbara, and Tinker, Jon, *The Management of the Southern Ocean* (International Institute for Environment and Development, 1983)

Mitchell, B., *Frozen Stakes* (International Institute for Environment and Development, 1983)

Orrego Vicuna, F. (ed.), *Antarctic Resources Policy* (CUP, 1983)

Rymill, John, *Southern Lights* (Chatto, 1938)

Scott, Sir Peter, *Travel Diaries of a Naturalist* (Collins, 1983)

Scott, R. F., *Scott's Last Expedition – The Journals* (Methuen, 1983)

Shackleton, Ernest, *South* (Century, 1983)

Shackleton, Rt. Hon. Lord, *Economic Survey of the Falkland Islands* (HMSO, 1976)

Shackleton, Rt. Hon. Lord, *Falkland Islands Economic Study* (HMSO, 1982)

Shapley, Deborah, *The Seventh Continent: Antarctica in a Resource Age* (Resources for the Future, 1984)

Strange, Ian J., *The Falkland Islands* (David & Charles, 3rd ed., 1983)

Sunday Times Insight Team, *The Falklands War* (Sphere, 1982)

Twistleton-Wykeham-Fiennes, R., *To the Ends of the Earth* (Hodder, 1983)

Walton, Kevin, *Portrait of Antarctica* (George Philip, 1983)

Watson, George E., *Birds of the Antarctic and Sub-Antarctic* (American Geographical Union, Washington)

Worsley, F. A., *The Great Antarctic Rescue* (Times Books, 1977; Sphere, 1979)

Priestley, R., Adie, R. J., and Robin, G. D. Q. (eds), *Antarctic Research* (Butterworth, 1964)

Index